MW01701288

Toward a Dialogical Civilization. Dialogues Volume 1

WEIMING TU

ISBN 979-8-9907702-2-5

English Transcripts: Huang Qi (黄琦), Tony Huang

English Editors: Misha A. Tadd, Jonathan P. Keir, Marek z Jeziorek

Photographs: Ai Bei, Marek z Jeziorek

Printed in the United States of America 2025

For videos, visit https://www.youtube.com/c/culturalchinafoundat

For information, visit https://tuweiming.net/

A Note From An Editor

Prof. TU's texts included here were created as transcripts from the videos. The videos were initially captured by Ai Bei and later by Marek z Jeziorek. Not every text included here has a corresponding video. If a chapter has an associated video, you might see a QR code at the end of it. When scanned on a phone camera, the QR code should take you to the corresponding YouTube video.

Before publishing this volume, we realized that to enhance the clarity of the text and make it more readable, we needed to edit some of the chapters. Jonathan Keir and Misha A. Tadd did the initial editing. Prof. TU is grateful for their work. Marek z Jeziorek performed the final edits while creating a consistent look and feel for the book. Additionally, some of Prof. TU's interlocutors requested to edit their dialogue. If you encounter a textual discrepancy between a video and this book, it is most likely due to our editing.

Marek z Jeziorek, an editor

TABLE OF CONTENTS

Dialogue With Michael J. Sandel 2004-04-13 5

Dialogue With Raimon Pannikar 2004-07-03................................37

Dialogue With Hossein Nasr, including William Chittick and Sachiko Murata 2004-07-06................................50

Dialogue With Ewert Cousins 2005-02-27................................61

Dialogue With Ioanna Kuçuradi 2009-09-17 75

Dialogue With Samuel Lee 2009-11-17................................89

Dialogue With Fred Dallmayr 2009-11-18................................101

Dialogue With Jerome Kagan 2010-04-09 113

Dialogue With Homi Bhabha 2010-05-20................................146

Dialogue With JC Kapur 2010-7-11 165

Dialogue With Fred Dallmayr 2011-06-10................................177

Dialogue With Gholamreza Aavani 2013-06-17................................199

Index................................232

Dialogue With Michael J. Sandel 2004-04-13

Bio: Michael J. Sandel (born 1953) is an American political philosopher who has taught at Harvard University since 1980. He graduated from Brandeis University in 1975 and received his doctorate from Balliol College, Oxford, as a Rhodes Scholar, where he studied under the philosopher Charles Taylor. His legendary course "Justice" was the first Harvard course made freely available online and on television. It has been viewed by millions worldwide, including in China, where Sandel was named the "most influential foreign figure of the year." His first book, *Liberalism and the Limits of Justice* (1982), offers a critique of liberalism in the tradition of Kant and John Rawls. His other significant works include *Democracy's Discontent: America in Search of a Public Philosophy* (1998), *Justice: What's the Right Thing to Do?* (2010), *What Money Can't Buy: The Moral Limits of Markets* (2012), and *The Tyranny of Merit* (2020). In *Encountering China: Michael Sandel and Chinese Philosophy* (2018, edited with Paul J. D'Ambrosio), leading scholars of Confucian and Daoist thought explore connections between Sandel's work and Chinese philosophical traditions. Sandel has lectured widely in China, at universities and public venues in Beijing, Shanghai, Shenzhen, Hong Kong, Guangzhou, Xiamen, and Xian.

Tu: This conversation is especially meaningful because your work is now available in Chinese.

Sandel: I've brought a copy of the Chinese edition of my first book to show you.

Tu: The title is *Liberalism and the Limits of Justice*. It's a good translation—the title.

Tu: You know, there are two translations of "communitarianism." One is more sociological, based on society. The other one is more philosophical and implies a shared body that is not just physiological but is the body politic.

Sandel: I see.

Tu: …a group of people share the same body politic.

Sandel: Right.

Tu: Some kind of sense of commitment.

Sandel: So, what are the two words? I'm just curious.

Tu: One is *shequn zhuyi* 社群主義. *Shequn,* which means social group. The other one is *gongtongti zhuyi* 共同體主義, the term about the shared body or shared community.

Sandel: I see.

Tu: I think that his translation is actually better, but the language is not that familiar.

Sandel: He used the second term.

Tu: Yeah, he used the second one. I think it's a new term. It will be like when they accept the idea of "identity." I think the translation of "identity" was in the '60s.

Sandel: So, how did you learn about it?

Tu: I probably put too much emphasis on the concept itself and not enough on the experiential side.

Sandel: I see.

Tu: The idea of identification, of an epistemological point of view on this. I feel that maybe it's better to do as a shared concern or experiential understanding of one's connectedness with a group and large community.

Sandel: Yes, so that issue is very similar to this translation issue.

Tu: Very much so, as it is the whole question about identity. When Erikson used the term earlier, I think for the first time in *Young Man Luther,* in reference to the identity crisis, he was talking about a particular stage in human development. He never really anticipated that the term would be so broadly used later. At the time, it was simply psychohistory, history, and interaction. Then, the term was used not just for personal identity crises but also for professional groups, identities of sociology, philosophy, and then national and cultural identity.

Sandel: Yes.

Tu: The first course I taught at my alma mater was "Cultural Identity and Social Transformation in Modern China."

Sandel: When did you teach that?

Tu: '67, back in Taiwan.

Sandel: What were some of the main texts that you used?

Tu: Basically, at the time, we used simply texts related to modernization and democratization. I certainly made reference to De Tocqueville's *Democracy in America*, and I mentioned Durkheim's *Division of Labor*. To a certain extent, I also employed Weber.

Sandel: Right.

Tu: Weber's whole notion from Gemeinschaft to Gesellschaft, that modernization is very detrimental to what he called "universal brotherhood," which can never be recreated. I think, in a way, your work is trying to say, "Well, that's not totally irrelevant."

Sandel: Yes, I am very sympathetic to that idea and to that work. Are these texts, the three texts you just mentioned of De Tocqueville, Durkheim, and Weber, translated into Chinese?

Tu: They're all available in Chinese. Maybe Durkheim's work hasn't been translated yet. 迪尔凯姆《社会分工》 中文有吗？[Is there a Chinese edition of Durkheim's *The Division of Labor in Society*?]

Voice off camera: 中文有，好像有。 迪尔凯姆已经有十本书了。[It seems there is a Chinese edition. There are already ten works by Durkheim in Chinese.]

Tu: Okay, so there have been a few of Durkheim's books translated. I actually was very much influenced by people like Talcott Parsons, who are not philosophers. When I first came to Harvard, I was particularly interested in three disciplines of philosophy: aesthetics, ethics, and philosophy of religion. Unfortunately, none of them were recognized by our colleagues here as important.

Sandel: We still have that problem.

Tu: We still have a problem, but it's better now. Everyone is dealing with ethics.

Sandel: Ethics. Yes, yes.

Tu: But the philosophy of religion is not so much.

Sandel: So those were the three subjects you studied when you first came here?

Tu: No. Those were the three subjects I wanted to study.

Sandel: You wanted to, but…

Tu: I was given a Harvard-Yenching Fellowship, so I could have gotten into philosophy or other disciplines, but Quine was so prominent. The whole emphasis was on logic, epistemology, logic of the mind, linguistic philosophy, and metaphysics. None of the areas I was interested in were even recognized as proper topics. They did invite Charles Stevenson from Michigan. Emotional…

Sandel: Right, emotivism?

Tu: Emotivism. He was the only one to teach ethics. The only other person who was interested in the areas that I was interested in was Morton White, but then he went to Princeton's Advanced Institute. The only person who later became very much interested in my studies at the time was Henry Aiken.

Sandel: Oh yes.

Tu: You know him?

Sandel: I know of him. He was at Brandeis, and I was an undergraduate there.

Tu: Oh, you went to Brandeis. He was the only tenured professor at the time who resigned from Harvard and went to Brandeis.

Sandel: Yes, that's where I was an undergraduate.

Tu: I see.

Sandel: I didn't study with him but knew about him.

Tu: Yeah. He joined this group called "History of Consciousness."

Sandel: Yes.

Tu: Right. He was very, very helpful, but he was so frustrated with his colleagues.

Sandel: I can imagine. Was it later that you began putting together Neo-Confucian thought with some of these Western philosophical views, or did you have that in mind when you began studying?

Tu: Well, when I first came, of course, I was already very deeply involved with Confucian humanism and people like Benjamin Schwartz.

Sandel: Oh, all right.

Tu: He was very, very supportive. Fairbank was less so, but he was a giant in Chinese studies. Still, he was quite sympathetic. John King Fairbank arranged for me to have lunch with Judith Shklar.

Sandel: My colleague and friend.

Tu: She was an Assistant Professor then. I didn't know she would become such a giant. She was very, very helpful. So, Fairbank helped, too. I met quite a few people; there was also Kenneth Galbraith. He's our neighbor now. That's his house.

Sandel: He's your neighbor.

Tu: Yeah. He's 95, and I just saw him.

Tu: I realized there are different liberal traditions: There's the Harvard school and the Chicago school.

Sandel: Yes.

Tu: Kenneth Galbraith put a lot of emphasis on the role of the government in terms of civil rights, whereas the liberal tradition of Chicago is totally…

Sandel: Anti-government.

Tu: I call them market fundamentalists.

Sandel: Yes, that's a good term for them, market fundamentalists. In fact, even the term liberal has such a different meaning in the United States and Europe. In Europe, to call someone liberal means to say that they are a Chicago-style market liberal, like Margaret Thatcher and Ronald Reagan. In Europe, that's what liberal means, whereas in the United States, liberal generally means John Kenneth Galbraith.

Tu: But I think people in Chicago, including Hayek, for quite some time, were marginalized and not considered the mainstream of American liberal thoughts.

Sandel: Von Hayek, yes. I think Milton Friedman, who is the great representative of Chicago, calls himself a liberal or a classical liberal.

Tu: Right, right.

Sandel: These days, we refer to them as libertarians or market liberals.

Tu: You mean like Nozick?

Sandel: Well, Nozick, Milton Friedman, and Hayek.

Tu: Oh, Nozick, oh I see. You're right, from the political point of view.

Sandel: In the justice class, we read the three of them together.

Tu: As the?

Sandel: As libertarians.

Tu: Oh.

Sandel: But that would really fit with what you're describing as the Chicago market liberal.

Tu: But you know the first name that slipped my mind, Buchanan.

Sandel: James Buchanan?

Tu: James, yeah. I went to George Washington University to give a talk about three years ago, and Francis Fukuyama and James Buchanan were my panelists. I was very surprised that James Buchanan had this classical liberal mind. He made the observation, "I used to think that freedom is the only quality that we need to underscore in the market. Now I think responsibility is indispensable, but is not enough." I said, "What is the other quality? Is it decency?" He said, "Yes, yes. If people are not decent, they can't be responsible and can't be free; they can be very detrimental to the public good." I don't know whether he changed his mind, or at least he felt the classical tradition was not enough. He is very much embraced by Southern political figures, senators, etc.

Sandel: Southern conservatives.

Tu: Conservatives, yes. They established a whole center to honor him. Yet, in his late 60s or 70s, he was much, much more open to new ideas, to our kind of ideas.

Sandel: Now I wonder what he would say if you put it to him. I think he comes from a very conservative view.

Tu: Very conservative. I don't know, but I still don't understand the meaning of decency, whether it is just a personal quality or something more.

Sandel: I wonder.

Tu: I wonder about that too, yeah.

Sandel: I doubt his notion of decency would lead him in social terms to support mutual obligations in citizens to care for one another.

Tu: Right, right. I don't think that he would go so far with this kind of policy issue.

Sandel: Right. Well, these different understandings of liberal can be confusing but also very revealing. In the United States, sometimes I think that political debate, for the most part, is dominated by those who share a premise, which is the premise of a very deep individualism, and they disagree about how that individualism should be applied. The libertarians, or the market liberals, say it should be applied to limit government, minimal government—Let the market decide! —whereas the more egalitarian liberals also start with the same individualist premise but think the only way to respect individual rights and individual autonomy is to have a fair framework of a social welfare state with a decent minimum public provision. They are both arguing within the same; I would say, relatively narrow but deeply individualist, premise. I think part of the work that you've done, and this may be a similarity in some of the work that we've both done, has been to challenge that individualism. Don't you agree?

Tu: I agree with you. I'd like to say that Robert Bellah is probably more sympathetic to non-individualism.

Sandel: Yes, yes. I think he is among those who have challenged the individualistic premise.

Tu: I must acknowledge that he had a rather defining influence on my early days. He is Talcott Parsons's best student, and yet he thought very differently and finally decided to go to Berkeley. He was already clearly very unhappy with the Lockean tradition.

Sandel: Yes.

Tu: That's clearly the problem that we may face. To think from that point of view of the original state as something with no history, no culture, and no social contact gets us headed in the wrong direction.

Sandel: Yes.

Tu: Maybe I'd like just to give you a sense of the issues we've been exploring both at the institute and especially my own concern. We have a project that we call "Reflection on the Enlightenment." Normally, the idea is that Enlightenment humanism is so powerful that the whole Confucian tradition in China was deconstructed because they wanted to be scientific, wanted to be democratic, and wanted to learn those great values from the West; the tradition was relegated to the background as the feudal past.

Sandel: Yes.

Tu: But in recent years, a few of us have begun to reflect upon Enlightenment not simply from the modernistic or post-modernistic perspectives but from the perspective of the Confucian tradition. This is done in the broader context because the Enlightenment tradition also affected Judaic, Christian, Hindu, and Islamic traditions. The assumption is that the most powerful ideology in human history now, especially in the modern period, has to be the Enlightenment: liberalism, capitalism, and socialism came out of this. It's secular, but it's powerful. The values embodied in the Enlightenment have now been recognized by people, including China, as universal values, not just universalizable values, such as liberty, rationality, due process of law, human rights, and dignity of the individual. I think we all cherish these ideas.

Sandel: Yes, of course.

Tu: But if you look at it from the Confucian point of view, while we accept all these values as universal values if we put them together, they are not enough for us to deal with the complexity of the human condition now.

Sandel: I agree.

Tu: So, from the Confucian perspective, individual liberty is a question of not just equality but justice as fairness. In addition to rationality, there is the question of sympathy or the Buddhist ideal of compassion. In addition to due process of law or legality, civility is essential, like the new notion of civic republicanism. In addition to rights, there is obviously responsibility. In addition to the individual, there is the whole sense of communal connectedness. We may have to sometimes argue that sympathy is superior. Our colleague, Jerome Kagan, believes that sympathy is more basic to moral reasoning than rationality.

So, these are some issues that we have been exploring, and this is the reason why we are very attracted to your work. We consider it a pioneering attempt to recover that tradition. So, tell us a little bit about your current thinking on this. We are familiar with *Liberalism and the Limits of Justice*, *Democracy's Discontent*, the whole question about the search for American popular philosophy, and other essays as well.

Sandel: Yes. Well, I find your project very exciting and intriguing. I want to learn more about it for two reasons. First, I agree completely with what you said about Enlightenment ideals being important, but also insufficient for an adequate ethic, that it is inadequate as individual ethic, but also as a public ethic. I think that is a very important starting point. Secondly, I think that the Enlightenment tradition, and those who live in societies where Enlightenment ideals are aspired to, have a lot to learn from traditions outside the Enlightenment understandings, including the Confucian humanist tradition that you have brought into dialogue with the Enlightenment understandings. For both of those reasons, I think that this is an exciting and important project.

I would also say there is a third reason, which is the most obvious and important one—most people begin with yet another reason, which is the importance of intra-civilizational dialogue and understanding—I would go further than that, that of course, is very important, but what you've raised is not just a matter of different civilizations and traditions understanding each other's so that there will be less conflict and more understanding, it is also that those in the West who aspire to Enlightenment ideals themselves have something to learn, even for their own understanding, from education and engagement with Confucian humanism and, I would say, with other pre-Enlightenment traditions. It's not just to get along better, though that's obviously important, not just to improve mutual understanding, but also to really improve, deepen, and supplement the respective ethical traditions themselves. For all of those reasons, I think it is important.

Now, to get into the actual content of the engagement between these two traditions, one of the great aspirations of Enlightenment moral philosophy and political philosophy is to see moral and political authority as self-sufficient. So, in some ways, I think Kant's idea of autonomy is the ultimate working out of this project. Kant's deep insight was that if we understand ourselves fully as free, it is not enough, as Hobbes, Locke, and the empiricist thought, to understand freedom as the absence of obstacles to the utilization of our desires, to be fully free in the sense of being an autonomous person or even to be governed by desires or a will that we legislate for ourselves. So, there is this idea of utter self-sufficiency of the liberal self, to be capable of freedom that consists in a kind of autonomy, to be governed by law and by yourself. So, that, in a way, is the ultimate expression of this liberal aspiration of self-sufficiency, but is that idea of freedom adequate? I don't think so.

Part of *Liberalism and the Limits of the Justice* tries to show the inadequacy of that Kantian idea of freedom as Rawls had worked it out in a contemporary version of the theory of justice. For Rawls, this notion of self-efficiency is in the idea that the principles of justice that define our rights don't need to depend for their justification on any substantive conception of the good life or of human flourishing. So, that's his version of this Kantian project of utter self-sufficiency. The great appeal is that in modern societies, people disagree about the good life, and so he tried to show that we can nonetheless have principles of justice that don't depend on any conception of the Good. But I think that project fails for just the same reasons that Kant's project of moral autonomy fails, that this idea of utter self-efficiency doesn't work. Then the question has to be, what are the moral sources that are available to human beings if we are situated beings? And we must ask situated how, in relation to what traditions, and with what critical resources with respect to those traditions? Those are big questions that are still being investigated, but at least at issue is the Enlightenment project of self-sufficiency, whether it's Kant's idea about autonomy or Rawls' idea of the "right" being prior to the good. If the project of the Enlightenment is inadequate and unsuccessful, then we have to begin to look for other moral sources. Charles Taylor refers to sources of the self.

Tu: Yes.

Sandel: I learned a great deal from Charles Taylor, who was a teacher of mine.

Tu: Oh really? Where?

Sandel: At Oxford, where I was a graduate student.

Tu:_He was here before, and we had a discussion.

Sandel: Yes. He's told me about his discussions with you. I studied Aristotle, Hegel, and liberalism with him at Oxford. So, I think he also would share this sympathy with your project because I think he shares this idea. He traces it to Hegel's critique of Kant on the grounds that a fully realized ethical life requires a *sittlichkeit*, a situated ethical life that is not totally detached from the human situation or the particular life history of an individual or a society. Once one sees the need to situate the self, and to connect it to the conception of the good life and the emotive life, then there is a lot more room for the kind of dialogue with other traditions that have a rich sense of the human situation. That is a great opening for this dialogue between Confucian humanism—among other traditions—and the Enlightenment idea.

Tu: I think we could probably include MacIntyre's *After Virtue* in this connection.

Sandel: Yes.

Tu: The one thing that worries me is why the Kantian project still has a lot of persuasive power in the world, as that is the reason why many people become really critics of either communitarianism, as you describe it, or Confucian humanism. The other one is something I learned from Peter Berger, the sociologist. He argues that globalization, among all kinds of other problems, is somewhat related to the question of liberalization of the individual. In other words, a person may have more choices and may have more possibilities. One is the Kantian idea of the independent autonomist self; human emotions are not even involved in this case. It is just a rational assertion about the categorical characters. The other is the major trend of globalization also underscores the individual, and we can see the persuasive power of that in a market-driven society like China right now. I think the question about the situated self now becomes more appreciated.

Sandel: Yes.

Tu: Then you have this, maybe, premature synthesis about how the communitarian project will safeguard the individual's dignity.

Sandel: Yes.

Tu: At the same time, that it would be able to overcome the obvious negative consequences, many of them probably unintended negative consequences, of this Lockean or Kantian idea of the individual.

Sandel: Well, the setting of globalization does pose these questions, because globalization consists fundamentally of the spread of market relations across national boundaries and other traditional boundaries, so that market relations come to be universalized and to govern spheres of life that were once thought to be protected from market exchange. In some ways, the ideal of the individual is carried to a logical extreme in a globalized market system. But there is a paradox because in many ways the effects of a globalized market system is to undermine the dignity of the individual, because what happens is that it's more and more difficult to govern or regulate markets at the level of the national community. That's what globalization means, that nation states have less and less control. The resulting effect is that corporations, market forces and capital markets govern larger parts of life. That actually has the effect of disempowering the individual, though markets are often invoked in the name of respect for the individual and individual choice. In Chicago, they will tell you that markets are about choice, respecting individual choice.

Tu: Liberalization of the individual.

Sandel: Liberalization. But there is another side to this, which is the actual structures of power. Large-scale market societies, that aren't governed by public ethics or national considerations of the common good, wind up swamping the individual. So, individualism has a doubled relation to globalized markets. In the second of those two relationships, markets are disempowering. I think the other effect of globalized markets is to crowd out those spheres of life, including particular communities and even religious traditions that provide a counterpoint to individualism and market relations. I think that is part of what creates the backlash against globalization; there is the disempowerment of individuals in the face of large structures of power in market societies, and there is the erosion of intermediate forms of community and identity. These things taken together create a sense of dislocation that fuel, very often, a backlash against globalization. This is the paradoxical relation of globalization and the individual.

Tu: In the classical period of Mencius, he is confronted with two challenges. One is extreme individualism in the so-called Yang Zhu 楊朱 tradition, and the other one is the abstract universalism and collectivism of the Mohists. The Mohists talk about universal love, and the idea that you have to be free from all the constraints of particular societies, so you can become a true citizen of the world to be able to serve society in the most impartial manner. Actually, in what happened in China is in the last 30 years, that idea played a very important role. That's why there is a form of kind of collectivism in this abstract universalism.

Sandel: That's a fascinating parallel.

Tu: I think it fits well with the notion that you have to free yourself from the feudal past, all the primordial ties: familial, communal, and so forth, so that you become a citizen of the world, of the nation, and of the tribe.

Sandel: This thinker was?

Tu: Mozi.

Sandel: Mozi. Is he evoked explicitly or only implicitly?

Tu: Implicitly. Often evoked in a more positive way against the Confucian "differentiated model."

Sandel: Yes.

Tu: So, the Mencian response to these two challenges, extreme individualism, and extreme collectivism, is the assumption of the person as situated.

Sandel: Yes.

Tu: The point of departure, thinking about a person is always concrete person in and out.

Sandel: I see.

Tu: If you construct something totally independent, you have to return. Otherwise, there would be something lost, or something basically destroyed.

Sandel: Yes.

Tu: Then the situated person is always contextualized in terms of family relationships, in terms of society and so forth. The major question is how you can extend or expand this vision of a person to involve continuously other aspects of the world, in terms of your consciousness and your concern.

Sandel: Yes.

Tu: So, the term they use is extension.

Sandel: Extension.

Tu: You start with the self or sort of binary relationship with your parents or your siblings, but that is the basis on which you expand. If you don't expand it, you will fall upon selfishness or suffer from nepotism. So, we need to always do it with a public-spiritedness.

Sandel: Yes, absolutely.

Tu: But this does not mean you have to get out of the niche in which you find yourself.

Sandel: Yes. Of course.

Tu: The thickness of that is not necessarily detrimental to your ability to extend further. So, I think in a sense of your local communities, all these turn out to be very meaningful for the ideal of the good life, but it's not in form of parochialism as how you defined it.

Sandel: Right, yes.

Tu: So, I think that has been a major struggle. It is not universal love as a form of abstract universalism, but the ability to have sympathy and compassion for human beings and maybe even beyond. At the same time, you never lose your own situatedness in order to build not only a family relationship, but also a communal relationship. My sense is that it might not be a solution, but at least the conception itself is more richly textured in terms of the kind of issues that we face today.

Sandel: That so well describes the challenge at the level of individual ethics and political philosophy, and also a kind of spiritual challenge to articulate an ethic that, on the one hand, is situated that avoids the abstract universalism, over detachment, and self-sufficiency as you described, but on the other hand does not lapse into parochialism. It gestures beyond itself towards horizons of concerns beyond the immediate particular. I think it is a great political challenge, probably the greatest political challenge of our time. I don't think we have very good solutions for developing political institutions, at different levels in forms of community and identity and different levels of association, that can inspire and nurture these multiple levels of concern and identity. It is so difficult. I think it is fundamentally a political project. I don't think this is something that could be worked out at just as an individual level or a personal ethics, because it requires a kind of differentiated or articulated public life with multiple identities, some more particular, some more universal, but held in a kind of tension that remains an integrated way of life. There will inevitably be a tension among the sometimes competing and sometimes overlapping identities on the kind of picture, this differentiated picture, but it requires intermediate institutions, forms of life, forms of community and identity that can draw people out of their own privatistic, narrow parochialism, but with forms of common life that don't immediately lapse into the pure universal.

Tu: Absolutely.

Sandel: This is a project that globalization requires but hasn't yet found an answer to. It points towards this universal market society, which can't sustain, if anything in it erodes and undermines, these differentiated and immediate forms of identity. In the United States, we haven't really come up with a very good solution to this problem. There's a long tradition of local government. Even in New England the township is a way that Thomas Jefferson saw we needed, and so he thought you had to have a decentralized political system in order to make people ultimately cultivate a national patriotism and not just so they would identify only with their town. De Tocqueville saw this.

Tu: Yes, as a great strength in America.

Sandel: Yes, yes. But now we've drifted from that, and the intermediate institutions are weaker, and for a century or so the drift was to the national level and a direct relationship between the individual and the nation state. This, in many respects, was terribly important because of the civil rights movement, for example. The intermediate forms of the states and localities were bastions of prejudice, and so the development of capitalism in the United States and also the struggle for civil rights worked to shift political authority, power, and responsibility to the nation and to conceive of the individual as a citizen of the nation. But that also had the effect, gradually, of diminishing the hold of intermediate sources of authority and community.

In Europe, we see now that wrestling with challenges to the nation-state from above and from below. On the one hand, there is a movement towards a larger Europe by ceding sovereignty and authority, but also a pull towards regional and local forms of political identity with language as a source of distinctiveness. There, we are beginning to see some differentiation in both directions, but I don't think any part of the world has found a solution to this.

Tu: I didn't know John Rawls very well, though I met him a few times. One thing I appreciate is your critical reflection on his project, and I find it difficult to appreciate his notion of public and private. I would consider many of the dimensions of human life that are essential for human flourishing to be extremely private.

Sandel: Yes.

Tu: For example, religion is private, the matter of the heart.

Sandel: Yes.

Tu: When I was involved in introducing the study of religion to the Faculty of the Arts and Sciences, making it not just a subject of the Divinity School, Burton Dreben represented the critique. He said, "Look, I am so much committed to my own religion. I'm a believing Jew, but that's a matter of the heart. I don't think it's doable, researchable; that is not something that needs to be discussed in a public domain." But that's one area. This whole distinction between public and private self is... Private enterprise, what does that mean? You have a multi-national corporation that is more public than even nation-states. There is the whole question of how this Confucian notion about compassion may seem, on the surface, too romantic. It is true that the situated person may, in terms of their own particular existential situation, feel more intimately related to the people who are close and emotionally more invested. Yet, the idea of commiseration or of sympathy, you can extend that in a very concrete and experiential way. You cannot ask someone who cannot feel intimately connected with someone to invest a great deal of energy and time, but you need to cultivate it. It is almost like elevating the level of concern, and then it will flow far. How far it flows depends on how you do it.

Sandel: Right.

Tu: More education can pay off, but also the underscoring of human potential for the care of others.

Sandel: Yes.

Tu: This is a very gradual process. So, one way to be human, being human in the broader sense, is to extend what you cannot bear to the area of which you can bear. The idea is that you cannot bear the suffering of those you are very close to, your children, your family, and so forth, but you sometimes can bear the suffering of a stranger somewhere because you are not emotionally connected. You can expend that very thick and contextual feeling gradually outward, then gradually your humanity will be extended, and hopefully, others will do the same so that you build up, on the surface, a kind of emotional connectedness, and each of these possesses a political implication.

What happened in China in the last thirty years or so is just the reverse. The reverse is, first of all, if you are the revolutionary, it is very important that you treat your enemy in the most absolutely harsh way because if you treat the enemy friendly, then your clear distinction between what is right and what is wrong becomes blurred. So, you begin with what you can bear, the suffering, and then you extend that. For example, if you have friends and colleagues who are not part of this party, you cut yourself from them. Gradually, you move to even your family members, even your parents. You really have to do that. It is a total reversal of the Confucian idea of extending your strong feelings toward those who are close to even strangers. You begin with the enemy and then extend that all the way. It is a total reversal, and now I think everybody is trying to recover a sense of situatedness. Of course, people begin to celebrate the importance of family relationships, and yet the structure of many such mechanisms, like community spirit and community contacts, all have already been destroyed. They try to recover that tradition and immediately face the problem of many forms of parochialism and how to move beyond them.

There is this intriguing notion about the relationship between public and private, which assumes that public spiritedness is always a positive of value. Following it, I consider myself private, vis-à-vis me and my family. If I become concerned about my family rather than just myself, this is a demonstration of public spiritedness. When my family is private, the neighborhood community is public. When the neighborhood community is private, the larger society is public. When the larger society is private, the nation is the public. When the nation is private, the international community is public. When the whole human species is private, then the much larger world involving animals and so forth is public. In that series of consecutive circles, you never move out of your private sphere. You don't give up your situatedness as an individual, with the dignity of an individual, when you become fruitfully and thickly connected with the family and so forth.

Sandel: You extend the bounds of the private as you enlarge the scope of compassion and concern.

Tu: And you even want to do it spiritually.

[Break]

Sandel: Here's my question. My account of this enlarged sense of the self that has a public significance and that gestures beyond the merely familial and so on is that it has to do with enlarging one's narrative or sense of life story and seeing one's own story in a larger narrative. It does have the effect of implicating me in the fate of the wider society with which my own life is bound up. I would be more inclined to describe this in terms of obligations of membership or solidarity, bound up with a certain narrative conception of the self as against a purely voluntary choosing self. I would see those obligations of membership as particular, but not merely individualistic, particular in the way you've just described. I would see them as flowing from a sense of identity or membership that goes with a certain narrative rather than extending the emotion or the feeling or the compassion. Though, that may be one effect that certain sentiments will have. Take patriotism as one sentiment with a certain emotional dimension, but what constitutes the obligation is a sense that I have a responsibility for those with whom I share a common life story.

Now, here is really where I have a question: am I just using different language to get at a very similar phenomenon, or is there actually a difference in the ethic here? I worry about describing this mainly in terms of compassion, feelings, or emotion for two reasons. First, I don't see compassion, feeling, and emotion as adequate for a public ethic. Second, I see that for the public ethic, I want there to be a shared narrative, a shared life story, and obligations of membership and solidarity flowing from that. I want there to be a kind of public education that cultivates and nurtures. That's why it is so similar to what's described, but to cast it in terms of compassion or feeling lacks a cognitive dimension that I think is necessary for the public ethic to sustain itself. It also lacks a kind of reflective dimension that gives a basis for critical reflection on the traditions. I worry that relying solely on compassion and feeling doesn't give the kind of critical reflective dimension, and that takes us back to the example of patriotism.

So, to go back to the example of patriotism, the deepest act of patriotism in some circumstances might be to dissent. Going back to an American example, the Vietnam War. There were those who said patriotism requires one to "Love it or leave it." Others were protesting the war. There are two ways of protesting. Anyone can protest in the name of justice. People in Sweden can protest the Vietnam War in the name of justice because the ware was unjust; however, the Americans who also protest against this injustice have a further obligation. I would say it is even an obligation of membership or patriotism to say that it is unworthy of our traditions. Americans could have a special obligation to oppose an unjust war fought in their name that even the conscientious Swede wouldn't have. Now, this patriotism is actually giving an expression of an obligation to dissent, to disagree with these certain policies for reasons that go beyond abstract justice or injustice.

Now, can compassion capture what's at stake here? I'm not sure that it would. That is where an obligation of membership of solidarity, in this example, might require it because it involves a certain telling of a life's story. Why is it unworthy of us? Well, you have to tell the story about how this is our story, our traditions, our values, in a way that requires dissent as an act of patriotism. So, here's why the language of narrative obligations, membership, solidarity, and even patriotism invite the possibility of critical reflection and dissent in a way that I worry--I may be wrong about this--that compassion, sympathy, feeling, emotion might not. Now, is my worry misplaced?

Tu: No, I don't think. I don't think so. It's a very, very critical issue. Before I respond to that, I think I'll take up a few points. I totally agree with you about these two very different senses of self. I also agree that the idea of individuality, the autonomous self, requires strenuous effort to become altruistic.

Sandel: Yes, we're both critical of that.

Tu: This is especially true if we extend the self not as an isolated individual, like an island, but the self as a center relationship, and at this center, dignity, autonomy, and independence are all very important. We can actually work from that centeredness to fight against injustice in society and the community. There's a question: if everybody is drunk, should I, as a sober person, join them or criticize them? This relates to the notion of the dignity of a person, but as relationships, these are not simply an extension. These are constitutive parts of myself.

Sandel: Constitutive, that is a good way of putting it.

Tu: Yeah. So, the idea is to have individuality on one hand and then try to be altruistic. Just don't simply reflect upon more complicated notions of this.

Sandel: Here we agree.

Tu: I think you'd probably also agree to disagree with Richard Rorty. You know, I've talked to him quite a few times. I just felt so frustrated because he had no interest in culture other than his own, and he had no appreciation for this particular, more nuanced idea of the self. He makes it very clear that you have to choose between self-realization and social service.

Sandel: Yes, we both disagree with Rorty on this.

Tu: "I'm a postmodernist ironist," this is his self-description, "and I'm committed to self-realization." That's fine. On the other hand, he feels that the market has made it. You don't learn from democracy anywhere else because we've done it. This is the best system in an empirical sense.

Sandel: An empirical sense, yes.

Tu: Okay, that's one. Then you have Levinas, who was extremely influential in terms of my own work, in terms of his notion about fidelity and care for the other. Still, I feel a little bit uneasy about this tremendous emphasis on the other as the first move in understanding who you are, that unless you care for others, you are not even your true self. Now, in the classical Confucian tradition, say in the *Analects*, learning is for the sake of the self. It means the self in terms of character building and self-realization, which sees the self as the central relationship in that learning. You don't learn for others, don't learn for your reputation, for your parents, or even for the betterment of society; you learn for your own self. But since the self is not an isolated person, the learning itself necessarily leads to human connectivity.

Sandel: Yes, I find that very appealing.

Tu: Okay. Now, I think the question raised is a fundamental question. It's not just for Confucianism, but also maybe for Buddhism as well. Buddhists ask the question. The interesting thing is this clear distinction. My understanding, say from Mencius, is there exists a clear distinction between emotions, like anger, joy, jealousy, emotions, or what we call passions, and the idea of sympathy, empathy, and compassion.

Sandel: What is the term for compassion, sympathy, and empathy put together?

Tu: It is *ceyin* 惻隱. One classic example is if you see a child about to fall into a well, you have a sense of alarm, and this is very spontaneous.

Sandel: It's spontaneous.

Tu: It's spontaneous, but it can be cultivated totally through public education.

Sandel: Now, when you say, "can be cultivated through education," how can spontaneity be cultivated?

Tu: No. That kind of spontaneous reaction itself is probably in nature.

Sandel: Yes.

Tu: But what can you cultivate is precisely the sense of having membership in the human community, this sense of obligation to the human community as a whole. The difference between human beings and the other members of the animal kingdom is precisely the ability to express ourselves in this kind of sympathetic resonance with other humans. That's something that can be cultivated as culture. A civilized person would do this, even though it's spontaneous. If it's not grown, it's just a spark of inspiration, not a defining characteristic.

Sandel: Right.

Tu: And this is true. This narrative has many dimensions. It's the narrative of the family, the narrative of the community, the narrative beyond. These different levels of narratives impose obligations understood through ritual, though not just ritual.

Sandel: Way of learning initially.

Tu: But I think the best way to understand ritual is not as a ceremonial act but as an expression of civility. Right now, people try to translate the word *liyi* 禮儀, often read as "ritual," with the broadest meaning of "civility." So first, vis-à-vis the other members of the animal kingdom, we are members of a civilized human community. Then, vis-à-vis any other countries, we are members of a group of nations. It imposes more obligations with kinds of membership solidarity. In terms of the nation, we are all part of the Chinese nation. We are all part of this Shanghai community, of the city. We're part of this locality. We're part of a school. The sense of commiseration or compassion is not just emotion. It is not an emotional attachment. It has a deep feeling, which entails a sense of connectedness and, therefore, entails membership solidarity. However, you raised one very critical point of view, which I think is absent and needs to be cultivated in the Confucian tradition. It is the alternative intelligence, in other words, a loyal opposition, which is related to your notion about critical reflection. For example, it's very difficult for the Confucians to imagine un-filial acts as positive. They've done it. There's a gap between what a father may be and what a father ought to be.

Sandel: Yes.

Tu: There's a gap because of the notion that a father should act like a father and son like a son. Fatherhood is not simply embodied in the actual thought, as in many, many examples where the fathers turn out to be very irresponsible. So, the son's obligation is to try to educate the father.

Sandel: To correct the father.

Tu: To correct the father, to right the father.

Sandel: That is the act of filial loyalty.

Tu: Absolutely.

Sandel: So, there are instances that these kinds of acts are built upon.

Tu: These are resources, though unfortunately, the politicization of the tradition, whether you see it in Singapore or China, precisely argues against that critical reflection.

Sandel: I see.

Tu: I think it's happening here. You love it, or you leave it.

Sandel: Yes.

Tu: If you're patriotic, you simply follow.

Sandel: Right, right.

Tu: But I think in America, or maybe in European societies, this critical reflectivity is very pronounced. There are just numerous cases where people become martyrs. It's attributed to Voltaire, "I don't agree with anything you say, but I will defend their rights."

Sandel: Yes. That's right.

Tu: That is to protect your right to express yourself. I think these concrete examples, especially of the Enlightenment period, helped underscore that dimension. I believe that, in the Confucian tradition, resources are there.

Sandel: The example you gave of filial loyalty requiring correction or improvement of the father…

Tu: … of the father. This is also true with the nation.

Sandel: Well, this is what I was going to ask. Has this resource, at the level of the personal example you just gave, been extended to the nation or the political level? And what does that mean?

Tu: I'll give you one concrete example, a historical example from the 15th century. When China was invaded by the steppe peoples and the emperor was captured, what was to be done? The emperor, everybody knows, is the symbol of national unity. The emperor was captured, and the defense minister said, "Look, this is a serious problem." So, in consultation with the royal family and the bureaucracy, a decision was made to establish another emperor. They nominated another emperor to say, "Look, we have an emperor." Then, they decided to fight against the invading forces. However, the enemy's leader decided to return the emperor unharmed to create an authority crisis.

Sandel: Yes, he did it on purpose to create a problem.

Tu: He did it on purpose! They then put the old emperor aside and considered the new emperor to be the real emperor, and the minister of defense was greatly honored for that act. But the old emperor launched a coup d'etat within the court to regain his power. The central issue is about this man, the defense minister. Is he disloyal to the emperor? After a major court debate, all the Confucian scholars accepted the view that he was patriotic. There's a major debate about this at the national level, and then later, they discussed the very interesting difference between the court and the state. They said we serve the state, not the court. Then, they said we serve the state, but even more, we serve the culture rather than the state. Then, they argued that the court is totally corrupt and the state is doing things against the well-being of the people as a whole, so we are identified with All Under Heaven. All these issues, whether you identify with All Under Heaven, with the state, or with the court, were debated in the 17th century or earlier. So, this is a very rich tradition.

In recent years, especially since the founding of the People's Republic, some of the rich resources are relegated to the background or can be sidelined so that any dissent is considered unpatriotic. Therefore, people worry because consensus formation is so powerful, and they worry about the lack of critical reflection. I think that you pointed out the extremely important arena. It's not enough simply to emphasize sympathy, compassion, or empathy as feelings for the construction of the kind of public sphere for debate and argument, but the idea of membership solidarity and a shared narrative, especially with continuous critical reflection on the sentiments themselves and on the critical issues confronting the nation. What acts are considered, in the long run, more beneficial to the nation as a whole? These are really crucial issues.

Sandel: It is interesting. So, you look at the resources initially in the filial case...

Tu: Then to the community.

Sandel: Mm.

Tu: So, whether you're part of a clan, an organization, or part of society, sometimes you support your community against the aggressive intent of the central government. So, you preserve your locality. This is true even in China today. The city of Beijing has criticized Peking University, but when that happens, the people of Peking University gather themselves around and say we've done the right thing. Your interference is not accepted. These are the major cities and are given local autonomy. But then, of course, the question has always been: don't be selfish; don't just protect your private interests. You have to look at the broader picture of the educational situation in China.

Sandel: Right.

Tu: These debates are going on. So, I think it's workable in terms of different domains of...I think in terms of the cultural resources. You may have a response to the question or a tentative answer.

Sandel: No, I found it very interesting. There is so much of this that I'd like to learn more about. Is there, in the recently mentioned 17th-century case that had a political significance, this idea of loyalty, but of a very critical kind? Is it a continuing theme or did it just become crowded out after the establishment of the People's Republic? Or is there a continuing tradition of this?

Tu: Very much so, but this is the whole question about the role of the intellectual. Should an intellectual be simply an integral part of the political machine, or should an intellectual always remain critical, not just in the political sense but also in the social and cultural sense, and continue to work as a feedback system? Should they be a group that can stand outside of the motives of the government itself? Of course, if you look at the situation broadly in terms of Cultural China, not only the People's Republic of China, but Hong Kong, Taiwan, Singapore, and the Chinese diaspora in Europe, Asia, Indonesia, and America, the whole question right now is about if patriotism means unity. Everybody should be considered part of the Chinese cultural unity. Patriotism means allowing the Chinese all over the place to flourish. And therefore, it's even the whole question about the two sides of the Taiwan Strait.

There is also the whole issue of minorities in China. Should the vision of being Chinese be broadly conceived to include all 55 minorities and not simply the Han Chinese? How about the Chinese Muslims? Can you be a Christian Chinese? For a while, it was believed you could not be Christian and be authentically Chinese. But now, the Christians, the Buddhists, and the Muslims define the spiritual landscape of China, and they certainly have stakes in this situation. This has been extremely fluid. Even during the thirty-seven years of Mao Zedong's rule, these issues never simply disappeared. They just continued to be voiced in different threads.

Sandel: Very interesting.

Tu: About the cultural resources you mentioned, you raised the example of Charles Taylor.

Sandel: Yes.

Tu: You also know MacIntyre?

Sandel: Yes.

Tu: You met him personally,

Sandel: I know him a little bit. I'm closer to Charles.

Tu: Who are the other contemporaries that you find, like colleagues or, let's say, intellectual comrades?

Sandel: Well, I think they would be the two major intellectual comrades.

Tu: Would there be anybody else?

Sandel: I'll give you another. This, in a way, takes us back to the Jewish tradition.

Tu: Yes.

Sandel: There is someone in Jerusalem, David Hartman. Have you ever heard or read things from him? He's trying to do for the Jewish tradition what you're doing for Confucian Humanism.

Tu: He's at Hebrew University or not?

Sandel: Well, he lectures there but has his own institute, called the Shalom Hartman Institute, in Jerusalem. For about twenty years, he has convened a summer conference on Jewish philosophy, to which a number of us have gone for a week to study Talmudic and other texts.

Tu: Oh?

Sandel: His project reminds me of your project. It is to bring a serious engagement between the Talmudic and Jewish traditions into contact with Enlightenment philosophy. Some of us who teach political philosophy and who are not trained well in Talmud, as I am not, have had the opportunity to study with him and other Talmudic scholars there.

Bringing, developing some links between the Enlightenment tradition and the Talmudic tradition to see whether there are resources within traditional Judaism for a public ethic, whether there are resources for pluralism.

Tu: I think it's really fascinating. Pluralism in Israel?

Sandel: Well, that's his hope. He's originally from Brooklyn. He was a modern Orthodox rabbi in Montreal, went to Israel, and has lived there for about thirty years. The purpose of his institute is to deal with the history of Israel and try to find common ground because, within Israel, there is a sharp split between the Orthodox, who came to be very almost fundamentalist Orthodox, and the secularists. There is very little connection between them, so he's trying to bring religion into the public sphere to draw on the Jewish tradition, but with critical interpretation, he wants to find resources for a kind of democracy and pluralism without having it be totally secular. He is trying to do the kind of thing that you're engaged in with the Confucian tradition. So, over the years, I have participated.

Tu: How many years has it been?

Sandel: We started twenty years ago. I haven't gone every summer, but we've been in touch and I've learned a great deal from him. Other people who have participated include Hillary Putnam, whom you now know; Sidney Morgenbesser from Columbia; and Michael Walzer.

Tu: Michael was there? Wow.

Sandel: Yes.

Tu: Who was that from Columbia?

Sandel: Oh, that was Sidney Morgenbesser. He's a philosopher at Columbia. One of the works that have grown out of this is Michael Walzer's. He has been spending his recent years developing two volumes called *The Jewish Political Tradition*, and it's grown out of Hartman's studies where he's had Talmud scholars assemble texts from the Talmudic tradition, and then he's had a number of us write commentaries relating those texts in the rabbinic commentary to contemporary political theory. There is a topic about justice, about community, about membership, about the common good, about the question of pluralism and so on. So, I think it'll ultimately be a three- or four-volume thing. This has grown to bring the resources of the Talmudic tradition into contemporary political philosophy.

Tu: This is so exciting.

Sandel: When you ask about other intellectual comrades, it includes that whole group, David Hartman and Michael Walzer.

Tu: You must have a lot of communication with Michael Walzer.

Sandel: Oh yes, he's a friend.

Tu: He's taught here before.

Sandel: He taught here. In fact, his last year at Harvard was my first year.

Tu: So, there's overlap.

Sandel: And he was on the hiring committee.

Tu: He hired you?

Sandel: Yes, he hired me in the first place, but we've been friends since then and participated in the Hartman Institute.

Tu: Yes.

Sandel: So that's another fruitful effort that's going on in relation to traditions trying similarly to engage the Enlightenment. Hartman's model for this is Maimonides.

Tu: Oh, yes.

Sandel: Because Maimonides had a full mastery of the Talmudic tradition but brought it into contact with Aristotle and Greek philosophy.

Tu: Yes.

Sandel: Hartman's observation is the last time this really happened, in a deep way, was back in the time of Maimonides. What Maimonides did in bringing the Jewish tradition into dialogue with Aristotle now needs to be done in bringing the Jewish tradition into dialogue with Kant and the Enlightenment. So, that's been the ambition of this project in which he's involved us.

Tu: I don't understand one thing. For years, I was very puzzled by Hilary Putnam because he was part of the Committee on the Study of Religion. We've even shared a few graduate students.

Sandel: Yes.

Tu: I don't know whether you met Gadea.

Sandel: She was very good.

Tu: Ok, so, before he [Hilary Putnam] retired, he continuously taught this course, I don't know how many times, before Judith Shklar.

Sandel: Uh, ah. I think it may have gone a little…

Tu: Maimonides, Rosenzweig.

Sandel: Yes.

Tu: Martin Buber and Levinas. Just imagine the mathematical logician, and also a very radical one in the '60s.

Sandel: Yes.

Tu: He was very radical.

Sandel: But this grew out of the Hartman conferences. In fact, each year we study Talmud in the morning and, in the afternoon, a particular thinker. Maimonides, we study all the time, but Levinas was among the texts we focused in the afternoon section.

Tu: Now, this is terrific. You know the person who actually introduced me to Levinas was Dreyfus [Hubert Lederer Dreyfus], you know the late Heideggerian scholar. He was at MIT. Then, he went to Berkeley.

Sandel: Yes.

Tu: He read my thesis and wrote, "I have to admit that it's not Heideggerian in any sense." I said, "Yes, you are right." He said, "There's someone you should read, I'll give you a book." That was Levinas, and that's how I became interested in Levinas.

Sandel: You know, sometime, I'd like to get you together with David Hartman. He's in his 70s now. Chuck [Charles Taylor] came to a few of these.

Tu: Oh, Chuck came?

Sandel: Yes.

Tu: Oh, wow.

Sandel: Mostly because he was curious about learning about the Jewish tradition, he came in early days to some of the summer events.

Tu: When you say the summer, how long did it normally last?

Sandel: It's normally a week.

Tu: Just one week?

Sandel: Yes.

Tu: I see, that's fascinating. I had something like this for many of my graduate students and also colleagues in Upstate New York in the Adirondacks. We will go there for one week—it was not as intellectually a powerhouse—and read one Confucian text.

Sandel: That's wonderful.

Tu: We did it on the *Great Learning*; we did it on the *Analects*, on Mencius, on Zhu Xi, on Wang Yangming, and on Liu Zongzhou. These scholars, for about a week, read and discussed in detail every summer. I think one week, we got stuck on the first line for about three hours.

Sandel: That's wonderful, that's the way to do it. That's very much like the Talmudic…

Tu: The Talmudic way.

Sandel: Exactly, line by line. In fact, I'd like to introduce you sometime to David Hartman. He would love to meet you and would be very interested. Sometime there will be a way to for you to visit his institute and have a kind of study of both sets of texts.

Tu: Together.

Sandel: Together, and it'd be very interesting.

Tu: I learned one thing about the Golden Rule stated in a negative voice instead of a positive voice: "Do not do onto others what you do not want them to do to you." I had a graduate student of mine who explained how Rabbi Hillel once asked his students if they could summarize the whole Talmud in the old tradition by standing on one foot. Then he said, "Do not do to others what you don't want others do to you." Then, he told them to study the Torah.

Sandel: Right, right.

Tu: You know, most Confucian and Jewish statements of the Golden Rule are in the negative, while the Christian is in the positive.

Sandel: I see.

Tu: The difference is this. In the positive assertion, you're given some authority to spread the gospel. It's my obligation to help you to understand it, because you're not exposed to true way of life. I need to do that. But in both the Jewish and the Confucian populations, it is considered as the spirit of reciprocity or the spirit of concern to realize that which is best for me may not be best for you. It's a passive observation, but it's important for inter-religious dialogue.

Sandel: Yes, very interesting.

Tu: There is a question I wanted to mention. I don't know whether this is correct, but did you single out John Stuart Mill and [Ralph Waldo] Emerson as important? I'm sure there are other important resources for civic republicanism. Is that not that right?

Sandel: Well, for liberalism.

Tu: For liberalism.

Sandel: Yes, but I'm somewhat critical of Mill.

Tu: Ok, and Emerson as well?

Sandel: As a liberal, yes.

Tu: I know John Stuart Mill, because his own personal privacy experiences, became very nervous about any kind of encroachment from the outside. But why Emerson?

Sandel: Well, Emerson is much beloved and celebrated.

Tu: Especially here.

Sandel: In the United States.

Tu: Especially here.

Sandel: Yes, and last year, it was his two-hundredth birthday. Lawrence Buell, an Emerson scholar, convened a group of us to do a panel celebrating Emerson's two-hundredth birthday anniversary. He was more than a literary figure, though. He's a quasi-religious figure for the American literary-philosophical world, and so the panel avowed just about everything about Emerson. They loved Emerson. There was a woman who's a literary scholar at Yale, Wei Chee Dimock, who'd read about everything of his. I was slightly embarrassed because they are great Emerson devotees. They love him, and here I was at the birthday party, the one who doesn't appreciate him. I was there as a kind of gentle critic of the Emersonian tradition. I see him as a source in a kind of literary-cultural way of American individualism.

Tu: Self-reliance.

Sandel: Self-reliance. Also, those who say, "No, he wasn't really an individualist," point out that he was part of the transcendentalist movement.

Tu: Absolutely.

Sandel: So, it wasn't just individual selfishness. He wasn't for selfishness, but the alternative for him, the higher spiritual reality for Emerson is transcendental universal. So, there in Emerson, as you described very well earlier in the discussion here, the spiritual life moves between individual self-reliance and the transcendental universal point of view with nothing in between.

Tu: Absolutely.

Sandel: That's why I don't celebrate Emerson, though he is terribly influential, and he's appreciated and venerated even among this group of colleagues whom I respect. So, I see him as a powerful American expression of this liberal individualist idea, including this universalist transcendental dimension that, in my mind, misses all the middle terms of the moral life or the spiritual life.

Tu: Also, there is the whole question about the lived world or life-world in terms of daily interaction, because one of the very basic assumptions in the Christian tradition is that the ultimate meaning of life ought to be realized in ordinary human existence. If you have this transcendental vision as something to aspire to without the lived concreteness, then all these levels miss out on something. Well, the reason I mention this is twofold. One is Stanley Cavell, a perfectionist.

Sandel: He loves Emerson.

Tu: Really, his description or at least an attempt to describe the good life of some kind. Second, I gave a few talks. That was quite some time ago. Often, people would come up to me and say, "Well, I don't agree with you," but then the people come and say, "Really appreciate it. This is very much what I believe in." Quite a few of them turned out to be Emersonian universalists.

Sandel: I see!

Tu: So, I said to myself, "My gosh, there ought to be something there." Now I realize you're absolutely right about this link between self-reliance on one hand and the sense of a transcendental universal spiritual life.

Sandel: Yes.

Tu: I'm not criticizing our colleagues in philosophy in general, but what has happened in America for the last thirty to forty years is that the discipline of philosophy as a profession has become so privatized. Only a few practitioners, like Church cardinals, are defining the turf. In a way, the great American tradition of public philosophy faded. At the time when I was a graduate student, the real public figures turned out to be theologians like Paul Tillich or Richard Niebuhr, sociologists like David Riesman, or economists like Kenneth Galbraith. These days, public philosophers have just disappeared.

Sandel: Yes.

Tu: They're not on national stages. Robert Bellah once told me, and maybe he was right, that the last public philosopher was John Dewey.

Sandel: Yes, I was just going to say John Dewey.

Tu: Who are some of these—not just in America—thinkers that you consider your predecessors or are standards of inspiration for the communitarian work?

Sandel: Well, the standards of inspiration for the role of public philosopher and for the content of communitarian ideas might not be the same. In the case of Dewey, you can argue that he was, to some extent, some of both. Rorty has claimed Dewey, by the way, for his version of liberalism.

Tu: Yes.

Sandel: But actually, that's a misreading of Dewey. Dewey was very concerned with creating a public, and he wrote about the eclipse of the public.

Tu: Yes.

Sandel: He thought that this was a great loss, and he was not a believer in either abstract universalism or unencumbered individual self. So, I would claim Dewey for the kind of tradition in terms of public. Well, his role as a public philosopher is…

Tu: … and also his emphasis is on the social dynamics.

Sandel: ... and the role and importance of the public domain.

Tu: Yes.

Sandel: Though, what is interesting, in retrospect, when reading Dewey, is that you could only be a public philosopher in an age when the public was fairly narrowly circumscribed and much more patient before the invention of the television. If you read what he actually wrote, he's a terrible writer. It's almost impenetrable. I wrote an essay about Dewey and made this criticism while at the same time appreciating the role he played as a public philosopher. But, as far as figures today…

Tu: Oh, just one thing with Dewey. You know he spent two years in China.

Sandel: Oh, that's right.

Tu: Including the May 4th period when, he gave an incredible lecture, and he gave a lot of talks translated by one of his best and most famous students, Hu Shi. It generated a lot of discussion on his ideas about education and so forth. Bertrand Russell also visited China.

Sandel: Right.

Tu: He and also Tagore, the Indian writer.

Sandel: Yes.

Tu: Dewey had the most impact. But in retrospect, Dewey's appreciation of either the current situation or the contemporary situation within Chinese civilization pales in comparison with Bertrand Russell's. He had a much deeper sense, and that's why when he came back, he decided to write a history of philosophy. He decided to write about Western philosophers, and he had a tremendous appreciation of Chinese and Indian cultures. Dewey's almost like a teacher. He represents the teaching civilization. I don't know how much he learned. His collected works and, later, all the lectures that he gave in China were very faithfully recorded. More than 50, 70 years later, people decided to have a portion of that be translated into English. The University of Hawaii published it. It had no impact on Dewey's scholarship in America because nobody considered any of those lectures as really significant.

Sandel: I see.

Tu: But the Chinese version turned out to be continuously important... I'm sorry [for the Dewey digression].

Sandel: No, no, no.

Tu: You mentioned Dewey and…

Sandel: If I pick a philosopher whom I admire or find inspiration from the post-war period, I'm staying with Isaiah Berlin in England. He didn't have a great impact on American philosophy, except later, in his essay "*Two Concepts of Liberty,*" he had a tremendous influence on political philosophers.

Tu: Is Isaiah the right pronunciation?

Sandel: Yes.

Tu: But in China, I don't know why, I tried to argue with because they always translate as *yisaiya* 以賽亞.

Sandel: Oh, right. But he was a major figure, and he addressed big questions that were not nearly the technical questions of the kind that preoccupy many other philosophers.

Tu: So, did you work with him?

Sandel: I didn't. He had retired by the time I was in Oxford. I heard him give a couple of talks, but I didn't study with him. I admired him for the breadth of learning.

Tu: Yeah.

Sandel: And for his willingness to engage big basic questions of political theory at a time when political theory was virtually moribund in the Anglo-American world. So, I admire those things about him. I don't agree at all with the two concepts of liberty. I don't agree with the negative, positive liberty.

Tu: Maybe a short note about the reason you don't agree with these two distinctions...

Sandel: He distinguished between the two, and then he defended negative liberty. He saw positive liberty as leading to totalitarianism.

Tu: And this relative to the background, in a way.

Sandel: Right, and so that he appreciates negative liberty, to celebrate negative liberty. It's very much in the tradition of John Stuart Mill, and it appreciates a public dimension of freedom. For Berlin, writing in the wake of Nazism and Communism, he thought the only way to protect liberty was to define it as simply the absence of obstacles to the individual and any notion of public freedom he associated with Nazism or Communism.

I think he overreacted; he drew too broad a conclusion. Of course, his worries seem right, but I think he let that completely crowd out the full understanding of the public dimension of freedom. In the tradition of John Stuart Mill and the best tradition of English liberalism, he drew a very sharp public-private distinction, which we've already discussed in relation to Mill. So, I disagree with that. Though, I admire him enormously as a person, as a public intellectual, as someone who addressed big questions that mattered in a public way, and with great learning; all of that I admire about him.

He was of an earlier generation. Of the present generation, the people I admire in this way, Charles Taylor would be and is a very great source of inspiration. Here's someone who is an accomplished philosopher who bridges Anglo-American and continental philosophy. He is not only an Anglo-American and continental philosopher, but he is also open to other traditions and other civilizations. You mentioned Dewey being a teacher. Was your teacher teaching rather than a learning philosopher? Chuck is very much the opposite. He's someone who learns as he teaches. They're connected. And so that's a lesson I hope

I learned from him. In any case, I greatly admire that openness. It is not an openness in the way of abstract toleration but the openness of engagement with other traditions.

The other thing that's so distinctive about Chuck and his work, which influenced me very much, is the openness to religious sources for political philosophy. It also goes very much against the grain of contemporary philosophy, which tends to be uninterested in religion of any kind. So that's why I have a kind of special admiration and derive a great inspiration, as well as a personal tie to him. We've also participated in ventures of this kind. We traveled to Russia together just when the Soviet Union was splitting apart to try to engage in discussions about the Russian constitution, and the Ukrainian constitution. We learned a lot through similar kinds of cultural engagements, he and I. So, he would be another one. I think in the contemporary scene, Jürgen Habermas is a public philosopher, a public intellectual within Europe of enormous standing, and I've learned a great deal from his work. It's mainly his example I admire, don't agree entirely with his work. He's still very much committed to a Kantian view.

Sandel: I admire him in the role public philosopher, and for the role he's played in Germany, which is a very unusual role. Though, I disagree with his actual Kantian view that he has, and the kind of procedural ethics, in some ways, very similar to Rawls'.

Tu: Later, maybe we can have a conversation why…

Sandel: Yes. So, I don't agree with Habermas' philosophical view, but I learned from him and admire the role that he's played as a public intellectual in Germany. He's been a kind of conscience for German intellectual life and in German public life. On issues related to the aftermath of the Holocaust, he's been very strong as a voice within Germany. And so I admire that a great deal. We talked about John Rawls. I've been a critic of his. I was a critic of his work, but I admired him as a person. In a way, is John Rawls a public philosopher? Yes and no. No, in the sense that his work is obviously written for other philosophers and scholars in law, political science, and so on. But he did take on and revived single-handedly, really revived political philosophy in the Anglo-American tradition. And that is a kind of great public achievement, even though the work itself has not been read so much by citizens generally, but it did have a great impact. So I have great admiration for him.

Tu: How about the people that contributed to your vision of the communitarianism …these are public intellectuals.

Sandel: Well. Charles Taylor and [Alasdair] MacIntyre. Another person I admire, though he's not a communitarian really, I studied a little bit with him in Oxford, is this Polish philosopher Leszek Kołakowski.

Tu: I've met him. We had a couple of meetings together. He's incredible.

Sandel: He's very, very interesting.

Tu: Right.

Sandel: And I was able to approach him when I was in Oxford to have a tutorial from him on religion and philosophy. He wasn't a main teacher of mine, but he was part of the group there, and I came to admire him very much. And I think he's a great figure of this post-war period among public intellectuals coming out of Eastern Europe. So, I would include him among the public intellectuals I admire, although I can't say he's a communitarian. He's a skeptic. He's very much a skeptic.

Tu: He's very much one.

Sandel: Although he is someone who believes religion has a private and public sphere, I suppose in that dimension, he would be…

Tu: One last question is that you are deeply concerned about civic republicanism and how to retrieve that tradition, to be sure, but also the problem we face, not just American democracy, but the negative consequences of globalization.

Sandel: Yes.

Tu: You had your debate with Thomas Friedman and all kinds of other debates on globalization …

Sandel: Yes, yes.

Tu: In the Confucian tradition, the major problem is civility because they strongly believe that even though society and law are absolutely necessary for social order and stability, but without a sense of shame or kind of ethical concerns in terms of human flourishing, without a vision of a good life, without these important spiritual resources, not only the meaning of life would be undermined, but the purpose of society would also be. I'm not talking about any ideology, but all these would be undermined.

Sandel: Yes.

Tu: I don't necessarily like the idea of Social Capital, but maybe operationally, there's something to measure so-called cultural competence, ethos, or ethical intelligence. These are non-quantifiable but absolutely necessary resources in a society. It cannot be easily tapped. If we look at a liberal tradition, the idea of the economic man as motivated by self-interest, a rational human being promoted by self-interest, trying to maximize this profit in the free market adjudicated by law. And if we look at it, such a person is certainly not a model of self-realization; it's not an example for any young people to admire. So this question, which, of course, on the surface may give the impression of being elitist, but it's a quest for excellence. It's an idea of human nature that could be perfected, and communally, we have a mission to educate the young to aspire to great ideas. And that, I think, is an integral part of civic republicanism.

Sandel: Yes, one of the central disagreements between American liberalism and the civic republican tradition is about the status of the formative project. Contemporary American liberalism is very uneasy with the idea that public life should have, as one of its purposes, the cultivation of character or the promotion of civic virtue, as the civic republican tradition asserts. For my part, I think it's a mistake to think that politics can be, or should aspire to be, neutral on questions of virtue and the good life.

DIALOGUE WITH RAIMON PANNIKAR 2004-07-03

Bio: Raimon Pannikar (1918-2010), the son of a Spanish Roman Catholic mother and a Hindu Indian father, was a Catalan-Spanish Roman Catholic priest and a proponent of interreligious dialogue. He was a professor of philosophy at the University of Madrid, and later a professor of religion at UC Santa Barbara. As a scholar and religious specialist, he infused his Catholic theology with Hinduism and Buddhism, and was a prominent proponent of inter-religious dialogue. He has written over forty books including, *The Unknown Christ of Hinduism: Toward An Ecumenical Christophany* (1981), *The Cosmotheandric Experience: Emerging Religious Consciousness* (1993), and *Cultural Disarmament: The Way of Peace* (1995).

Tu Weiming: You were in the forefront of thinking about the question of world spirituality and future directions. I think you, more than anyone else, have been extremely prophetic. When the issue is raised, what actually comes to mind?

Raimon Pannikar: The right term is pluralism and not globalization. When you understand that old word of globalization was to work as a catalyst…

Tu: Yeah, to be ecumenical.

Pannikar: …to embrace the whole. However, the movement to embrace the whole means I reduce the whole to my own small little categories, and that's problematic. Also, I wish to note that religions need transformation.

Tu: Each one of them?

Pannikar: Each one of them. In fact, during the last five thousand years religions have been either locally or culturally limited.

Tu: Right, right.

Pannikar: Without the Greek heritage, you cannot understand Christianity. Without the Indian ways of thinking, you cannot understand Hindusim, well maybe only as a caricature. What we need now is a transformation of religion, but not a disrupting of it, not a destroying of it. Here the word "spirituality" is a symbol. Consider its role in a tripartite anthropology. The body is mine; it's not your body. If my body suffers you have sympathy, but your body doesn't suffer. In the soul, we commune with something in which we agree upon; it is in this intellectual world, through our psyche, that we commune. But the spirit is the third element in the Jewish tradition, in the Christian tradition, and in the Indian tradition as well. It's something, which encompasses or "en-globes" all of us. That is our spiritual understanding. The English word allows me to articulate this with word play. Understanding is to "stand under" the spell of the things you understand. You are not under the spell of the thing that you don't understand. You comprehend it, and then you dominate it. I think that world spirituality today is in this quandary of not destroying religions, but overcoming them by discovering something, not the common grounds, not common denominator…

Tu: Not the lowest common denominator.

Pannikar: …not the lowest common denominator. You mentioned that in the local you can discover the universal. If you dig deep down into the local, you will discover something in which you had no control, but you feel that thing agrees with you. The deeper I am a Catholic, the deeper I understand the Atheist or the Chinese or whoever. That's a challenge of the world we trade in. The very word "world" is ambivalent. Is it the spirituality of the entire world? No.

Tu: I feel if we use the term "Second Axial Age," it is a much more complex situation because of the interreligious communication.

Pannikar: Absolutely.

Tu: Also, I think in the Confucian tradition, especially in Mencius, there's this idea of digging the well deeply into your own ground. If you do that, if you dig deep enough, you will reach a spring and the water will flow. At the same time that deepening self-understanding, self-knowledge, is globally significant, even though it's highly local.

Pannikar: Provided that I dig deep enough in order to understand your soul.

Tu: The fascinating thing for me, then, is the relationship between body, heart and mind, soul, and spirit. One position, that is a kind of transcendent vision, is where you move beyond the body to the soul and to the spirit. But a more complex approach—you use the word encompassing in the spiritual realm—is represented by one word which has gained a lot of currency in the modern times: embodiment.

Pannikar: Embodiment, yeah.

Tu: Now the question is a different conception of the body. The body is not given; the body is an attainment. We don't own our bodies; we become our bodies.

Pannikar: Yes, absolutely.

Tu: In that sense, Charles Long mentions about the spirituality of matter. This is the whole Chinese notion of *qi* as a vital energy: it is both material and spiritual. So, I think, you'd probably agree that the Cartesian dichotomies would have to be overcome.

Pannikar: Absolutely. I have written a couple of books now on this, like *The Cosmotheandric Experience.* The cosmotheandric intuition is comprised of "cosmos," "theos," and "anthropos." Cosmotheandric is trinitarian. We are cosmos, we are theos (divine), and we are anthropos. The anthropos here mean man not just a rational animal, but as something more. The word I have coined is cosmotheandric. Cosmos, theos, and anthros are three dimensions of reality, so God is not the God over there. That would be simply too simple. That kind of God does not exist. The idea of the Trinity in the Christian way is that God is not a substance. If God were a substance, you would have three Gods. Christianity never allowed that.

Tu: What contrasts with substance? Is it process, transformation?

Pannikar: It is relationship.

Tu: Relationality, relationship.

Pannikar: Speaking in a very orthodox Christian way, the father is father only when he fathers. Without the father, or the father being a father, there is nothingness. It's absolutely *sunyata*; it does not exist; it's not a substance. And the son is a son only when it's begotten, not before it is begotten. We have lost this kind of relational thinking. Here's something which for the Chinese tradition I think is very important. For the Greek tradition, they have harmony. It is not just intelligibility, where you cannot present two things at the same time. It is not just the elective of either or, where there's that, then that, and then you see the relation. No, the harmony is the two together, but the two together are not intelligible. You have to discover another thing, the heart, the sentiment you feel, the sense of beauty you feel, that belongs together, but without chopping it off on one side or another side. That's why I am for the harmony of religions, but not for the unification of them. My only quandary with the word "globalization" is that we tend to homogenize. That's not what you mean and not what I mean.

Tu: For a while, modernization was conceived as homogenization, as convergence, but pluralism in our sense moves beyond exclusivism without falling into inclusivism. We recognize pluralism, and pluralism involves not only the caring for the other or respect for the other, but also considering the existence of the other as constitutive parts of my self-understanding. Apparently, you have a vision of Trinity, in terms of three religions?

Pannikar: The Trinity is not monotheism. That's the Jews' word. They were not silly or unintelligent to condemn the Christ. He really was stating that in Christianity there is no God. That's why the first Christians were considered Atheists.

Tu: When you said it's not monotheistic, you are…?

Pannikar: That one God does not exist.

Tu: In this particular sense, Christology, or the Trinity, can be understood in terms of three inter-related religious perspectives.

Pannikar: Not even three.

Tu: Maybe more?

Pannikar: No. In their capacity of bringing the things to one as an intelligible single body, the three belong together, and not the one before the other and the other before the one. For that, you need to open up, to overcome your reason and open up to those spirits. That's why the great divorce in modernity is the dichotomy between love and knowledge. Knowledge without love is cut loose. Love without knowledge is empty memories. The two belong together, but not as a synthesis.

Tu: It's a primal existence?

Pannikar: Exactly.

Tu: You also mentioned, specifically, in terms of major religious traditions that they may have different perceptions or perspectives on the same primordial unity.

Pannikar: Exactly.

Tu: You also mentioned that Hinduism or Christianity and other traditions can actually be understood in the same context of this primordial.

Pannikar: Yes but understood not in the rational sense. It's an enrichment of your own perspective that I share your vision. Here again the language helps us. If I see one thing, I see one thing and you see another thing. But I can hear you say something, which the eye doesn't see, and this is hearing that you are in harmony, although I do not understand. You see, I cannot say, "I understand you that you don't understand me." But you can say, "I'm aware that you don't understand me." Not that I understand you are wrong. I understand that you don't understand me. I am not irrational, but I try to see that reason is not the ultimate instance of humanness. We are moved by something that is not just reason. Reason has veto power.

Tu: I think a kind of sympathetic resonance.

Pannikar: Yes.

Tu: I think Werner Jaeger has made the distinction between the Greek mode, which is very visual, and the Judaic mode, which is very aural. God never reveals Himself or Herself as God visually to be seen, but always as a voice or a sound. Therefore, the art of listening becomes in a sense deeper.

Pannikar: Much deeper. I don't know the Chinese word, but the Japanese word for "listening" is *kiku* 聞く. The word *kiku* according to some experts, I am not an expert in these things, can be written with three ideolograms, hearing, seeing, and heart.

Tu: It's also very revealing that the Chinese character for "sage" involves the ear and the mouth, so it's very much aural. Also, Confucius said, "At the age of forty, I had no delusions; at the age of fifty, I knew the mandate of heaven; but the at age of sixty, my ears became obedient." This means he became particularly receptive to the sounds from the outside without judgment, just receptively allowing the sounds to come in.

Pannikar: To enrich me.

Tu: To enrich me, yes. I think in that sense maybe reason had something to do with visual, with seeing.

Pannikar: Like the word "evident" which is from the Latin *videre*, to see.

Tu: Right. With the aural, it is kind of a sympathetic resonance, which relates to the idea of compassion.

Pannikar: There is a sentence of Paul the apostle: *pistis ex akoes* in Greek or *fides ex auditu* in Latin. It means "Faith comes of hearing." It does not come from seeing or learning, but from hearing. If you don't hear the inner voice, you are not a believer. You're just indoctrinated, you don't believe.

Tu: I think in the modern times everybody's overwhelmed by all kinds of sounds and overwhelmed by information…

Pannikar: Information is not an art.

Tu: …the art of listening is being undermined,

Pannikar: Totally.

Tu: …along with the face-to-face communication. Another thing that is undermined is the wisdom of the elders, after all the transmission of wisdom in indigenous traditions and other traditions was through aural perception. In China, children were often instructed by the mother about how to behave, and it was a kind of exemplary teaching. Many of the mothers were illiterate and yet culturally extremely sophisticated because of orally transmitted wisdom. If we return to the issue of future directions of world spirituality, the first word you utter is pluralism, which means the coexistence of quite a few of religious traditions.

Pannikar: Without synthesis à la Hegel.

Tu: Without synethesis. You don't use the word "fusion" either. It's not the fusion of horizons.

Pannikar: No, it's not the fusion of horizons. It's about sharing horizons. You have your horizons, and I share a little bit of your horizion.

Tu: Overlapping consensus.

Pannikar: It's certainly an overlapping consensus. That's why I make the mental distinction between faith and belief, everybody's faith. The distinction between the human being and all the other animal species is that man has faith. Animals have awareness, many other things, but not faith. Faith is existential openness to transcendence, to immanence, to mystery, to the unknown. Then because we are rational people, we try to interpret that kind of thing, that belief. Beliefs are many; faith is one.

Tu: Is faith, in this sense, shared by all religious traditions?

Pannikar: Atheists have it as well.

Tu: And that sense of faith is not faith in the radical otherness? It's a faith as a way of life?

Pannikar: Absolutely, it manifests itself into how I live. Faith is not the interpretation of faith. My interpretation and understanding of faith are a belief. Beliefs are many, contradictory. Faith is not. It belongs in another category. Is not "faith in." It is simply faith.

Tu: When you say it's not "faith in," are you assuming there's no object?

Pannikar: No object. That's idolatry.

Tu: What is the relationship between faith and the dialogical man?

Pannikar: In faith I cannot understand myself, for my attempts to understand my faith generate my belief. My belief is the conceptualization, or the interpretation rather, of what I discover. In English you cannot say the verb "faith" is "belief;" it's a grammatical imperfection. Then when I try to understand my belief, not my faith, I word it out with a belief. That's my belief.

Tu: That's reconceptualization: my understanding of faith through my own conceptualization.

Pannikar: This is, in the philosophical sense, a transcendental relationship. You cannot have faith without a belief, but my belief is my belief and not your belief. In my belief, we share. All my contingency, all my counsel, and my God tells me to express my beliefs, but I cannot express my faith. Then you said "pluralism." The very word "pluralism" is pluralistic. We cannot have one significant pluralism. Pluralism is not "right;" it's not tolerance; it's more than that. In my way of speaking, it is the awareness of our contingency. I am not absolute. I don't have even a direct connection with the absolute. The absolute overwhelms me, and then try to somehow react to it.

Here's where the more feminine attitude enters into the picture. I do not absolutize my beliefs, except in trying to enrich myself through your beliefs or to contradict you even. In this play, we teach one another. I discovered that what I did believe is not a total thing, although for me it helps. But I will not put that on you.

Tu: The link to pluralism is the awareness or the recognition that there are so many different conceptualizations of faith through beliefs. Yet, it seems faith is deeper and more mysterious. We can never fully comprehend it. So, the dialogical dialogue among the different religious traditions exists.

Pannikar: Exactly. The dialogical dialogue is among persons not among ideas. I listen to you, I try to learn from you, I try to say that you're wrong, but you as you can't be wrong. In that sense we enter into communion, which is deeper than intellectual engagement.

Tu: That personal communication, in terms of the dialogical dialogue, can that be extended to the inter-civilizational level?

Pannikar: Yes.

Tu: My sense is that between the level of personal dialogues, that happen almost on a daily basis, and the level of the so-called dialogue among civilizations there are many, many intermediary structures at the regional or the provincial levels. So, we can think in terms of future directions, we can think in a pluaralistic world that dialogue, hopefully genuine dialogue that is not just tolerance but involves recognition, mutual learning, and collaboration, continues.

Pannikar: It enriches me.

Tu: The big question there is the celebration of the order. In many religious traditions, partly because of the spirit, but also partly because of the strong sense of identity, there is the desire to say, "I enjoy so much of the bliss of my religion, and I need to share it with others." That urge to share is related to, sometimes implicitly, sometimes explicitly, the feeling that what I have is so unique that I want to share in such a way that someone, who at least on the surface, fails to take part in the sharing.

Pannikar: There's a Spanish saying that says, "*hay amores que matan*," "There are loves which kill." An overwhelming mother can suffocate her children.

Tu: Let's say it's not that common, it's not love that kills, but it's a genuine care. A genuine care is to say they are passionate, but sometimes they've destroyed the appreciation of my belief, my conceptions.

Pannikar: I would like you to share with me, but not to put it on me.

Tu: Pluralism is not relativism.

Pannikar: Absolutely not. It is relationality. I call it relativity, not relativism.

Tu: What's the difference?

Pannikar: The relativism is a value. Relativity is...

Tu: There's no judgment.

Pannikar: ...there's no judgment, and this is again a contradiction in itself. Relativity is the awareness that anything I say is related to my context, and I have a third to be my hermeneutical key. There's a third element for hermeneutics to know the text, whatever it is. You can't know the text without the context. You have to go to university and study all the aspects of context. However, the third thing is missing. A pretext. What is the pretext? That which led you to say what you say.

Tu: Pretext, is that also pre-understanding?

Pannikar: No, no, no. Pretext is entering into another level of understanding.

Tu: After context?

Pannikar: After context. I have to know you. Your pretext is the part of you that can be very noble or very bad. Your pretext can be any other thing. In order to know pretext, I have to know you as a person and not as a machine of ideas.

Tu: You use the term pretext, though pretext normally gives the sense of "before text."

Pannikar: No. That's pre-text. Pretension is more Latin than that. The pretext is that *which I pretend of, what will be the purpose*. That would be the real meaning of pretext. That's more of the old Latin word "*praetextum*." It's not "before the text," but is "the purpose I have."

Tu: To find out, to go through the contextualization of the situation and to have a better understanding of...

Pannikar: The pretext can be very psychological. I can only know the pretext if I know your intentions. In order to know your intentions, I have to know you, not what you say.

Tu: I've been thinking about how a kind of dialogical relationships involves two persons. First, there is recognition, which means the ability to recognize someone, but then through respect and mutual learning there is a mutual benefit involved. I cannot understand you if you do to want to be understood.

Pannikar: Absolutely.

Tu: There's no way there.

Pannikar: There's no way.

Tu: There has to be a two-way traffic in this. Also, the two-way traffic is not only at the behavior level or even at the belief level, but also at the level of the encountering, of the shared...

Pannikar: ...intellectual level.

Tu: Yes, but I think intellectual understanding is also embodied in the experiential understanding of this. I think if we use that as a way of thinking...Normally what we do is to abstract from the concrete and look at formless or abstract universals that we become so much obsessed with.

Pannikar: I don't know Chinese, but in the languages I do English has "thinking," and in all the Latin languages there is "*pensare*." "*Pensare*" means "to weigh beside the love of a thing that has to move to its proper place." That is "to think." To weigh how that idea wants to go to its proper place.

Tu: So, a very creative act is implicit in thinking.

Pannikar: Exactly. Absolutely.

Tu: A creative act. One thing that has always bothered me, and I have been thinking about you often in terms of this idea in regard to how different on the surface your view is from other Christian conceptions, is the notion concerning the part of a human being in reference to the Chinese word Heaven and the idea that it is omnipresent and omniscient, but not omnipotent.

Pannikar: "Ominpotent" is the wrong translation. In the Catholic creed it is "*omnia potens*," and in the tradition of the Greek it is *pantokratopa*. This refers to a kind of king or monarch who cannot do anything he likes, but has enormous power, *krato*. His strength is overwhelming. When they translated the New Testament into Latin, they used "*omnia potens*." But this doesn't mean he can do anything that he likes: he is not omnipotent.

Tu: This suggests the notion of partnership, a kind of joint effort. One notion is that the human is aesthetically attracted to creation, to the world, and that aesthetic attraction links to a particular inner purpose.

Pannikar: Because I am part of it, because it is not a foreign being,

Tu: You have a sense that you are situated in it as home. There is a very powerful Confucian thinker by the name of Zhang Zai, who said, "Heaven is my father, Earth is my mother. Even such a small creature , as I, finds intimacy in their midst." That perception is so different from the existential tradition with Heidegger's notion about, "Throw me into the world," and Sartre's notion about, "Throw me into the nation." It's a very different take on the person. I use the term anthropocosmic, but I think that the missing part...

Pannikar: ...theo. Theo-anthropocosmic.

Tu: Now, the "theo," because of Atheist that is related to the "theo" ...

Pannikar: Of course. Today, sociologically speaking, one of the most powerful religions is Atheism because most of its so-called believers have made their God an idol: a golden idol that God doesn't exist. Of course, the Christian intuition of Christ, of Jesus, is why he was condemned to suffer his fate because...

Tu: In this particular sense, with pluralism, with the dialogical dialogue, and with theological cosmological and anthropological Christian fused into one, using your terminology, the future direction of world spirituality is not synthesis. It's continuous dialogue. It's that unfolding.

Pannikar: It's an unfolding that I am not complete without you, without the unknown, without the other. You know that in Latin there are two words for "other" and in the English and vernacular languages they are confused. "The other" can be the "*alius*," the other, the foreigner, the foreign, the strange, the stranger. Or it could mean the "*alter*," as in "*altera pars*," the other side of me. The "*alter*" is the other side, unknown to me. It is the other part of me.

Tu: I need to encounter this dimension of my existence that is forever elusive, but at least for my own self-reflexivity and self-realization I need to do it. I need the presence of the other.

Pannikar: One is not there without the other: within and without.

Tu: That sense of the other is the created world or the other is the human?

Pannikar: I don't believe in creation.

Tu: You don't?

Pannikar: I believe in the Trinity, but...

Tu: ... creation, like creating something *ex nihilo*?

Pannikar: Well, no. That is evil, historically biased, because "*ex nihilo*" came out of a dialogue with Plato. Plato believed that the *demiourgos*, Deminurge, created the world out of the primal matter to explain the problem of creation, and the Deminurge "*ex nihilo*," came from nothing. But "*ex nihilo*" doesn't mean of nothing nothing comes. That's why Genesis 1:1, according to Christians, has to be completed by John 1:3. "Everything through Him has come out to be" "*ingenito*," to submerge, to be. That's why the Creator is not an appendix of God. God is intrinsically creative if we are to substantialize God.

Tu: So, creativity...

Pannikar: ...is a sharing in this unfolding of the universe.

Tu: That sense of sharing, if not diametrically opposed, is radically different from the sense of total self-sufficiency.

Pannikar: Absolutely.

Tu: If you say you are totally self-sufficient, then how does the sharing, the existence of the others, and the importance of the other for one's self-understanding work?

Pannikar: Because the other is not the other in the sense of *alius*, but in the sense of *alter,* the other side of the self. The self is not the self in contradiction to the other. We belong together. The radical unity is not unity; it's harmony. The I and the Thou. The Thou is not the other. Even the language is not the he or she. The he or she may be the other. The Thou is neither you nor he or she. It's a part of that mystery of love.

Tu: You don't use the word between.

Pannikar: Yes. There's a sentence from Luke, "The kingdom of God is *entos* (in Greek)" The more mystically oriented theology says, "The kingdom of God is within you." The newer theology of liberation says, "The kingdom of God is among you." Neither say, "The kingdom of God is between you." That is something different. Between is between she and you; between is between us. It is not within individuals, not a kind of sociological thing, but between us. There is a Japanese word for "between" that probably comes from the Chinese. What is it?

Tu: I can't recall, but the Chinese has this notion of relation as *jian* 間 that suggests space…

Pannikar: …in between. We created the between.

Tu: There's also one term I feel uneasy about. The term is complexification. That notion is to certainly produce a certainty, but complexification is meaning the relationship is still center-to-center.

Pannikar: My gut reaction is that complexification is too complicated. It implies the ideal of unity. No, to me, the given is precisely the relationship. That's the primordial thing. It's not that God was alone and then at some moment created the world. God, world, and man are coextensive.

Tu: So, the idea of partnership.

Pannikar: Exactly. Partnership.

Tu: Can human beings then be considered, in some limited sense, as co-creators?

Pannikar: As co-creators and St. Paul says this using that very word. We are co-creators.

Tu: St. Paul says this in the…?

Pannikar: In the *Epistles to the Romans.*

Tu: I see. This notion is very close to my heart.

Pannikar: We are co-creators. That's the dignity of any human being: we are of infinite value. Here is my philosophical criticism of democracy. Quantity is important but is not ultimately definitive. Five is less than six, but why should a thing of beauty be with the six and not with the five? Our ways of thinking are so quantified that we think that the majority is a technical way by deciding many things, but it has no value at all. The number, the quantity is not the quality, and the quality is not even the thing. That's why this kind of mixture of cultures will help us to overcome our limitations.

Tu: I suggest that each religious leader in every single tradition presently has to address two very different situations. One is within the faith community and uses the language that is familiar because of the books or the traditions, but the other involves a different language related to facing the universal challenges of the human condition. So, a religious leader, in some way, has to be a public intellectual.

Pannikar: He has to be. He has to be. Totally. Totally.

Tu: It is possible, in your sense, that the cosmological, theological, and anthropological vision is to think that a human being can never be fully comprehended in the anthropological context, let alone the anthropcentric context.

Pannikar: Never. I have this kind of thing about which I laugh at myself. I have been engaged in, and still am now, helping a lot of people with spiritual direction, and sometimes I find myself saying "A" to my first visitor and saying "B," just the opposite, to the other one. It has to be tailored for you. I cannot reuse one thing for the two. I can't just say, "The doctrine says that" and I repeat it here, and I repeat it there. I say one thing here and a totally different thing there, because it's relationship. You need to hear that, and the other person needs to hear just the opposite.

Tu: It's not at all a strategy. It is simply a spontaneous response. It is about appropriateness.

Pannikar: Yes, appropriateness. Which is to say the *proprium*, the specificity of yours. What in South India we call "the meeting of the eye."

Tu: That's terrific.

Let me change the subject a little bit. Do you know that you and I talked very extensively about the possibility of revitalizing the conversation on "World Spirituality: Future Directions."

Pannikar: Oh?

Tu: "World Spirituality: Future Directions." Remember we have a volume in mind, and so your active participation and leadership is very important for this. We may have to all come to Barcelona.

Pannikar: If I'm still alive.

Tu: I think it will be very nice. We want to organize it soon. You remember we did it in Honolulu. We did it earlier and it's been going on a long time. I think now that the time is right to do something.

https://www.youtube.com/watch?v=M8Oqqhqv8JU

DIALOGUE WITH HOSSEIN NASR, INCLUDING WILLIAM CHITTICK AND SACHIKO MURATA 2004-07-06

Bios: Seyyed Hossein Nasr is Professor Emeritus at George Washington University and has lectured and written on subjects such as philosophy, religion, spirituality, music, art, architecture, science, literature, civilizational dialogues, and the natural environment. Born in 1933 in Tehran, Nasr was educated in the US at MIT and Harvard in geophysics and the history of science. His early research focused on the history of Islamic science. After attaining his Ph.D., Nasr worked as a professor at Tehran University and became the president of Arya Mehr University. In 1974, the Empress of Iran, Farah Pahlavi, appointed him as the head of the Imperial Iranian Academy of Philosophy, where he held discourses with many scholars, including William Chittick and Sachiko Murata. After returning to the US, Nasr was a University Professor of Islamic Studies at George Washington. Having written over fifty books in Persian, English, French, and Arabic, his major works include *History of Islamic Philosophy*, edited with Oliver Leaman (1995), *Islamic Spirituality,* Vol. 1 & 2 (1987, 1990), *Traditional Islam in the Modern World* (1987), and *The Heart of Islam: Enduring Values for Humanity* (2002).

William Chittick is a Professor of Asian and Asian American Studies at Stony Brook University. He received his Ph.D. in Persian literature at the University of Tehran under Seyyed Hossein Nasr in 1974. His work focuses on Rumi and Ibn 'Arabi. He is known for *The Sufi Path of Love: The Spiritual Teachings of Rumi* (1983), *The Sufi Path of Knowledge: Ibn al-'Arabi's Metaphysics of Imagination* (1989), *The Vision of Islam* with Sachiko Murata (1994), and *The Sage Learning of Liu Zhi: Islamic Thought in Confucian Terms* with Sachiko Murata and Tu Weiming (2009).

Sachiko Murata 村田幸子 is a Professor of Religion and Asian studies at Stony Brook University. She received her PhD in Persian literature at the University of Tehran, where she was the first female student to study Islamic jurisprudence. Known for her work on Sufism and Chinese Islam, she has written *The Tao of Islam: A Sourcebook on Gender Relationships in Islamic Thought* (1994), *Chinese Gleams of Sufi Light: Wang Tai-yu's Great Learning of the Pure and Real and Liu Chih's Displaying the Concealment of the Real Realm*, *The Vision of Islam* with William Chittick (1994), and *The Sage Learning of Liu Zhi: Islamic Thought in Confucian Terms* with William Chittick and Tu Weiming (2009). She was a 2011 Guggenheim Fellow.

Tu Weiming: …In that period of time, the great Daoist philosophers are gone. This is Daoist religion. Daoism's religion is popular, but it's also basically the cultivation of longevity.

Seyyed Hossein-Nasr: And also, a lot of magic…

Tu: There are two traditions. One is alchemy, external alchemy, and the other is spiritual discipline, but both of them are really related to the whole question of longevity and happiness.

Hossein-Nasr: Whenever this question of alchemy is asked, and I have studied works in European languages on Daoist alchemy by Nathan Sivin and the like, I wonder if there were any Muslim writers who began using Chinese alchemy or tried to bring Islamic alchemy into a synthesis with Chinese alchemy? Nothing like that?

Tu: Not really…

Ai Bei: Oh, we had one, Zhang Chengzhi 张承志.

Tu: No, this is a contemporary phenomenon where you have a novelist from the Muslim community. He became very popular as a novelist, and also now some Muslim groups actually consider him as their prophet. This kind of prophetic voice made the government very nervous. When he traveled to parts of China, some people would follow him not as readers but as his followers. However, I am not aware of earlier examples of this fusion of Chinese and Islamic alchemy.

Hossein-Nasr: You know Wang Daiyu 王袋輿 came a thousand years after Islam arrived in China.

Ai: Really?

Hossein-Nasr: Sure, the earliest Muslims were in Guangdong in the very first Islamic century.

Tu: The first generation.

Hossein-Nasr: Yeah, the first generation in the 7th Century was almost a thousand years before.

Tu: Roughly the first century of the Islamic calendar. Buddhism came into China roughly in the 1st century, and Nestorian Christianity also arrived in the 6th or 7th century. At the time when Wang Daiyu and Liu Zhi 劉智 were alive, the Buddhist Pure Land sect was popular, and Zen was very powerful. In the works of Wang Daiyu, we can detect, in a critical sense, a conversation with the great tradition of the past that even precedes Confucius with its notion about Heaven, its notion about the creator. In contrast, the Neo-Confucius tradition, Zhu Xi in particular, is much more of a kind of naturalism. It is natural philosophy with its idea of pattern or principle, and there is no longer a personal God. The principal is the ultimate pattern for all realities. That mode of philosophizing seems to be very much in conflict with the Christian orientation. His whole project, we realize, is to undermine Neo-Confucians and try to return to earlier Confucians.

Some scholars before simply characterized Matteo Ricci as a kind of priest who tried to learn Confucian ethics and tradition and styled himself very much like a Confucius scholar as a way to persuade scholar-officials to become Catholics. More recently, a doctoral student is working on a dissertation—I'm part of her committee—with the title "The Hegemonic Mind" or something of that nature. She is from China, but she did some work on medieval Western thought, and so her Latin is very good. She studied the correspondence between Matteo Ricci and the Vatican and concluded that Matteo Ricci, in his communication with the Vatican, was very clear that he was not going to change his way in order to accommodate himself to the Chinese situation. He didn't want to totally restructure anything, instead arguing, "You've lost your own tradition, and I'm helping you to..."

However, Liu Zhi and Wang Daiyu believed that there was so much of the Confucian tradition that they really claimed as their own, and so what they accomplished was not simply to say there's something deficient, that you really have to go beyond it or get rid of it, but to show their reasoning in working out a very comprehensive philosophy of life, and also a very detailed argument about cosmology. Of course, it's a kind of anthropocosmic vision unfolding in their ideas.

Then the question is, is that enough? Some dimensions are not there. So, it's not to say you have to go back to your own tradition to get it. It is to say we have something that you don't have, though we can fully appreciate what you do have; then suggest why don't you also think about this particular dimension? So, this way of doing things is very sophisticated and very different.

Hossein-Nasr: Is there anything in the Christian Chinese writing that would correspond to this type of engagement that you want to see?

Tu: My sense is that Matteo Ricci's work was previously considered as the most sophisticated inter-religious dialog between East and West. Now with Wang Daiyu and Liu Zhi, I think scholars, at least scholars who specialize in China, will have to reconsider that decision. I just don't know why such sophisticated formulations didn't catch the imagination of the contemporary scholars.

Hossein-Nasr: Well, because he was Islamic. It is quite obvious. The other one was Christian, and most of the people who started doing scholarship in the West came from a Christian background.

Tu: No, I mean at the time they were written.

Hossein-Nasr: Oh, at the time, yes. I see.

Tu: I just imagine that someone very well-seasoned in Neo-Confucian thinking would have been extremely impressed by what's going on there. It's the unfolding of what I call the anthropocosmic vision, which is very much compatible with the Neo-Confucian mode of thinking.

Hossein-Nasr: I think there's an assertion here...

Tu: Did you see the diagrams?

William Chittick: We've shown you the diagrams.

Hossein-Nasr: Yes, they're wonderful.

Tu: How many are there altogether?

Sachiko Murata: Seventy.

Tu: Seventy. Is that very common in Islamic thought?

Chittick: No, it's not very common.

Hossein-Nasr: Not very common, but there a few examples. They aren't really many.

Chittick: Ibn Arabi has a dozen diagrams, but that is in the whole of the *Al-Futuhat*, which is an enormous work, so...

Tu: Well, we have the Korean T'oegye's *Ten Sagely Diagrams*.

Chittick: Yes, you showed me that book.

Tu: It is Michael Carlton's book. I think what we have here is the most comprehensive vision in that particular way of presentation. I don't think I've encountered another example.

Hossein-Nasr: The book that you brought out together, has that had any echo in China?

Chittick: Oh, yeah.

Tu: Is it translated in Chinese or not?

Murata: Someone in Ningxia is working on it…

Tu: They might have a major meeting sometime next year in Ningxia, which is in the central part of China. There's a major Muslim community there. I think there's a great deal of excitement.

Hossein-Nasr: People like Wang Daiyu achieve. You see the interaction, because when you have interaction, you first-off have two things there and then they interact. These people know there are Neo-Confucian texts in Chinese. They are Neo-Confucian, obviously. Now they are getting to know Wang Daiyu, and people like that. It's also important to know where this work came from. There are a few books on Islamic cosmology or Islamic metaphysics that would be very good to have these in Chinese. Maybe there are some, I don't know.

Tu: No. Right now, there is such a gap. The tradition is transmitted among Muslim communities in China. The one material they do have are called the little classics. These are teaching manuals based on the teachings of the *Quran*.

Hossein-Nasr: How about translating into Chinese the *History of Islamic Philosophy* that I wrote up with Oliver Leaman, which is now the most complete work on the history of Islamic philosophy? Or some books on cosmology? Or the two books in our series on Islamic spirituality about the Sufi orders and Islamic metaphysics? In fact, the Sufi are all over China, the Naqshbandi order, and so forth. There would be a body of knowledge in Chinese for Chinese intellectuals to know what the Islamic intellectual tradition and Sufi tradition was, and then to see how people like Wang Daiyu issued from that. You have to know that. You have to know Jami, and to know Jami you need to know Ibn Arabi, and to know Ibn Arabi you have to know early Sufism, and to know early Sufism you have to know the *Quran*. They're all connected. They are part of the same tree. That would be wonderful if that could be done.

Tu: I think there is a project. The Academy of Social Sciences, the section on religion, could do this sort of translation. I think they are now considering translating the two volumes on Islamic spirituality.

Hossein-Nasr: That would be very good because it would open up the deepest things which affected through Central Asia, the Naqshbandi order, the Qadiriyya, and so forth, and how the coming of these ideas manage to flower as the philosophy of Wang Daiyu. Was Wang Daiyu a Naqshbandi?

Murata: No.

Hossein-Nasr: No one knows?

Chittick: Nothing is known about his affiliation.

Hossein-Nasr: There must be some news.

Tu: How about you two? Nothing? No news whatsoever? How about Liu Zhi?

Chittick: No, it's just not known.

Hossein-Nasr: Unknown, but he must have a connection to it Naqshandi or...

Chittick: It could have been like the *ulama* "scholars" tradition in Iran, where there is no formal *silsila* "chain of transmission."

Hossein-Nasr: No Apostolic Church in Iran would do philosophy. It's mostly among Shi'ites. Among the Sunnis, there were people belonging to Sufi *tariqas* "orders" who are Sufis.

Chittick: No doubt they had masters. The question is, is it a named order? If we go back, yes, we might find them. But the people who do the history of the orders in China have been able to find no connection, at least so far. But so little is known. In fact, they've been taking this position that these people are *ulama* types, who don't have anything to do with

Sufism. Of course, it is nonsense because as soon as you look at the contents of their works, one cannot deny they were involved with Sufism.

Hossein-Nasr: As soon as you say they're *ulama* and they're Sufis out there, that means you're saying they must have been Shi'ite. It's the only manifestation in Islamic history like this. In the Sunni world...

Chittick: These are the typical historians I'm talking about, the typical historians who have no idea of what Sufism is and simply identify Sufism with the orders. If it's not an order, a formal order, then it's not Sufism. If they're doing *Quran* or hadith, then it must not be Sufism. It is this type of simple-minded classification of Islamic sciences.

Hossein-Nasr: A typical case is Jami himself.

Chittick: Yeah.

Hossein-Nasr: I mean these two are translating the work of Jami.

Chittick: Of course.

Hossein-Nasr: Jami we know...

Chittick: The four works translated into Chinese are all Sufi texts.

Hossein-Nasr: Sufi texts, yes. It's not accidental.

Chittick: No, no.

Tu: I think in Liu Zhi's work there is much more than simply translation or exegesis. It is also a way of presenting, very comprehensively, Liu Zhi's level of philosophical reflection, both in the context of Chinese philosophy on the one hand and in the context of Ancient and comparative philosophy on the other.

Hossein-Nasr: That sounds great.

Tu: That will be very significant and will generate interest among even younger scholars to really look. The originality and the sophistication are not clearly appreciated. The genealogy you pointed out will certainly be a scholarly enterprise, but there is a certain kind of excitement that this is original thought at its best. The next step is to move beyond simply the exegesis and translation and have people begin to do more graphic studies of these figures, as there is motivation for making some very important general statements.

Hossein-Nasr: That's really like discovering a new branch of Neo-Confucianism. It's like how there's a Latin Averroism in relation to Islamic philosophy. Averroism goes to Europe and was in another universe, but it is using the language of a very important Islamic philosopher. From the point of the pure Chinese philosophical tradition this would also be an important discovery.

Tu: Yes, very. My impression is that before the 19th century no major contribution to Islamic philosophy was done in languages other than Persian and Arabic.

Chittick: Well, Liu Zhi is 18th century. Are you excluding Liu Zhi?

Tu: No, no, no, yeah. We don't mention Liu Zhi.

Chittick: Outside of the Chinese.

Tu: Outside of the Chinese.

Chittick: There's nothing going on except in Arabic and Persian, maybe Turkish a bit, but no major contributions.

Hossein-Nasr: There are two other languages, as that period was also the beginning of Urdu. But you have to start with theology, and there are one or two treaties in Urdu.

Chittick: Yeah, but all that stuff is secondary from Persian. They translated and popularized Persian works.

Hossein-Nasr: They translated it, but it is nevertheless philosophical discourse done in Urdu. The main languages of course are Persian and Arabic.

Tu: That's by original thinkers?

Hossein-Nasr: By people who are thinkers. Yes, there is some originality. They're not completely new schools of thought, like how Neo-Confucians also have new Neo-Confucians in the same tradition with different formulations here and there. For example, there is a very important Indian-Muslim philosopher whose name is Maulana Ashraf Ali Thanvi who lived in the 19th century and into the early 20th century. Mainly a 19th century writer, he's the most important philosophical critic of Western philosophy that the Islamic world produced in the 19th century. He was an incredible writer. Of course, he wrote mostly in Persian, but also many things in Urdu. He wrote over seventy or eighty books that are very popular in India. While we're on books, I have a student of mine named Fuaad Nadin, Pakistani, who after being smothered by Bruce Lawrence has just left Duke. Bruce Lawrence said to him, "Become a deconstructionist or you have to leave." He just resigned as a student.

Chittick: Unbelievable.

Hossein-Nasr: He was going to do his PhD. Anyway, there are a few figures like that, but the main language is Arabic and Persian.

Tu: Yes. I think what we have here are very original thinkers within the Chinese tradition no matter how we compare them.

Hossein-Nasr: It's also a new branch in Islamic philosophy.

Tu: It's also a new way of thinking about the Neo-Confucian tradition. That is not something Matteo Ricci attains. By comparison, what Matteo Ricci has done, is not only not that distinctive, in fact, it's not really that sophisticated. We expect East-West dialogue at his level, but now with this group it's very...

Hossein-Nasr: I see a very important issue involved here, which you have been able to bring out. It is that only like meets the like. Ricci came from a moment in Western intellectual history in which Christian cosmology was already eclipsed, medieval cosmology was already practically gone, and pure metaphysics was very hard to come by. Whereas these people came from a tradition that had a parallel depth as the Neo-Confucians in the 13th century, and so they came prepared to be able to penetrate more profoundly into this. I think you understand what I mean. Today when some Protestant theologian who's trained in some Protestant seminary makes a study of Al-Ghazali, he simply doesn't have the depth within his own tradition to reach that depth in Al-Ghazali. There are so many studies like that.

Ricci belongs to a period of Western intellectual history during which you cannot expect the same metaphysical and intellectual depth that you would have in these Chinese Muslim thinkers who belong to a living metaphysical tradition which is parallel with that of the Chinese. That's the problem, and that's something which has to be done in comparative philosophy.

Tu: I think you're actually right. For Matteo Ricci, the contribution is simply the possibility of contact between two radically different traditions. Symptomatically, anyone who is able to do that is of significance. What we find in Liu Zhi...

Hossein-Nasr: Seventeenth and the eighteenth centuries?

Tu: Early eighteenth, right? Seventeenth is Wang Daiyu.

Murata: Early eighteenth for Liu Zhi.

Tu: The period was important to do it right. Without very rich, live, and ongoing pure metaphysical thinking as the motivating force to challenge the most original minds, neither the originality nor the brilliance of the thinking is possible. I think that kind of intersection both deeply...

[Break]

Hossein-Nasr: They deconstruct not only Western philosophical thought, but also non-Western philosophical thought, even in a comparative mode. I'm not putting too much hope in the main philosophical activity in America and England, in the Anglo-Saxon world, except for individual philosophers here and there. That's not going to change so quickly because, basically, they do not accept the reality of metaphysics. They do not think it's possible to know the real. Both Neo-Confucianism and Islamic philosophy are based on the premise it's possible to know the real. Philosophically, that's the basic fundamental issue. We have to do our own thing. There is a seminar here, seminar there; we'll see what happens to the philosophical scene in the next decade or so.

I was hoping ten years ago that as interest in non-Western philosophies increased, it would also deepen the philosophical interests in the Western in serious philosophy. It has occurred, as there are certain people like Robert Neville, your friend in BU, or a few people here and there. But in many cases, it's Foucault and Derrida, people like that, being applied to Islamic thought, Indian thought, and so on. A lot of that is going on.

Tu: Yes, you're absolutely right. The irony is this. At the time when some of the best analytical philosophers, much more sensitive analytical philosophers, begin to be very serious about questioning their own premises—look at Derrida in terms of his best in analyzing Logocentrism and so forth—these scholars in China and in Japan and other places, came up under the influence of this particular line of thinking.

One of my students, Lionel Jensen, did this book called *Manufacturing Confucius*. *Manufacturing Confucius* is precisely the result of Foucault's line of thinking, raising questions about how nothing could be asserted. Everything is always manufactured. It's a cultural production because the term Confucianism itself is misnomer. It's a great tradition, but especially in the last thirty or forty years in China the attack on this tradition became the most powerful movement. This only changed in the last twenty years, since 1980 when open reform policy began, and young scholars, when they can, do the kind of work that we try to do.

I think people can appreciate it very well now inside and outside the academy, but often for the wrong reasons. It is either for patriotic, chauvinistic reasons, or for holding on to a kind of outdated intellectual tradition. So, the people that try very hard to support you, be very suspicious of them.

Hossein-Nasr: In Classical Chinese, what term would most correspond to the philosophic notion *Sanatana Dharma* in Sanskrit, that kind of perennial wisdom? What would you use in Chinese? What will we use for wisdom?

Tu: In the name of Liu Zhi, the second word *zhi* 智 is the functional equivalent of wisdom, true wisdom.

Hossein-Nasr: And prayer wisdom? Internal wisdom?

Tu: In the Confucian tradition, the cardinal virtue is humanity; some translate it as benevolence or sympathy. The idea is that it's possible to have someone that is wise but not humane, but it's not possible to have someone who's humane but not wise.

That is your philosophy in the land of the prophet. You have a human quality, which is certainly part of the perennial wisdom, but it's not simply the power of argumentation, or the power of reason, or even the power of the Socratic dialogue, it's a kind of tacit understanding or embodying of not just the truth from outside, but the internal truth as well.

Normally, the Confucian learning is characterized "learning of humanity." The perennial wisdom is the continuous renewing of the sense of humanity.

Hossein-Nasr: How would you say that in Chinese?

Tu: *Ren* 仁.

Hossein-Nasr: What term do you use in Chinese? We offer it in classical Arabic, classical

Persian, Sanskrit, many other languages, not only in Latin.

Tu: The Hindu word is *Dharma*

Hossein-Nasr: *Sanatana Dharma*, the "Eternal *Dharma*." They use the word *Dharma* for wisdom in this context. Wisdom has always been eternal *Dharma*. *Dharma* exists in Chinese. I know that.

Tu: In modern Chinese now, they call it *yongheng de zhenli* 永恒的真理. It is the Eternal Truth.

Hossein-Nasr: What is that term?

Tu: *Yongheng de zhenli*. *Zhenli* actually means the "true principle," which means Truth. *Yongheng* means "eternal."

Hossein-Nasr: I'll have to get a transliteration of that from you.

Tu: I have to think about which one I... I don't know.

Hossein-Nasr: When Raimon Panikkar and I looked into Buddhism, who was it with? Ahmed?

Tu: Ahmed Mashal, no. I don't know.

Hossein-Nasr: Armstrong died.

Tu: Armstrong also, yes.

Hossein-Nasr: A number of them have died. It was 20 years ago. It's been such a long time. The original plan was that each of us would write an essay. Unfortunately, I did it. I spent a long, long time on that.

Tu: Mine is already published.

Hossein-Nasr: To limit yourself and discipline yourself, the anthropocosmic view that you have expressed, all of this is just brushed aside by groups who have their religion now, and they're modern at the same time. There are no constraints left. It's going to make the push back against the destructive environment much more difficult.

In the whole world, Protestant evangelical Christians are the group least interested in preserving the environment. I had a debate the other day with someone. There's at least two of these people have written three books on the idea that Christ is going to soon come, and the faithful are going to be uplifted, and everyone else is going to be destroyed. They make millions of dollars all the time, these evangelicals on television, and so forth.

These books have sold 60 million copies, and they're written exclusively about when Christ comes, and how the flesh of all non-Christians will be torn from their face, the burning of animals who try to flee, their flesh will tear apart, and bones will break. Really very, very graphic, gory descriptions, and these have sold 60 million copies in the United States, more than any other adult book. Still, they criticize the preachers in Saudi Arabia for being extreme. This is really a joke. What is going on?

When you talk to these people, they say, "Oh, you should not talk about conserving nature. God will soon take care of it. It'll be up in fire, and destroyed, and ashes, and we're going to be lifted up to Heaven." They're totally mad, totally mad. It's this form of Christianity that is spreading all over the world.

This is what happened with these churches that were blasted in Iraq. The Christians had lived in harmony with Muslims for centuries, but all these missionaries on the back of American tanks, with all the money from Texas, were trying to convert the Muslims of Iraq to Christianity. So, they were very angry at these missionaries, these illiterate idiots who don't know anything from Oklahoma or Texas or someplace like that. They offended people, but they also have the military force behind them. They have protection. So, they are firing these churches. Of course, all the Islamic religious leaders were against it, saying that it's against Islam, but the level anger is so high. This had been unprecedented. They do it, unfortunately. It's going to destroy all of Christians in Iraq, who will migrate and go. They're very worried.

Tu: That situation is…

DIALOGUE WITH EWERT COUSINS 2005-02-27

Bio: Ewert Cousins (1927-2009) was Professor of Theology at Fordham University. He was a Jesuit theologian who was an advisor to the UN on global spirituality. He was also a member of the advisory board of the Monastic Interreligious Dialogue, was co-convener of the Commission on World Spirituality and was consultant to the Pontifical Council for Interreligious Dialogue. His research focused on St. Francis, Bonaventure, world spirituality, and the Second Axial Age Period. Having worked on the Rosebud Sioux Reservation, he developed a strong interest in Native American spirituality and later also studied Hinduism. His major works include *Bonaventure: The Soul's Journey into God, the Tree of Life, the Life of St. Francis* (1978), and *Christ of the 21st Century* (1994). He also was chief editorial consultant for the 107-volume *The Classics of Western Spirituality* and was General Editor for the 25-volume *World Spirituality: An Encyclopedic History of Religious Quest.*

Ewert Cousins: You were speaking about the Second Axial Period as a possible focal point for discussion. There's a place I could begin, which would call for some flashbacks to a conference.

Tu Weiming: That was the first one of a series or just the only one?

Cousins: This was a once-in-a-lifetime conference. The Temple of Understanding had a number of conferences in Calcutta, one that Thomas Merton went to when he made his famous statement, "We are already one." They also had about three or four other conferences in the United States. All the while, Juliet Hollister, who was the foundress of the Temple of Understanding, wanted to do something at the UN. She always had connections with people. She had a very good connection with C. V. Narasihan, who was the office director for Secretary-General Kurt Waldheim. Finally, after much probing C. V. Narasihan told her that the time was right for a conference at the UN. This was unprecedented in terms of the things we were talking about because the UN was set up as a secular organization. Other than to the religious NGOs, the UN didn't have any connections with that dimension of the world's population.

Her idea was to have something at the UN in the General Assembly. That's what she wanted. That was the plan. My friend Jean Houston was working with Juliet at the time. She asked me to join the planning committee. We had about five people. I was given the task to be in touch with the office of the Secretary-General. I would meet with his spokesman once a week, and report to him about how things were going.

Henri Levain, in the great French tradition, was the person I spoke to. He was not only the public spokesman of the Secretary-General, but he was also the one who went on troubleshooting missions around the world. He was completely absorbed in that dynamic. I just fell in love with UN right away, with these people I met. I'm a reincarnated diplomat, I think, because I just loved it. I learned a lot about the structure of the UN. That was the context.

Eventually, the conference was held for five days at St. John's Cathedral in New York. Then for one afternoon, on the premises of the UN, we wanted the General Assembly, but we lost it. We wanted conference room number four, but we lost conference room number four. There was always tension from the Russians and the Chinese because the Chinese had just come in.

I'm not going to repeat all this, but that was the context. It was at this conference that thirty major figures in Native American culture in the United States appeared on the first day. I got word that there are thirty Indians here. What do we do with them? For the whole week there were tensions, including the Native Americans, people from the other petitions, and this was getting resolved in various ways. It was in that context that my understanding of the Second Axial Period emerged.

Tu: I remember. I attended one meeting at the event.

Cousins: That was later.

Tu: Oh, yes. That was in the '80s.

Cousins: That was in the '80s.

Cousins: This was in '75. We started putting together that package for the world spirituality project at that time in the '80s. Then I realized that because we had quite a resource in the editors, and we could do it twice at the UN. I remember when you came...

Tu: So, they're talking about the first one in 1975...

Cousins: This is '75, almost 10 years earlier. But for me, that was the real crystallization period of whatever ideas I have now. It was there that it crystallized. What I was suggesting is that one part of the narrative would be to begin at that spot and do a few flashbacks to my own experience with it, with the Native Americans, and then how that played into what was going on in this big conference for the UN. Does that make sense?

Tu: Sure.

Cousins: But tell me what you think.

Tu: Well, I think the central issue is really the possibility, at least the imagined possibility, of the Second Axial Age. What is the meaning of it?

Cousins: Yes. Well, that's where it emerged from, because I was dealing with both the indigenous people and with the Axial Age religions. I was just floating around in a context of the secular institution of the UN. That's where it all came together.

Tu: The intriguing thing for me is that the Axial Age civilization, that notion as developed by Karl Jaspers, was very much out of the Greek tradition of reflection. He's, of course, much broader than just that. Another issue that the Chinese are particularly interested in is this question from Max Weber. Max Weber's definition of modernity in terms of rationality is quite different, on the surface, from Karl Jaspers' notion about the possibility of the confluence or communication of different kind of Axial Age civilizations. But Max Weber became an important interpreter of modernization because of Talcott Parsons's introduction of Max Weber to the American scene, and he translated *The Protestant Ethic and the Spirit of Capitalism*. That became a key book for understanding modernization. The Max Weber that most people knew in the United States in the '60s and '70s was the Max Weber as interpreted by Talcott Parsons, who wanted to formulate a general interpretation of modernization.

For 10 years in the '80s, some German scholars, Schlukta in particular, wanted to recapture the foments of Max Weber's conception of human civilization by identifying Max Weber as a comparativist because he did work in early Christianity and Judaism. He wanted to work on Islam. He didn't have a chance to do it. He certainly did a lot of extensive work on China, basically Confucianism and some Daoism.

He was also interested in exploring Hinduism and so forth. In other words, the German attempt is what they call the de-Parsons-izing. In a way, there was some kind of implicit conversation between Weber and Karl Jaspers. I think your way of conceptualizing this Second Axial Age may be, in terms of the initial stage, very much inspired by Karl Jaspers.

Cousins: That's true, and it deals with consciousness itself.

Tu: I think your own approach is not just Jaspers, because you're involved him with many others...

Cousins: What came through to me in Jaspers was his reading of the crystallization of the major cultures of the world in that time frame in which he was researching. It meshed perfectly with what I was doing at the UN, or at least I thought so. Yet, it went beyond the framework of Karl Jaspers and got into indigenous people. That was the way I went, partially because I already knew the indigenous people. I was always interested in how they fit in. The other reason was very practical. Here we had all these people coming from around the world—we flew in a hundred people to do a Japanese ritual. This was in this big cathedral, the biggest Gothic cathedral in the world, and all that's going on. It was something. I won't get into all the details of that.

Then right on the first day, somebody said, "There's a bunch of Indians." That's how they said it. They said, "You better go over and see them, because they have concerns." I already knew some of them personally. I knew the others, most of them. We had the *crème de la crème* of the Native American population in the United States right there. They weren't just a token Indians. They were the heavy-duty stuff. Then for a whole week one of the major concerns—was the only one orchestrating it—was to work out a rapprochement with the indigenous people who had a very clear task to bring their vision of the world to this forum at the United Nations.

I was the one, or at least I was a major figure, in saying that you can't do that. I had to say that because I had been working with the office of the Secretary-General, that's through Henri Levain, for eight months on delicate negotiations. Who's going to speak with Hinduism, who's going to speak with...We tried our best to get someone to speak for Chinese religion. At that time, we just didn't know enough. If I had known you...well we didn't connect. Henri Levain went out of his way, but it just couldn't happen. We didn't have a Chinese presence there because almost anything we'd do Mainland China wouldn't accept.

They had just got into the United Nations. The point was it just was impractical. Pretty much at the last minute, we had to leave them out. We had the other representatives. It was all symbolic: one person for Hinduism, one person for Buddhism, and what not. Then the Native Americans wanted to be in on it. I was the key person negotiating with them and telling them it was impossible and so forth. We put them on the stage and made a lot of...They didn't riot. That was one of the main concerns about this whole thing. They seemed happy about it.

That's the way the thing unfolded. What was going on in my mind all the while was a picture of the history of the human race from indigenous times through the great civilizations, and right into the middle of modernity. That's what was going on in my mind. That might give you a sense.

Tu: The one substantive issue is the cultural, spiritual resources you had already accumulated when you encountered them, not that they suddenly opened your eyes to a different dimension.

Cousins: You mean the indigenous people?

Tu: The indigenous people.

Cousins: That went all the way back to what we talked on before about my activities on the Sioux reservation. I already had that. That's why I was interested in inviting them. When that matter came up, I knew that I could invite at least one of the Sioux because I had connections with them. We did, and he was on a panel. Then the first day of the conference, we had thirty-five of the leaders of the Native Americans from the United States. It was wonderful. I was very happy about it. Then we had to solve a lot of diplomatic problems. That's the story.

What I was trying to say is that what led me then to have a deeper understanding of the role of indigenous people in the history of culture was that the United States was a locus for this kind of encounter, especially at the UN. It was there that my understanding went beyond the Axial Period. I knew that Jaspers didn't deal with indigenous people, at least significantly, and you had to deal with them because here they were. That was my sense. I had the greatest admiration for them, from my own contact with them.

It was during that week that these things fitted together. That's when I came up with my own idea of the Second Axial Period. My understanding was that the Second Axial Period was involved with a recovery or an awakening of the Axial Age religions to what was before them, which Jaspers never did. I thought too, when I formulated the Second Axial Period notion, that it was the indigenous people who were bearers of wisdom that the world needed very much. That's exactly what they thought about themselves at the time. That's why they were coming to the UN, doing dances all around the country, and everything. To be heard.

There was always a prophecy, and you probably know about. It was a Hopi prophecy. The Hopis are great prophetic, conscious people. There's a Hopi prophecy that the Native Americans would be invited to come to a house made of mica. They would give a message to the world. They've been trying to do this. When they met in 2000 at the UN, there was a big meeting. You were there for that. They were still interested in getting this message out. You were maybe there in the evening when all of them were gathered on the stage, from all around, from arctic, and whatnot. Up came Oren Lyons, who is a leader. He's Iroquois. There must have been on stage that evening about 100 or 150 of them.

They had this sense of urgency, of a message for the human community. Usually the prophecies are very dire, that if they don't measure up, then things are going to go bad. This was a major element in my understanding of the Second Axial Period. It was that these people are still around. I used to check with Robert Muller and get data on them. He said he thought there were at least 300 million on Earth. He may have data on that. They're growing. That seems to be the case. They're past that point of just disappearing. Not only that, but they have a voice, and they carry their wisdom, their forms of consciousness that we don't have; the whole package that goes with that.

My understanding of the Second Axial Period was that the clock had not ticked too much to make them disappear. At this point when the whole human race is threatened with ecological disaster and so forth, there needs to be some voice in the human community that really involves a transformation of consciousness. That's the essence of my understanding of the Second Axial Period, that consciousness is capable of retrieving what has slipped into unconsciousness, and that this can be evoked in some way.

I sometimes like to use the notion that the indigenous people are the prophets and the catalysts, simply because they have the consciousness. I thought that the Axial Age civilizations really just did not have that consciousness, all the way back to 800 BCE. I just thought that they just didn't have it. My understanding of the Second Axial Period was...Well, I did think that this consciousness, although we're not conscious of it, is somehow within us. It's not completely unavailable. Also, the feeling is that if crises are so great, then these latent dimensions of consciousness can come to the fore, and there will be this witness, and so forth. There was a small group of people on Earth who retained a form of consciousness that the whole human race needed at this time.

They're constantly going to meetings to spread their message and whatnot, and they do attract a number of people into their community in different ways. I'm always hearing about this, all around the world. Anyway, that was my understanding of the Second Axial Period.

Tu: In the '70s and up to this day, maybe under the influence of Axial Age civilizations but I think rather more under the influence of one particular Axial Age civilization that in the last 300 years crossed the Atlantic, the mentality is simply that human history progressed from religion to metaphysics to science. In the area of science, where even metaphysics is relegated to the background, religion certainly is not only going to be very insignificant, but it also may be considered as an archaic mode of thinking. That is very strong. That is still going strong, the notion about modernization as rationalization.

A distinctive feature of rationalization is secularization. In a secularized world, all these other dimensions of human experience would not be as significant as economy, politics, social science, and so forth. I think we also have to accept the fact that all the major institutions that we serve on, the various kinds of organizations connected with universities and research institutions, all of them, including some universities very much devoted to theology, including Fordham, could all be considered as part of this movement of enlightenment rationalization.

In this particular context, I know a few people that were particularly sensitive to cultural legacy, much more than simply the evolution of instrumental rationality to science and technology. You also know Mircea Eliade.

Cousins: Yes, I know him personally, a little.

Tu: I think he counts certainly because of the emphasis on the archaic man inherent in the human experience, and I figure in perennial philosophy, for example...

Cousins: By the way, Richard Paine and I went to visit him and asked him if he would be the editor of the indigenous volumes in the series. He said he was busy with that big publishing project for MacMillan, *The Encyclopedia of Religion*. He said, "But I suggest Chuck Lawman to you."

Tu: He was at Chicago.

Cousins: Yes, he was at Chicago. I must say that Chuck was a good man for it, but, on the other hand, he wasn't. We had lots of problems with Chuck. I wanted to bring out the first two volumes, but that was another whole story on account of Chuck.

Tu: Also, Raimond Panikkar. I don't know when you first met him.

Cousins: I met him in 1960. I've known him for all these years.

Tu: Maybe we will talk a little bit about him too. How about Huston Smith? You know him?

Cousins: I know him very well, too. I'm the one who brought him in because I thought he ought to be in the project, but he didn't qualify to be an editor. That's an interesting thing. I think our norms are so strict, and appropriately so. In fact, I sometimes say that when they got conferences together if they could find a Hindu down the street, they would get him. But we didn't have a slot for Huston. I asked him to come to the first conference at Fordham because I thought he was a major figure.

Tu: Would you consider yourself as a perennial philosopher in that sense, or no?

Cousins: Well, there's a whole group of perennial people. No, not in that sense, but I think I accept what they're doing. The reason why he didn't fit into a real slot in our structure was that he was a Westerner. Our editors had to be from the tradition. Granted that he didn't quite fit, but he was a major figure. That's what I thought. He's a wonderful person. I always got him in whenever I could. I just asked him to come.

Tu: Returning to that notion about your sense of the Second Axial Age civilization or Axial Age Period, the ethos is basically totally against it because of secularization, rationalization. Now we mentioned a few people, you must know a number of other people you could consider as your conversation partners.

Cousins: There are a lot of people who might be writing for the different volumes, but I didn't make that choice because the editors made that choice. It's safe to say Nasr would be a good case in point because he certainly is a global figure. Also, he had established that center in Teheran. That was a major phenomenon, as far as I could tell. I never did get to it but used to hear about it. First, Richard and I got him to be involved with the Islamic volumes in *The Classics of Western Spirituality*.

It was just one step over when we put together the world spirituality package just to keep him there because he was global. Because of his Sufi connections, he was not completely universally part of the Islamic world, but, on the other hand, he was not so Sufi that people wouldn't take him seriously.

I thought it was OK to go with Nasr in that case because we were dealing with spirituality and the Sufi tradition, and they wrote that. He did an excellent job editing certain segments on Islamic material. I thought he fit it in well. Besides, he's the first one to give the Gifford lectures.

Tu: He's probably the first non-Western philosopher to be included in the living philosophy series.

Cousins: When that meeting was held at the end of the 1990s in Boston, the International Philosophy Conference, he was in the newspaper. I don't know if you remember, there were about five people. I don't think were you there? I can't remember. I don't think so. But Nasr was there, and Nasr represented all of the classical traditions of Islam and everything else; all that he stands for. None of the other people had anything like it. They looked like these poor little people who thought they were great, but they had no tradition.

Tu: Oh, you mean talking about the panel on the living philosophers?

Cousins: Yeah. Do you remember that?

Tu: Sure. Sure.

Cousins: Nasr was the only one who represented anything that hadn't been thought of maybe in the last 200 years, in one way or another. It doesn't faze him. He just goes ahead and does his thing, and he has a lot of support from the traditional school. The traditional school is a special thing, you know the people in the school, and, of course, Huston Smith is part of that. You have a lot of crossovers from these different places, but I thought the names you've mentioned right now were very appropriate for our purposes in the world of spiritualities because of what they have to teach. All of them would fit in.

Tu: Your sense on secular spirituality?

Cousins: We have a volume on secular spirituality, and it's already published. You were one of the people who kept Nasr going. Remember that time we had a discussion. Nasr was not happy about having that volume in the series, but Richard and I thought it ought to be there. It was so funny because I asked you to speak out of your background and you had that dialogue with him. I remember that well. As a matter of fact, he was convinced that we ought to have that. You saved the volume.

Tu: You've heard indigenous people's prophecy, but do you consider them as prophets?

Cousins: Yes, I do. I think they're prophets for our time if that's what you mean?

Tu: Yes. I think the questions in the ethos of secularity is that ever since Thomas Kunhs' notion about human progress, and Karl Marx, Max Weber, and the modernists, all these scholars assume that the situation is very different. I'm sure you're critically aware that your position itself, and mine included, is very much of a minority position.

Cousins: Oh, yeah. That's right. Yeah.

Tu: Is Teilhard de Chardin one of the most important inspirational sources for you?

Cousins: Yes, he is, and I think he breaks through the impasse. That was one of the reasons I think I was attracted to him. In fact, when I read *The Phenomenon of Man*, which was in the late '50s, I had an interesting reaction. I was really very much excited and moved by his total view of evolution, etc. I said the thing that I like most about it is that he opened up a space for the Native Americans and the indigenous people. Teilhard is not famous for his knowledge of indigenous peoples, accepting their bones and studying their cultures, but to this day, I'm not puzzled by that connection I made. I think it was authentic, but it was intuitive at the moment. I wasn't able to put it into a package.

When I'm now looking back at Teilhard and all of indigenous in my life, between reading *Phenomenon* and the present, I would say that that was a valid insight. Teilhard's whole going back to origins of human consciousness really had a continuity that moved forward. I tend to think too that the human mind has capacities that flow over, you might say, some of the particular perceptions that you just described, secularity and society and so forth. In other words, I think there's more to human consciousness than those secularizing trends. That's just my general perception.

There's another reason that I have been involved in researching states of consciousness. I don't know if I've talked to you about that. Do you know Jean Houston?

Tu: Mm-hmm.

Cousins: I think she's a pioneer in doing research in consciousness. There are layers of consciousness that she explores, and I was a subject for that research.

Tu: A subject in what sense?

Cousins: She would explore my going to different states of consciousness. Other people, too. She found out that I was an apt subject for that. For about fifteen to twenty years, I was involved in that research.

Tu: Is the research a psychoanalytical one or...?

Cousins: Well, it is. Modern psychoanalysis is encountered in that. I guess you'd have to put it together with Freud, Jung, and what is called transpersonal psychology that developed from the time of William James to the beginning of the '60s when people started doing more research with LSD at Harvard and MIT.

Tu: Timothy Leary.

Cousins: Yeah. Huston Smith was involved in that, too. As a matter of fact, I always thought that that research at MIT and Harvard was bizarre. I was just getting into another part of that research, which is what Jean Houston did. She published the first book on that, *The Varieties of Psychedelic Experience*, but then she gave up using drugs because you don't really have to have drugs to do this kind of research. In fact, it's probably better not to. At any rate, that I found it very helpful. I thought it was exciting and so forth. Also, I think it gave me a sense of the dimensions of the psyche that really resonated with a lot of indigenous peoples, not just myself. Actually, I'd say that I love modernity and I think it's a marvelous achievement, but I think it doesn't touch all of the levels of the psyche.

That's why I'm inclined to feel that when we were doing the kind of work, we did in the World Spirituality Series that it wouldn't be right to filter these other predictions through the modernity lens, because there seems to be "More in heaven and earth than dreamt in you philosophy," that line from "Hamlet. I just had a sense of the scope of human, not only individual, but collective consciousness. Much of my sense of optimism, and I feel that I'm an optimist, really has to do with those capacities, those vast capacities. Also, I feel eternally indebted to indigenous people because they've opened up so much for me.

I really did feel that at the time of the conference at the UN, that this is something I could do to return the gift, in a sense, that they gave to me. That's why I was really strongly motivated to give them an appropriate place. Anyway, this is a sketch of the landscape, the way I look upon these things. I think I do embrace modernity, but I don't believe that some of the forms of modernity with their limitations to consciousness are broad enough and deep enough to sustain the power of consciousness. In other words, I think that consciousness is just so powerful.

Now, I have a lot of funny statements that say, "You can't keep a good psyche down. It's going to come back." "Be careful of what you try to throw away because it's going to come back in your dreams." It really is part of you. You see, part of my understandings of where we are as a global community is that we are at a number of impasses right now, and also on the edge of big transformations, social transformation, all kinds of transformations, building a global community.

I tend to say one of the big problems of global community is the nation state, because it's a nation state, it's a problem. How do you resolve it? Like I said, when there's only one nation state, then you have a global community. These are just brainstorming things, but I think we're at impasses like that. Usually, at great impasses, everything's about to explode and maybe it's OK for everything to be about to explode because of the latent resources of the human being. I think at that meeting we had it was marvelous to have those Black Africans there. Really. I think that was a big jump forward. Anyway, I'm just brainstorming here.

Tu: If the Axial Age civilizations themselves were in a way instrumental in marginalizing the archaic, primal, or indigenous consciousness, and let's assume that that's the case, then this means human civilization, as Karl Jaspers and people like him understand it, is a form of forgetfulness. I think you used the term.

Cousins: I have used that term, yes.

Tu: So, the distinctive feature of the Second Axial Age is an attempt to retrieve...

Cousins: Not so much an "attempt," because I think consciousness operates out of the bounds of consciousness. You know what I mean?

Tu: Mm-hmm.

Cousins: I think it has happened without our knowledge, in some sense. Anyway, that's a particular, specific aspect, but I agree that's a formulation of what I hold.

Tu: Consciousness without self-consciousness.

Cousins: Yes. In other words, we are talking not so much about consciousness as unconscious. I'm so used to that in psychoanalysis and so forth. I think creative people don't always operate from consciousness, but they know how to orchestrate and bring to the surface these deeper levels. I think that's probably true for the greatest intellectuals. I'm so curious about consciousness, as you might gather, and it has been a major focus of my attention. It's not easy to talk about all of this.

Tu: One way of getting at it is to identify specific features of Axial Age consciousness that advanced way beyond the earlier ones. Certainly irrationality, self-consciousness, reflexivity or...

Cousins: What I find interesting is—and this is not just intuitive—that after many years of researching the levels of consciousness, I think that the human capacity in the realm of consciousness is more layered and much richer than our everyday consciousness. We have these capacities. However, I certainly have the highest respect for modernity because I think it's a permanent achievement of the human race.

Tu: Can you say that achievement is the outcome of the Axial Age?

Cousins: Yes, that's the position I've held. There are different ways of looking at it, but I think I know the issue you're raising. I thought that modernity was a peak, in a certain perspective, of the Axial Age civilizations. It wasn't going to come any other way except through what Karl Jaspers calls the Axial Age Period, because without that you couldn't have modernity.

Tu: That I understand, but I think the more intriguing question is whether modernity, as it emerged out of the Axial Age consciousness, was a natural and inevitable outcome, or a very strange kind of development. In other words, that it was something nobody really anticipated.

Cousins: My response, and it's not simply facetious, is all of the above because I think that's how consciousness works. You have individual and collective consciousness. It tends to go through people who are creative in their approach and others who are more rational in approach. They operate in different ways. There are always geniuses around who represent these several different modalities. I guess that one of the characteristics of my understanding of the human capacity is just a great admiration for indigenous people. They're somehow bearers of forms of consciousness that have existed in human consciousness going back to the caves of Lascaux. These things do not die; they are somehow always available. They may emerge in a great burst of creative energy like modernity.

Tu: If we focus on that form of modernity, we are both beneficiaries and also victims.

Cousins: We're the victims, yeah.

Tu: The question is that if we consider the Axial Age civilizations in a differentiated way, consider it in terms of the whole spirituality thing, then the rise of modernity is an expression of human consciousness, and that expression may be the outcome of something totally beyond human understanding. Historians are now deeply involved in the whole debate on whether this involved all the other civilizations. For example, Robert Bellah addressed this in his earlier work on the religious orientation, but I think he changed his mind.

Cousins: Yeah, I didn't realize it. I didn't know him particularly well.

Tu: The question is if, of all the Axial Age civilizations, only one managed to move from the historical period to the pre-modern and then from the pre-modern to the modern. This is not just the view of Dr. Bellah, but it's also of Talcott Parsons, Max Weber, and many others. But the question from your point of view concerns why Christianity or Western civilization may have been the last one to go through this process.

Cousins: Well, I think that Islam was last.

Tu: Islam is last?

Cousins: Yeah, historically.

Tu: The question is about how modernity has been characterized as the outcome of what was earlier called Westernization.

Cousins: I know they say that, but I was never completely convinced.

Tu: How would you perceive modernity in the context of the consciousness within the axial civilizations?

Cousins: I have great respect for India. Most of my research is involved with India, so when I suggested that last evening I had more of an agenda than I expressed. I said I think it would be good to have someone from India in our project, and I suggested a person I know, the last *maharaja* for Kashmir.

Tu: Karan Singh?

Cousins: Karan, yeah. He's a major statesman; you probably know some of his career. I said that because I think that we ought to have India and its heritage present in our enterprise. That's all I was thinking.

Tu: I totally agree.

Cousins: There is no problem with that? I'm not being outrageous?

Tu: No.

Cousins: My point was that my immersion in India is something that still makes me think that India, in the way I'm presenting it now, has maybe the broadest kind of consciousness that the human race has ever had. The kind of consciousness that someone like Karan has. He was at the UN event. He's very learned, etc. He is a very good politician, in the good sense, and very creative. I think he represents a dimension. I'd hardly call it modernity. In a certain sense, it is modernity, etc., but not in the sense that we are talking about. Somehow his scope, and I think it's somewhat characteristic of the Indian version of the original Axial Age, somehow can deal with dimensions of consciousness in a rich way.

I really have had a great affinity for Hinduism. The more I get to do studies and work with people, I'm constantly aware of the scope of consciousness that seems to be available in some way. Now, it didn't emerge in a way to produce modernity as we know it in the West. I'm saying that the Western emergence of consciousness is a unique phenomenon. It shares in some of it, the modes of thinking of the Hindu tradition.

Now, why didn't the Hindu tradition have that breakthrough with its modernity aspect? It's an interesting thing to speculate on. Certainly, if you were to have a little gathering here of some of the great thinkers of India, even in spite of the burden of colonialism, which it suffered and profited from a great deal, they now have their own identity. That's one of the reasons I suggested Karan, because his consciousness is interesting.

Tu: You mentioned that Indian consciousness is particularly comprehensive.

Cousins: The Hindu

Tu: The Hindu, right. The Western mode is exceptional; it's unique. What actually happened is that uniqueness of the Western mode, we sometimes talked about Western exceptionalism, historically become the most dominating, the most powerful.

Cousins: Again, in that modality I understand it. Yes, I think we're getting to a point of clarity. I think that consciousness is much vaster than Western modernity acknowledges. You could say, "What are these other dimensions?" You can just say the spiritual consciousness of India or the particular consciousness of indigenous people. You want to put them on a showcase or something. I would feel that they're all wonderful because I have this sense of the exploration of consciousness. Also, I feel that any time that a major breakthrough comes in consciousness, it's available throughout all history. It's a little hard to justify that.

Tu: It would take the Western case. It's a form of breakthrough.

Cousins: I think it's a breakthrough.

Tu: Many people say that that's the only one that broke through the historical mode and moved into the pre-modern and modern.

Cousins: You can say that, but that's not too meaningful for me. It's clear that they left things behind. Here's a funny thing I say, "You can't keep a good psyche down. You can't throw away what you leave behind. It's going to grab you." I think we see that going on in the world. You want to say, "What goes on in the world now?" Some of the most bizarre things have emerged when you're talking about politics and administration. It's a little hard to sort all of that out.

What I mean is that even breakthroughs aren't purely positive and have a general gift to give to the present and the future—like modernity—these breakthroughs of consciousness, they're so powerful and so energizing that they engulf the people who are the bearers of it. These people may lose other dimensions of consciousness, may lose contact with other dimensions of consciousness that they already had. I think that's a tradeoff. My basic understanding of consciousness is this silly statement, "You can't keep consciousness down." It keeps coming back and back and back again, even though the Axial Age people just forgot their whole past. There's no difference, as far as I know.

DIALOGUE WITH IOANNA KUÇURADI 2009-09-17

Bio: İoanna Kuçuradi was born in Istanbul, Turkey in 1936 and is of Greek (Rûm) descent. She studied philosophy at Istanbul University, from where she graduated with a B.A. degree in 1959 and earned a Ph.D. degree at the same university in 1965. Kuçuradi worked as an assistant professor at her alma mater and Atatürk University in Erzurum, and she was founder and head of the Department of Philosophy at Hacettepe University where she also taught as professor of Philosophy. From 1997 to 2005, Kuçuradi was founding director of the Centre for Research and Application of the Philosophy of Human Rights at Hacettepe University. She is also holder of a UNESCO Chair of Philosophy since 1998. Since 2006, Kuçuradi has taught philosophy and acts as director of the Centre for Research and Application of Human Rights at Maltepe University. She is a founding member and eventual president of the Philosophical Society of Turkey and has been the president of the World Philosophical Federation, the International Institute of Philosophy, and the International Federation of Philosophical Societies. She is the author and editor of many books including *Ethics and World Problems* (2016), *Human Rights: Concepts and Problems* (2013), and *The Concept of Knowledge: The Ankara Seminar* (1995). She has received many honors, including Goethe-Medaille, UNESCO Aristotle Medaille, and the Council of Secular Humanism's Planetary Humanist Philosopher's Award.

Professor Tu Weiming: It is your idea that if philosophical knowledge is sufficient in clarifying many of the conceptualizations of ideas, then the work of the human rights movement will be greatly enhanced and the various problems of human rights will be much clearer, even though they express themselves in different cultural traditions differently.

Professor Ioanna Kuçuradi: This is one of the conditions, but not the only one.

Tu: Not the only one. This is the philosophical test.

Kuçuradi: Yes, and it's also very important for practice. Now, I think, for the protection of human rights three things are very important. One is the sincere will, and this is mostly missing.

Tu: It has something to do with attitude and belief.

Kuçuradi: Yes, attitude and also, I think knowledge helps in the formation of this will. This is why a kind of education in human rights is very important. The third one is to be able to make right evaluations about the situations in order to find what one has to do in the existing conditions for the protection of human rights. This is where I think we can solve the problem of cultures. In different cultures and in different conditions we have to do different things to protect human rights. This is not that because human rights are different here and there. Human rights are always the same. We must have the clear concept of each right and in general what are human rights. This is not clearest in their minds because in the international instruments there are rights that are to me not basic rights.

They are rights, but not basic rights. This makes for confusion and is one of the reasons that leads people to say that in different cultures they are different. This is not the only one. Of course, there are the separate ones like political reasons, when people you say, "No, it's not in our culture." But I very severely oppose that. Human rights bring demands for a special treatment of all human beings. So, if you say that it doesn't belong in our culture, then you don't consider yourself as human beings. It's for every human being. You are a human being; I am a human being; he's a human being.

Tu: Not at least the idea of civilized human being.

Kuçuradi: No, not even a civilized human being.

Tu: Just a human being.

Kuçuradi: Just a human being.

Tu: There's a debate now concerning the instruments used for promoting human rights, say from the United States or from Western Europe, and how they put a lot of emphasis on political rights, freedom of speech…

Kuçuradi: Now, according to my criteria that I developed, economic, social, and political rights are not basic rights.

Tu: Not basic rights?

Kuçuradi: Not basic rights. However, there's a difference because the right to education is included in government, social, and economic rights, but education is more fundamentally a basic right. The right to work is a basic right, but the right to have syndicate is not a basic right.

Tu: The right to have syndicate?

Kuçuradi: Yes. It's a social right. It's a way to protect some rights in the existing conditions. This is a social right. Social, economic, and political rights are rights through which we can protect basic human rights. This depends on the way limits are drawn to the citizens. It's important how these limits are drawn. If they are drawn by taking into consideration their implications for all the citizens of the country, then they protect these rights. Otherwise, if these limits are delineated by other determinants, mostly group interests, then they don't protect human rights, and there is a gap between basic rights and social or economic rights.

Tu: In addition to education, what are some of the other basic rights?

Kuçuradi: Education, health, and freedom. There are two different kinds of them: the right to education, the right to health, the right to food, the right to basic standard of living, and, of course, the right to life. Then there are ones like freedom of thought and freedom of opinion. These are basic rights.

Tu: Normally, the first set, not education, but right to life, right to food, right to maybe clean water…

Kuçuradi: They are included.

Tu: How are different kinds of rights like the right to education and the right to freedom related? China argues that right to life and right to food are things that we've done in only seven years. More than 400 million people were lifted out of abject poverty, so they've said, "We've done a lot." On the other hand, their attention to not only right of thought and right of speech, but also right of religion are not…

Kuçuradi: I don't think the right to speech, if it's separated from the freedom of thought or freedom of opinion, is a right.

Tu: How about assembly? Right of assembly?

Kuçuradi: The right of assembling is something at the borderline between individual rights and collective rights. It's an assembly that requires a group, so it's not directly a right like the others.

Tu: So, the basic rights are rights related to the individual, or the dignity and economy of the individual.

Kuçuradi: Yes. Group rights, in my classification, are not basic rights, but they are very important when there are implications of basic rights of individuals in existing conditions. They are interests. It's very easy to confuse interests and rights. Group rights are not basic rights, but implications of basic rights. One of them is the so-called cultural rights. It's a very confusing concept. The right to culture is something different; it's an individual right. But cultural rights are group rights. We have to be very careful. Group rights are important. Using the mother tongue is an important group right.

Tu: What about the question of privacy, privacy of my diaries? Is that basic?

Kuçuradi: It is basic, but there are problems. In Germany, I was asked about this. They wanted to know if when someone is beating his wife should the police enter or not? We had such a case in Turkey where there was someone killing his mother, or his sister, and the police didn't go in. If they had gone in, people could have lived.

Tu: So, this is violation of human rights because life has been threatened?

Kuçuradi: Yes. I also say human rights should not be taken by heart or understood by heart.

Tu: It's based on rationality, or rational calculation?

Kuçuradi: No. It's based on right evaluation of the situation, and, of course, the will to protect rights and no other intentions. But if I were a policeman, I would go in. The law does not prevent this, but people don't know even the law. They confuse things. Police may in this situation enter the house. It is not against the right of privacy.

Tu: Right. What is the distinction between ethics or cultural morals and basic human rights?

Kuçuradi: Let's describe the first distinction of culture and morals. What I call cultural morals are the value judgments and empirical norms prevailing in a group.

Tu: Specific to that group?

Kuçuradi: Specific to that group, but changing, of course.

Tu: Of course. It's fluid.

Kuçuradi: The problem is that now we have the so-called multi-cultural society, and in the same place we find different cultures living together. There are different value judgments developed to protect the order of this group. If they were deduced with sagacity, they play an important role in our social life. They emerge from the condition where they are deduced, but when the conditions change…

Tu: Your understanding in application of rights will have to adjust.

Kuçuradi: They no longer have a base. But people say, "It's our culture," and they try to keep them going. In the meanwhile, there are new norms on the same issue, new approaches to the same issue, and clashes come from this. So, I say they are norms of empirical origin. If we see how a cultural value judgment is formed and how it changes in time, we see that they have an empirical origin. They are usually deduced by a kind of induction.

Tu: Yes, yes. Now, if you look at the situation between migrant workers from Turkey and the people of Germany, the migrant workers have been bringing a different set of cultural values, but the Germans would like to protect an order. The Germans, for some time, had this outmoded idea that ethnicity was the most important criteria. This means a Turk who has lived in Germany for ten or twenty years will still not be considered a German, or if someone in Russia has German origin, they would still be considered a German. Yet right now they are opening up, and society is changing very rapidly in Germany, in France, and in England because the population of these societies now include other ethnicities. In Germany, it is about 80 million, and in France, Italy, and England it's something like 50 million. So, the situation is changing very dramatically. For a long, long time, the conception that the criteria and basic values in the West...

Kuçuradi: Basic values, or basic value judgments? We have to be very careful to distinguish them.

Tu: Yeah, basic value judgments from the West are voluntarily accepted by a number of societies as universal.

Kuçuradi: They are not universal.

Tu: That's my question.

Kuçuradi: Cultural morals and norms are not universal.

Tu: I know. But the truth of the matter is that these values, local knowledge, or local values, have become globally significant.

Kuçuradi: For example, which ones do you mean?

Tu: Some the basic ones, like the idea of liberty, or the idea of due process of law, or the idea of Enlightenment rationality...

Kuçuradi: What is rationality?

Tu: There are many forms of rationality now.

Kuçuradi: Then if we speak of rationality, we come to the result that there are many rationalities. I'm strongly against this debate.

Tu: You are against...?

Kuçuradi: I have a paper on it, "Rationality and Rationalities."

Tu: I see. What about Habermas' notion about communicative rationality? Would you consider that as a variation of rationality?

Kuçuradi: What is rationality? What do we mean by rationality? It is the opposite of metaphysics in the popular sense, and this is the trouble. Metaphysical-rational, metaphysical-rational, we have to overcome this duality.

Tu: Let's say that empirical science, either as way of deduction or as way of reduction, is a rational discourse that is very different from the romantic notions or the so-called Oriental mysticism. There is this very strong sense in the West that science has a unique position, and there's no way you can do science without a certain kind of rational procedure. Would you consider this as a specific case that is universalizable?

Kuçuradi: No. This is the positivistic approach to science.

Tu: I agree with you on that.

Kuçuradi: What is important is knowledge, and we have not only scientific knowledge. Philosophical knowledge is also knowledge, as is everyday knowledge. But what is knowledge? Knowledge is every proposition that has an object independent of the person who puts it forth. So, we have different kinds of knowledge.

Tu: So, there's always an empirical and objective side to knowledge.

Kuçuradi: Knowledge is objective, but what I mean by "object" is not an ontological object, but relations.

Tu: Sure, sure. I don't know whether this make sense or not, but I make a distinction between private and personal.

Kuçuradi: Private and personal?

Tu: You know we have Michael Polanyi's notion about personal knowledge or the tacit dimension. The private is something I don't want to share with anyone, and I hope the public would protect my privacy, but the personal is something about which I feel very strongly, a kind of existential commitment. I want my personal beliefs, my personal sense of the importance of something, to be debated and to be discussed. So, they are also transparent. Using the rather awkward expression, they are "embodied knowledge." The personal is experiential knowledge.

Kuçuradi: Now we have to be very careful in using the words. I would never use the word "belief" for knowledge. Knowledge is not a belief. Although pragmatism and neopositivism take this unit of knowledge as belief, this is mistaken because belief is personal. My beliefs go with me to the tomb.

Tu: The distinction I try to make is that although belief as something personally felt is not rational, it's still debatable or arguable.

Kuçuradi: Beliefs should not be debatable.

Tu: It's just a commitment which is dogma.

Kuçuradi: But so far as I can see, there are two kinds of belief. One includes those beliefs that create their object, and another involves the beliefs where we believe in the truth of a proposition. This proposition maybe true, maybe false, maybe absurd, but for the believer it makes no difference. Belief can be belief in the truth of a proposition, but this is by coincidence.

Tu: Yes. The first kind of belief that creates its own object is different from the second one. The second one is religious belief?

Kuçuradi: Religious belief is mostly the second one. But let's say for Muhammad his belief is the first one.

Tu: The first one?

Kuçuradi: Yes, they create their object, and then the other believers take their beliefs and say, "Muhammad is the seal," "Jesus is the Truth," or "Confucius is…," or whatever.

Tu: Both of them will not be classified under the category of rationality?

Kuçuradi: I don't like the word "rationality." What is rationality? I don't use the word rationality. I can speak to how people understand rationality, which is as the opposite of metaphysics. Personally, I don't use the word rational *ever*.

Tu: Do you use anything as a functional equivalent?

Kuçuradi: I say "knowledge." Knowledge is very important because if it's knowledge, directly or indirectly you can justify it. It's not easy to justify a proposition of this or the past. It's not easy. It's difficult. But theoretically, it's verifiable.

Tu: So, it's also falsifiable?

Kuçuradi: Also falsifiable, of course. Verifiable and falsifiable.

Tu: Do you make a distinction, in this sense, between knowledge and wisdom?

Kuçuradi: Yes, yes, yes.

Tu: Can we say that you cannot simply reduce wisdom to knowledge, just as you cannot reduce knowledge to simply information or data?

Kuçuradi: Wisdom is a personal characteristic. There are wise people, and this specific characteristic they have is what we call wisdom. Knowledge is something different; knowledge is propositions.

Tu: Can we say a person who is considered wise is not necessarily very knowledgeable?

Kuçuradi: In which sense?

Tu: For example, a guru, or a sage. I think in the Confucian tradition there is a distinction: you really don't have to have a lot of knowledge because knowledge itself is…

Kuçuradi: Just a moment. We have to have a clear concept of knowledge. Knowledge is not information.

Tu: Certainly not.

Kuçuradi: You don't need much knowledge to have learned a lot of things, but knowledge is something that is gained through direct contact with the object.

Tu: Will you say that internalization of values in the Aristotelian sense of virtue ethics is a form of moral knowledge?

Kuçuradi: No, it's philosophical knowledge. To know justice or to know any virtue is philosophical knowledge, but to become virtuous is something different. Knowledge is very important in this respect because if you don't know, then you are not aware of what wisdom is. There is a very important Aristotelian notion: *phronesis*. It's an intellectual virtue; in fact, it's not an ethical virtue. If you don't have knowledge, then you do things by chance. But in the case of the examples you gave of the sages, they have an empirical knowledge, which is gathered over time as they reflect on things. Still, it's difficult to be consistent, but if you are aware and you have the knowledge of this, you can also be consistent.

Tu: In the Confucian tradition, the ultimate meaning of life is not only realizable but ought to be realized in ordinary human existence. Each and every human being is aware of something that is not virtue ethics in the strict sense. Mencius argues a position that life requires empathy or sympathy or an ability to know or will.

Kuçuradi: This is practical wisdom, which is important for life.

Tu: Yeah, but these forms of practical reason…

Kuçuradi: Wisdom.

Tu: Wisdom. Can these forms be understood as naturally and necessarily human? Or do they have to be learned?

Kuçuradi: They have to be learned and they have to be evaluated. Before we try to spread them, they have to be evaluated philosophically because this sort of wisdom can be a human virtue, but it also can be a value judgment related to the times. We cannot take for granted that the sages or prophets conveyed timeless wisdom, though they did say some very important things.

Tu: They have to be evaluated and based upon the empirical situation. In this particular sense, the philosophical knowledge about human rights is pre-condition.

Kuçuradi: No, no, it's not a pre-condition. I say that human rights are ethical principles, but all ethical principles are not human rights.

Tu: Sure, sure.

Kuçuradi: There are many, many questions now, especially the confusion of ethical questions and human rights questions, like in bioethics now. Every question is not a question of human rights.

Tu: Sure, I agree.

Kuçuradi: The opposite is true because ethics is the basis of human rights.

Tu: Sure. Ethics covers a much larger range than human rights, which is very specific.

Kuçuradi: They are not specific. What do you mean by specific?

Tu: There's a realm that we considered human rights, including basic rights, and other forms of rights.

Kuçuradi: When I say human rights, I mean only basic rights. Not the other rights.

Tu: OK, right. The ethical realm is much larger than basic human rights. I agree with you that if you focus on the basic rights, then the possibility of global or universal ethics can be established. It's not universal ethics in the general sense of the term. It's very specific to the basic human rights, but these basic human rights, as they express themselves in different cultural traditions…

Kuçuradi: No! They shouldn't express themselves in different traditions.

Tu: No, no, no. I agree with you. I think they are universalizable, and they are…

Kuçuradi: No. We have to be clear on the concept of universal. Universal is used to mean that something is varied everywhere, but this is wrong. I say that for human rights, and for all practical principles, universality means they bring demands for every human being.

Tu: Yeah, but you agree with them…

Kuçuradi: Whether they are enforced or not everywhere.

Tu: Yeah, but you are basically in agreement with that position, right? You mentioned that you feel a little bit uneasy about Hans Küng's approach to human rights.

Kuçuradi: Yes, yes. Not human rights, ethics.

Tu: Universal ethics, yeah.

Kuçuradi: I said that with the first principles. For me, ethical life is based on knowledge and not on norms. Norms can help us, including human rights, when we are not able to make right evaluations in a given situation. They increase the probability to protect value, but it's not absolute. The important thing is to be able to evaluate the situation correctly, and then do what should be done so that values are protected or at least not damaged. It's not easy. Still, human rights are important for public life and for legislation.

Tu: And order, social order.

Kuçuradi: Yes. The order has to be based on human rights, but for personal relation with others, ethics is important. I don't understand ethics to be sets of norms. Ethical knowledge is very important. Ethical norms can help in the case of all professional ethics; they can help to protect value when we do not have sufficient knowledge of a situation, but they don't guarantee it.

Tu: Sure. Because our knowledge about particular subjects can be deepened, can be broadened, and sometimes considered as ethical…

Kuçuradi: But for legislation, it's important to take them as a basis. However, in given situations, one has to be very careful to make right evaluations. Otherwise, why do we want human rights? In order to protect value and human beings.

Tu: Yes.

Kuçuradi: If we, by using the rights, don't do that, then why use them?

Tu: Sure. You actually have a lot of reservation about the idea, which is not just Confucian but also Jewish, "Do not do to others what you do not want others do to you" …

Kuçuradi: Yes, the so-called called Golden Rule.

Tu: No, the golden rule is normally understood as, "Do to others, what you want others to do to you."

Kuçuradi: Yes.

Tu: But the Confucian...

Kuçuradi: "Don't do."

Tu: Yeah. But you have some reservations about that.

Kuçuradi: I have great reservations that it should be considered the most important ethical principle because it's a typical example of a hypothetical imperative, to use Kantian language. It's easy to understand each other with this Kantian term. "If you want this, do that," or "if you don't want this, don't do that." So, it's not a categorical imperative. There is going to be a workshop where I will speak on "human dignity," and I plan to start with a story of how I was once on a live television program. At that time, the journalist who I was speaking with said, "Professor, you made a connection between philosophy and torture." I was shocked, and said, "There is no connection between philosophy and torture, but when you look at the fact of torture with philosophical and ethical knowledge you see the following. People think that the tortured person is degraded, but I say 'No, the degraded one is the person who tortures.'" In all ethical relations, we protect our human dignity by what we are doing, not by what we suffer. Even the title of the convention is "Declaration Against Inhumane Degrading Treatment," which suggests torture is considered to be a degrading treatment. "No," I say, "degrading for those who torture, not for the tortured." In all ethical relations what is important to say is, "I don't do that." We had this summer camp for children on human rights, and we called it "I Don't Do That" in Turkish. This is why a kind of human rights education is very important.

Tu: Sure. So, "I don't do that" is specifically "I don't do that to someone or to animal too."

Kuçuradi: Not to an animal. In general, if I use my vote, it's not against someone, but just against an action of mine.

Tu: Wow, that's terrific. Now I think it's very critical when understanding your own style of reasoning to identify your philosophical resources, and it seems Kant is extremely important. What are some of the other great minds, philosophically, that inform your own philosophy and how you do philosophy?

Kuçuradi: Kant is very important, but he is not sufficient for me. I start my own ethics with a saying on "good will" that comes from Camus' *The Plague,* "La bonne volonté peut faire autant de dégâts que la méchanceté, si elle n'est pas éclairee." Goodwill can cause as much damage as ill-will if it's not enlightened."

[break in recording]

Tu: The whole Buddhist tradition is based upon compassion, which is a form of sympathy, and another tradition that I'm…

Kuçuradi: Sympathy and compassion are the same word etymologically.

Professor Tu Weiming:

Sure. For example, right now there is this declaration of compassion, that's a declaration of human rights. Now, in practical terms, your sympathetic responses to the people very close to you are often more intense than your sympathetic responses to strangers, and the idea is that you really need to extend the sympathetic responses beyond just those to your parents or to your children. Without this expansion, that sympathy suffocates and becomes totally constrained. The extension of sympathy involves an ever-expanding network of people, and that's commonly considered an important ethical evaluation of the human.

Kuçuradi: It's normal to start from our nearest people, and then go to the world. This is important. Yet, we have to be very careful not to confuse this wisdom with philosophical knowledge just because it has an epistemic basis, this attitude to care for people around you, and then for your compatriots, and then for the whole world. It's very important. But why can we justify it? It's not because it's said by a Saint or by a wise man.

Tu: Because it's common experience.

Kuçuradi: No, it's because we can evaluate it and see why it's important. It's not sufficient that it is said by someone who we admire. We have to justify it.

Tu: More recently, first in French and now in many languages, Pierre Hadot writes about philosophy as a way of life, and the subtitle of his book is "Spiritual Exercises from Socrates to Michel Foucault."

Kuçuradi: It's not philosophy; it's a way of life based on philosophy. People confuse worldviews with philosophical knowledge, and I'm strictly against that. Worldviews are not philosophy, though they are important. Some of them are important, but perhaps not all of them. Still, we are not to consider them philosophy.

Tu: If you look at the evolution of philosophical thinking as it has changed since the 19th century and into the 20th century, there's a professionalization of philosophy among the people who are themselves philosophers or teachers of philosophers. This professionalization helps to establish standards, especially in the analytical school.

Kuçuradi: The analytical school is a very narrow school.

Tu: Yes, OK. Of course, you also have phenomenology.

Kuçuradi: It's very important up to a point; they try to analyze concepts. It's good, but it's not the aim of philosophy. It is a tool.

Tu: Yes, yes. But what is your view about professionalization? We say they are philosophers or sociologists. My sense is that in all the other disciplines they have their own criteria, and they do their job well, but if philosophy turned out to be a profession, the reflexivity of the philosopher in understanding his own work must continue. So, I agree with you that analytical tools are significant, but will you consider continental philosophical thinking, phenomenology and so forth, as a much more appropriate way of trying to use the tools, and to think philosophically about everything?

Kuçuradi: Phenomenology, of course there are different branches for phenomenology, is important because of its attention to the object. From this side it's important, but not from every side. The analytical school uses the dichotomy that something is either science or its metaphysics, and its starting point is propositions and not the objects. So, it's good, but we should never forget why we do sciences and why we do philosophy. It is for a better world, for a better life, for a more humane life. We must never forget that. A philosopher is one who brings new knowledge in this area; it's not a profession like the others. If you are a teacher of philosophy, this is a profession. But a philosopher is the person who brings new knowledge.

Tu: What is your evaluation of contemporary philosophical thinking like Nietzsche. Nietzsche has become a very powerful resource for the people who consider themselves deconstructionist. Or what is the evaluation of Heidegger?

Kuçuradi: I do not have a good relationship with Heidegger, but Nietzsche is very important and very easy to misunderstand. I have a book on Nietzsche; I read the whole work. The Schlecht edition, I read everything.

Tu: You know Walter Kaufmann? He's done the translation.

Kuçuradi: Walter Kaufmann uses somewhat of a psychoanalytical approach. He [Neitzsche] is a dangerous thinker. You must be careful in distinguishing who makes him speak. I distinguish between three types in Nietzsche, and you also can find contradictions. He's very important, but you have to know him as a whole because he's not a systematical writer. You have to systematize his ideas…

Tu: What are the three aspects?

Kuçuradi: He speaks of, the so called, *Die Herde*, the "mass man."

Tu: The over-man or the super-man.

Kuçuradi: No, no, the mass-man. Then he speaks of another type, who tries to become free from the morals of the society of his time. Some manage to do that, but they stay until the end of their life either protesting permanently or becoming ascetics. The third type becomes the *übermensch*: the creative person in any area.

Tu: What is the difference between the master-man and the so-called over-man or super-man?

Kuçuradi: He enumerates the characteristics of the super-man. He's creative, and in *Thus Spoke Zarathustra* he has a very nice metaphor to explain this: "I'll speak to you of three metamorphoses of the mind. How the mind, or the human person, becomes a camel, how he's become a lion, and then a child."

Tu: I see. Thank you very much. I've taken a lot of your time.

https://www.youtube.com/watch?v=H2WI77WaFAg

DIALOGUE WITH SAMUEL LEE 2009-11-17

Bio: Samuel Lee is the Secretary-General of the Korean National Commission for UNESCO. He received his Ph.D. in Social Science at the University of Gottingen, Germany, and taught philosophy at Soong Sil University in Korea for over 20 years. After returning from Harvard University Divinity School, where he was a visiting scholar, Samuel Lee was appointed the first Director of the Asia-Pacific Centre of Education for International Understanding (APCEIU), where he remained from 2000 to 2004. During that period, he created the annual teacher training programs for education for international understanding in the Asia-Pacific region. He is a Presidential Commission on Sustainable Development member in the Republic of Korea. Having once worked as a Central and Executive Committee member of the World Council of Churches, he is also recognized as a leader in Korean Christian society. He has authored several books, including *Philosophical Thoughts on Jurgen Habermas* and *Philosophy of Peace and Praxis of Unification.*

Professor Tu Weiming: Professor Lee, I understand you're interested in Asian values, but as far as I know, you're one of the most cosmopolitan philosophers because you spent 15 years in Germany. Also, I'd characterize you as a public intellectual because you're politically concerned, socially engaged, and very culturally sensitive here and abroad to student protests. You've also held very important positions in promoting the study of philosophy. I was greatly honored to participate in the World Congress of Philosophy in 2008, organized by you and your colleagues, where the congress was held in Asia for the first time since 1900. Obviously, even if philosophy is not an Asian term, there is a profound interest in it in Asia. The question of Asian values was debated in the '80s with Japan and the so-called four little dragons, but now you are revitalizing that discussion with a view toward the future. I'd like to know a little bit about this.

Professor Samuel Lee: Yes, Professor Tu Weiming. I'm very pleased and honored to meet you. Both of us have been executive members of FISP (Fédération Internationale des Sociétés de Philosophie). We are both East Asians who have a good dialogue with Western philosophers, as well as African and Latin American philosophers.

Tu: Yes.

Lee: They're talking about intercultural dialogue very much. I think understanding other cultures is important, but to have efficient dialogues with other cultures, one must know one's own culture first. As for Asians, we have had many good Asian traditions of philosophy and values, but we are very lost concerning what our identities are as we have suffered very much under the Westerners' influence and colonialism. We have had quite an inferiority complex as a result. However, in the '80s and '90s, especially in East Asian countries like Singapore, Taiwan, South Korea, and Hong Kong, which achieved some industrialization and economic development, people began to talk about Asian values in relation to industrialization and economic development. In the 1990s, I remember you coming to Korea to talk about the revival of Confucianism and discuss Asian values in relation to Confucian democracy or even Confucian capitalism.

But after 1997-98, when the Asian financial crisis came again, these Asian values were devalued. They were very much blamed for this so-called cruelty, for the corruption and failures of the rest of the societies, so for some time, we did not talk much about Asian values. Nowadays, I again find in Korea the revitalization of these discussions and not just in relation to democracy or capitalistic economy. Asian countries, including China, following industrialization and competition with Western countries, are faced with a kind of crisis both economic, environmental, and social. So, we need to find a real alternative value system to overcome this kind of crisis. So, why not take our Asian philosophies and values from some Daoistic or Buddhist sources, some naturalistic ideologies, or some spiritual thoughts? We have enough resources, but they have not been understood that well or interpreted well. Now, we have to discover these resources once again. In this regard, Professor Tu, you have done a lot, and I know you are still doing much digging into these resources.

Tu: Well, thank you. I think for a long time, ever since the May 4th generation of 1919—of course, it was March 1st in Korea—there has been a concerted effort to try to learn from the West to strengthen East Asia, mainly in terms of wealth and power, and that process continues even today. For a long time, the overall concern was how we could modernize. This means how can we learn from advanced industry societies like the United States and the European countries?

Now I think a new horizon, a new issue is arising. We've learned from the West, but when we begin to tap our own cultural resources, as you've pointed out, we must ask whether these cultural resources will only be mobilized to emulate the West. In other words, these cultural resources are judged in terms of their values only in reference to the utility of the modernizing process defined in the Western terms of wealth and power. China, for example, has been successful economically since the reforms of the opening-up period thirty years ago, so its voice, China's voice, has been heard. But what is the cultural identity? Is the cultural element simply an imitation of some important ideas from the West, or can the identity develop into a certain kind of fusion between so-called Asian values and Western values?

I will simply say that universal values should be understood as originating geographically in some specific areas. Some values, such as human rights, have deep roots in Western civilization, but the local cultures have become globally significant. At the same time, some Asian values, such as compassion and sympathy, were originally rooted in Buddhism or Confucianism, and now they have also become globally significant. So, a new challenge for us is probably the dialogue between core values on an equal basis, sharing ideas rather than, say, an asymmetrical situation, which is just learning from the West to gain their confidence in us.

Lee: Asians, especially East Asians, have come through the modernization and democratization process. Learning from the Western and European model of democracy, we have been seriously criticizing our traditions and customs. Of course, we've had to overcome our feudalism, traditional authoritarian rule, suppression of women, and many kinds of irrational and undemocratic remnants of traditions that still remain in our society.

Tu: Absolutely

Lee: So, through this modernization and Westernization process, we already have a critical view of our traditional values, especially Confucianism, as Confucianism has ruled over our countries. In Korea, for at least 600 years during the Joseon Dynasty, Confucianism was the state religion that suppressed Buddhism, Daoism, and Shamanism and fought against Christian and Catholic missions, which were completely crushed under this Confucian rule. In some sense, it was quite a reactionary ideology.

Tu: Absolutely intolerant.

Lee: Yes. Still, in our intellectual discussions, many say that we have to overcome the rituals and customs of Confucianism. Some even say, "Confucianism must die to make our people and country live." These are very provocative words, though still some are very much in agreement with Confucian ideas. The question is, have we really, rightfully understood our traditional values? That is the question. There have been many, many distortions. Under political rulers, the ideologies have often been negative. Even the Christian countries and the Christian religion have been very reactionary and very suppressive, but there are also many positive values that we have to respect in Christianity. In this regard, it was not very fair to completely devaluate our traditional values. In this regard, you have done much to recover these lost values of Asian traditions and philosophies. So, what is your reflection now? You have been at Harvard teaching Westerners and Americans for a long time about these Chinese and Asian values. I hope you can continue, but I want to learn more from your experiences.

Tu: Well, I think of all the East Asian countries (China, Korea, Japan, Vietnam)—not forgetting the Chinese Diaspora traced all over the world, the Korean Diaspora (cultural Korea), the Japanese Diaspora—Korea or cultural Korea can be considered the most Confucian of all societies. There's no question about it. It's Korea.

I first visited Korea in 1967, and I met Professor Yee Sangen. I was getting a collection of the complete works of Yulgok, and that is when I began to read Yulgok. Then I visited Korea in 1978 at the International Society of T'oegye Studies invitation. Ever since then, I've been back to Korea many more times. My study of Korean Confucianism, especially Yulgok and T'oegye, was absolutely critical to my understanding of Confucian history because Korean Confucianism is significantly different from Confucianism in China or Japan. I also think that the development of Confucianism in Korea is the most thought-provoking step in understanding the modern transformation of Confucianism. Again, the first conference on "Confucian Ethics and the Modernization of East Asia" was held in Pusan. Professor Yee Sangen actually organized it, and it was even before the so called "Hakone" conference in Japan.

There's no question about the fact that people can critically embrace the negative features of Confucianism: lack of transparency, a sort of collusion between the government and companies, nepotism, factional strife, authoritarian mechanisms of control, and the domination of the male over the female. But I think that, ever since the late 19th century, Confucian scholars in China, Korea, and Japan began to reflect critically on their own traditions. They used criteria from the West—liberty, rationality, equality, due process of law, rights, running ideas, science, and technology, these great Western values—to transform Confucian theories and practices to adapt to new situations. Korea has done a great deal in doing that. There are very powerful moral sentiments among the Koreans to establish Korea as an independent, autonomous, and forward-looking country vis-à-vis the colonialism and imperialism of the West and, more seriously, of Japan. Of course, China shared the same fate. So, in that process, the Confucian tradition has been radically transformed.

Now, we're talking about Confucianism in the 20th century with a view toward the 21st century. A modern Confucian can't accept the authoritarian mechanism of control in terms of male domination or authoritarianism and so forth. However, in terms of the "habits of the heart," these negative features still exist. So, I fully understand the notion that "Confucius must die so that the country can live." There's another position of course; Confucius will have to exist or live so the country can flourish. These are two very different positions.

China, for a very long time, really believed that unless the Confucian tradition was eliminated, China could not become modern, could not become progressive, and could not become a democratic system. Recently, because of the quest for cultural identity, many scholars, people, and indeed students began to question and reevaluate the Confucian legacy. My position, which I've held for the last three decades, basically involves trying to understand. My purpose is not to promote. Promotion, propagandizing, or evangelizing is something that I consider a negative. I need to understand, but understanding is predicated on the belief that, on the one hand, you're critically aware of the limitations, but at the same time, you need to recover the core values, especially those values that will continue to be meaningful and transformative in modern times.

The appropriate way to criticize the negative features is to retrieve some positive values. If you use ideas from totally alien sources and you believe you can simply eliminate your cultural tradition, it is too easy, too naive. If you do that, the "habits of the heart," those unreflective habits, will continue to haunt you. What we need to do is to retrieve the cultural values and critique them. That will serve as a basis for understanding the West and simultaneously rejecting and stopping its negative features. I think we're now in a new joint venture looking to the future, and Korea is perhaps the most important example. China is very much behind. China is trying to catch up.

Lee: I don't know...

Tu: If you look at common phenomena, I often use the example of the one thousand-*won* bill with T'oegye, a cultural symbol. This is unimaginable in the Chinese cultural context. It would take quite a while.

Confucian values, both positive and negative, are an integral part of Korean everyday life in terms of leadership, in terms of human relationships, and relationships between humans and the world beyond. Even now, Korea is very pluralistic; in terms of beliefs, it is 30 to 40 percent Christian, with probably even more Mahayana Buddhists. Shamanism continues to be important, and Confucianism is intertwined with all of them. A Korean Christian is very different from an American Christian. A lot of Korean Christians now go to the United States for missions because they don't believe that Americans are truly authentically Christian.

Lee: The Bank of Korea has produced new money, a 50,000-*won* bill, the highest currency. On it, they have printed the portrait of Yulgok's mother, Shin Saimdang.

Tu: Yes, she's a famous poet.

Lee: Yeah, she has been a very important and popular poet and educator who deeply influenced Yulgok. She is the first woman on the paper money.

Tu: But Yulgok? Maybe the 5000 won bill has Yulgok.

Lee: Yes. I am not a Confucian philosopher or any type of philosopher. I have a greater interest in Western philosophy and grew up after independence from Japan. I needed to know what direction our country should go. At that time, Korea was divided between capitalism and socialism, which was the key ideological conflict. So, democracy, social reform, and unification were the goals and targets of our generation from my childhood.

I had to go outside to learn, and I went to Germany, where I learned the philosophical traditions of Kant, Hegel, and Marx and the critical theories of Frankfurt Schools and Habermas. But now, since we are looking for our own identities, I am reflecting on my philosophical learnings from my teachers. When I was a student at Seoul National University, I was very much influenced by Professor Park JongHong. I don't know whether you know him. He was my teacher, and he was an expert in both Western and Oriental philosophy. He has seriously studied traditional Korean philosophy. I listened to his lectures for over three years on the history of Korean philosophy, which was when he had just started teaching. He taught T'oegye and Yulgok and compared them to Kant and Hegel.

He explained that traditionally, Korea also has rationalism, empiricism, and positivism. He compared both sides and questioned why we should only learn from Kant or Hegel. He was especially interested in the *Yijing*. He was going to write a book about the dialectical philosophy based on what he learned from the *Yijing*, the philosophy of *yi* [change] as a kind of Oriental dialectical methodology. He had not finished it at the time.

We are now just slowly learning about these kinds of resources, but we can find in Korean traditional philosophy enough resources to think about these modern and dialectical problems, conflict resolutions and mutual life, and ecological sustainability. Even though it's late, let us learn something!

Tu: You spent 13 years in Germany?

Lee: Yes, at the great University of Göttingen

Tu: You received one of the most thorough educations of any Asian scholar. Because of your familiarity with German idealism and its giants and interest in critical theory that follows the philosophical development of the West all the way to the current situation, when we begin to reflect on your own cultural identity and address issues of Asian values, your perspective is significantly different and valuable. So, we manage to raise new questions and offer new insight into this whole process. I sense that an overwhelming majority of philosophers in East Asia are familiar, though not necessarily fully seasoned like you, with what's happening in the West. Whereas some of the most brilliant Western minds, including Habermas, Derrida, Foucault, and many other contemporary scholars like Levinas, are basically ignorant about the rest of the world.

This is, of course, a historical movement that's difficult to change. I have to say their ability to dig deeply into their own cultural tradition, no matter how radically they were against their own philosophical traditions, such as Heidegger, each of them was totally seasoned in the whole Western philosophy from Plato and Aristotle all the way to modern times. That's part of their genealogy. That's why their philosophy is so moving, thought-provoking, and inspirational. Whereas many scholars in East Asia are overwhelmed by the West, have no confidence whatsoever in what their own tradition presents, and rejected these traditions in a very proud and arrogant way. So, what happened is that they received some wisdom from the West just secondarily because that great Western tradition from Plato to the modern times was somewhat absent; moreover, they also abandoned their own tradition. In that situation, it isn't easy to be creative.

I think philosophical creativity is not like something being created *ex nihilo*; it's not from nothing. So, I think one lesson we learned is that we don't return to our own tradition for its own sake. We have a different problematique. We know we must learn much more about the West to enrich our "life of the mind." At the same time, we know we have resources, and whether we study them or not, they are part of our life. These resources now need to be elevated to the conscious level. I think what you're doing is precisely this, with your very deep and profound involvement in Western philosophy and how you begin to think about these core Asian values. You raise thought-provoking questions for scholars in East Asian studies while at the same time challenging Western scholars. I believe that local knowledge that's in the Confucian tradition, the local or regional knowledge of East Asia, can become globally significant through effort. It won't do it if there's not enough philosophical input into the process. Part of the reason why an overwhelming majority of the forms of local knowledge that are globally significant originate in the West is that the known schools developed in Paris, London, or Cambridge, Mass., and they have become universal.

I think the time is right for some Asian scholars to begin to believe that some of their forms of local knowledge, relatively rooted in nature, can also become more than Chinese, East Asian, or Korean, that they can be shared with the larger world community. I sense that they are now ready to listen. Habermas is a good example. He said, "Well, we have many, many things in common." He also said, "I know you are in the Neo-Confucian world, but there are still differences." For example, he feels that the Neo-Confucianism with which we are familiar makes it difficult for the Confucian tradition to develop indigenous democratic ideas, constitutional democracy, or the idea of the person's dignity linked to human rights. I agree with him regarding the genetic reasons because, historically, that was the case; however, I don't believe that's the whole story. Another part of the story is that if tradition is like a flowing stream, other possibilities can open up. We've confronted something radically different, so the notion that they're fundamentally different, having faced radical otherness, will be a liberating experience for us. I think we are more or less bilingual or trilingual, and we need to take advantage of that, though not in any patriotic or nationalistic way. I think I agree with many people that we must go beyond China-centered or Confucian-centered work. We still need to enter our dialogical mode with not only self-confidence but also a certain kind of preparedness for this kind of encounter.

Lee: I have been motivated to learn more about this, especially through my work at UNESCO. I have worked for UNESCO for the last eight years, originally as the Founding Director of the Asian Pacific Center of Education for International Understanding. We have brought teachers and civil society leaders from 45 Asian Pacific countries to educate them and discuss international and intercultural understanding. Now, for the last four years, I have been the Secretary General of the Korean National Commission for UNESCO, involving myself in many…

Tu: By the way, you deserve to be congratulated because it's one of the most vibrant and comprehensive UNESCO programs worldwide, not just in East Asia.

Lee: Oh yes. This is especially regarding the issues of cultural diversity and the popularization of philosophy. I have traveled to many countries in Asia talking about cultural diversity, and I feel that East Asians, especially Chinese, Koreans, and Japanese…I am very proud and thankful to our forefathers, who have kept these good traditions. You know, we have our own letters, languages, and literature. In many Asian countries, they have lost their languages, their letters, and thus their philosophical traditions. Without these, it's very difficult for them to develop and understand their own identity; they are monopolized, really overruled, by foreign thinking without having the power of self-reflection.

In this regard, I think the East Asian tradition, including our long traditions of Confucianism, Taoism, and Buddhism, can be a good model for coping with monopolized globalization in this new world. In cooperation with each other, we need to discover our commonalities and traditions of Asian religions and philosophies.

Last year, when we hosted the 22nd World Congress of Philosophy in Seoul, Korea, for the first time in Asia, I was very glad many philosophers from China, Japan, and other Asian countries came. Over 800 people came from East Asian countries. We also have had special meetings and seminars among the East Asian territories including Taiwan. We decided to meet annually but have not followed up on it yet. I hope we can strengthen our networks and dialogues among ourselves. Even between China, Japan, and Korea, though we have influenced each other, we do not have much transnational research on the different manifestations of our shared traditions.

I think it's now time to strengthen these networks and collaborations, maybe through FISP or scholarly cooperation. We can identify and recognize good values and traditions that we did not previously recognize.

Tu: Following World War II, the United States rose to become the most powerful military and political system, which was also culturally quite vibrant (people have said America is the combination of Rome and the Greek civilization). One thing that happened due to this history was that all East Asian societies, maybe all Asian societies, began bilateral communications between themselves and the US, including Korea, Taiwan, China, Singapore, and India. In a way, the horizontal communication of all these countries, even though we call them part of the Confucian cultural area, is not good enough. Right now is the time to do more.

An attempt was made a few years ago when the Presidents of four universities, Peking University, Seoul National, Tokyo University, and Hanoi University, decided to have a meeting of the four presidents, and they used their own four languages with translations without English. Everyone spoke their native language during this effort to try to form some joint projects, and this is the beginning of what you have talked about as a "network." Of course, some scholars in Japan, like Shimazno, are attempting to develop a network of East Asian religious studies.

So, I think I would like to see not only more communication, but a new problematique: why are we doing this? We are not doing this just as a response to the challenge of Western law; that's only part of it. We do it with a view towards the future and hopefully as a joint enterprise. We hope to make some positive contributions and make this joint enterprise become universally significant. Amartya Sen published the book entitled *The Argumentative Indian*. If I would do something comparable, I would call it *The Dialogical East Asian* and discuss two important features. One is all these societies are learning societies. This is deeply rooted in the Confucian tradition; as you know, the opening line of *The Analects* is "To learn." Two, these societies also cherish dialogue rather than dialectic. Dialectic means you have to overcome the two sides to get to a higher level. Dialogical means I recognize not only the integrity of your existence but I also respect that you serve as a reference of mutual learning. I don't want to overcome or try to change you as you. So, the more I understand you and become self-reflexive, the more I can expand my horizons, and I hope you do the same. You know, that kind of interaction.

Some scholars believe, historically quite verifiably, that there was an international community in East Asia through maritime engagement, through the so-called ritual system called *chaogong* 朝貢. Of course, now Japan has begun to talk about what we call *Dongya gongtongti* 東亞共同體, "the Common Community of East Asia." They're very worried about this East Asian co-prosperity sphere. Now, they're willing to do that. I think if it is done in a proper way, and so like the ASEAN countries, not just ASEAN plus 1, 2, or 3, but an East Asian community economic collaboration that reduces tension. Of course, there is still tension between China and Japan, Korea, and Japan. I think culturally, they serve as a very important vehicle and hope that Confucian methods will become a new vision of ethics rooted in East Asia. This does not just refer to Asian values rooted in East Asia but applied as universal values, just like some of those rooted in the West have now become universal.

I have this vision, maybe wishful thinking, that a new dialogical civilization will emerge through various intra-civilization dialogues. This civilization is characterized not only by unavoidable competition, conflict, and casualties but also by both willingness to have dialogue and the actual experience of practicing dialogue at all levels: personal, national, regional, and civilizational. So, I think this is a new situation that merits a great deal of attention.

Lee: Yes, we have a very rich tradition of this good harmony.

Tu: Yes. One last point: I'm very moved by your recent decision to be involved in a very important ecological project in China. You may want to talk a little bit more about this attempt with a very large American NGO.

Lee: Yes, I am involved in what they call Ecopeace Asia, which was born from anti-desertification work. We are planting trees and vegetables in the dry sea lake in Inner Mongolia, China, which will attract hundreds of my students in the summer. This is very meaningful, but I wanted to tell you that I heard that you are returning to Peking University.

Tu: Yes

Lee: I think it is very symbolic and significant that after such a long time in Western countries, you are returning to your own country to pursue your goal of finding our traditional philosophical thoughts. I wish you all the best results, and I have high hopes that you can build an excellent focal point to connect and network in Asia, especially East Asia, to connect and network with other countries. Maybe we can hope that in East Asia, especially in China, Japan, and Korea, where we have shared some good common traditions and philosophical grounds, we can meet and establish some good Asian values and traditions.

Tu: I was happily surprised that it's only about a two-hour flight from Beijing to Seoul. We could also fly to Tokyo to have lunch there and return afterward. So, indeed, it is geographically a new realization for me. My decision came after I'd been teaching at Harvard since 1981, so we're talking about nearly 30 years, and I realized that I was approaching 70 years old. In this period of time, I really want a new kind of self-education. I know there are many things I can contribute, and that may come, but I think the real focus is self-education. The time is right to think in a more integrated and hopefully more profound way about how the many things I've been involved in can be brought together as a new mode of thinking. I look forward to a new style of philosophizing, to do philosophy, not simply to study philosophy or Confucianism, but to do philosophy with a view toward the future. I want to take human survival, human flourishing as deep concerns, personal concerns, and not just consider the abstract idea of the human species. In doing that, there is the possibility of tapping spiritual resources from the traditions that I know well, but I want to do it in an open, pluralistic, and self-reflexive way. I will say, "I'm doing this." This means a Christian, a Jew, a Buddhist, a Daoist, someone committed to Shamanist tradition, and even someone from the Indigenous traditions will be able to do the same. There will be real intercultural communication. This is now doable; I really believe it is doable. But I know if I don't do it, someone else will have to do it. If I am committed to doing it, there is no guarantee, even though there is always hope, that it can be fully realized. In any case, I want to do it. This is the motivation.

Whether something significant or efficacious will result, that's something that you can wish for but you cannot anticipate or expect. What you can expect is what you are able to do. In some way, you know it. I began studying this as a teenager, so I've been doing it for a long time. Now, it is time to reflect upon it. When I was studying at Harvard, I became quite aware that if I had no understanding of what was happening in the People's Republic of China, no matter how hard I studied the scholarship of Taiwan, Hong Kong, and Singapore, it would not be enough. It would still be very marginal. I returned to China in 1978 for the first time, and then, in 1980, I lived there for a year. That was also the year I visited Korea to study T'oegye, and there, I realized Confucianism is much broader than Chinese culture.

Of course, it's part of Chinese culture, as is Daoism and other elements. Still, at the same time, no matter how you broaden the idea of cultural China, it is not broad enough to accommodate the whole Confucian tradition because there are also Korean, Japanese, and Vietnamese manifestations. I began to realize if I didn't study Korean Confucianism, my study would be very superficial. If I ignored the Japanese or the Vietnamese traditions, my education would not be complete. I think this is still part of a journey. At least I know that my generation's view of Confucianism is much broader because none of my teachers, though they're great at understanding some of the major figures of Confucianism, took T'oegye seriously. None of them did any major work on Japan or Vietnam.

If we consider the Confucian tradition as the local culture of "Qufu" that became mainstream Chinese culture and then spread from China to East Asia during the 11th to 19th centuries, it is now time for it to go beyond East Asia. Still, to take this last step, you must be rooted in "Qufu," China, and East Asia while at the same time transcending all this rootedness. I do believe that.

I've talked with many, many brilliant Western philosophers. I've even had the chance to speak with Gadamer and got to know Paul Ricoeur very well. Fred Dallmayr is a terrific political philosophy scholar I've known for decades. I know quite a few people in the United States, and I believe that the time is right for a true dialogical relationship to be established. However, the precondition is that you must do work comparable to what they have done in their own culture. So, it's not just that you communicate with your colleagues in Confucian studies; you need to communicate with somebody in Christian theology, and you know the depth of Christian theology, or German idealism, or Heideggerian thinking, or Heidegger and Habermas themselves. You really need to have some sense of your limitations, as well as your own strengths.

That will be the beginning of a certain kind of revival that is basically very personal. I make a distinction between personal and private. It's not private because it's accountable, it's open and it's publicly debated. So far, I've been doing philosophy by developing discourses, like Cultural China, East Asian Modernities, Reflection on the Enlightenment Mentality, and so forth, but now the time is right to create more than simply discourses and have a focal point and to try to do the kind of philosophy some of the most brilliant minds in the West have done. It's not to emulate what they do but to have it serve as a reference and spiritual resource, as well.

Lee: Maybe Jesus was right in saying in the Bible that "Prophets are not welcome in their hometown." You may be right that Confucius had a bad influence in China and other countries, and in his hometown, he was criticized and neglected very much. We even saw in the Cultural Revolution that they destroyed Confucius' tomb. That could not happen in Korea, Japan, or even North Korea. In that sense, we have preserved some of the good traditions of Confucianism. Every year, we celebrate Confucius' birthday, and the music and instruments are original. Now, the Chinese have come to learn from us because they have lost all that. This has become a UNESCO heritage site. So, I think we have to share between China, Japan, and Korea. Confucianism and Buddhism went from China and Korea to Japan, and they have kept and maintained them very well and systematically. We also need to learn from the Japanese how they dealt with and developed this ideology. So, I think developing this kind of interrelation is very important.

Tu: I edited a book entitled *Confucian Traditions in East Asian Modernity*. I hope the forms of East Asian modernity can also serve as a reference for the imagined Southeast Asian modernity, South Asian modernity, Islamic modernity, African modernity, etc. That's the reason why I talk about multiple modernities. In any case, I do believe that a new vision of humanism or a new wave of understanding the human or rethinking the human is right now one of the significant philosophical tasks we must confront, and the Confucian tradition has a kind of spiritual humanism to offer. In a way, it's more suited to this new challenge than secular humanism, which ignores nature on the one hand and the spiritual realm on the other. The work is painfully difficult and must be done not only systematically but also with imagination and persuasive power.

Lee: Well, we can talk all evening, but I think we must return to our session!

Tu: Ok, thanks so much.

Lee: Thank you very much.

https://www.youtube.com/watch?v=UA7S87UvE-Q

DIALOGUE WITH FRED DALLMAYR 2009-11-18

Bio: Fred Dallmayr is Emeritus Packey J. Dee Professor in the Philosophy Department at Notre Dame University. He is a political theorist specializing in modern and contemporary European thought with an additional interest in comparative or cross-cultural philosophy. He has been a recipient of NEH and Fulbright fellowships and has been a visiting professor at the New School in New York and at Hamburg University (Germany) and a Senior Fellow at Nuffield College in Oxford. Among his recent publications are: *The Other Heidegger* (1993), *Beyond Orientalism: Essays On Cross-Cultural Encounter* (1996), *Achieving Our World: Toward a Global and Plural Democracy* (2001), *Dialogue Among Civilizations: Some Exemplary Voices* (2002); *Hegel: Modernity and Politics* (new ed. 2002), and *In Search of the Good Life: A Pedagogy for Troubled Times* (2007). He is past president of the Society for Asian and Comparative Philosophy (SACP). He is also a member of the International Coordinating Committee of "World Public Forum: Dialogue of Civilizations," and of the Scientific Committee of "RESET: Dialogue on Civilizations."

Professor Tu Weiming: Fred, I was very impressed and inspired by your attempt to return to philosophical anthropology. For a while, people characterized my work in the Confucian tradition as in the spirit of philosophical anthropology, but I never previously noticed any powerful movement in the West after Scheler.

Professor Fred Dallmayr: Yeah. Philosophical anthropology was very strong in Western philosophy during the 19th century and the early 20th century. There were some major figures, like Max Scheler, who was a student of Husserl, and also Plessner. These were major figures in philosophical anthropology, and they developed a conception of the human which overcame the Cartesian tradition of splitting the human in mind and body.

Tu: Yes.

Dallmayr: That was a very significant effort, and it continued until the mid-20th century. But then for a number of reasons, it became unpopular. One reason, as I tried to point out, is the up-surge or the rise of post-modernism and the idea of the end of man, the death of man, the death of the subject. So, much of French philosophy was very anti-humanist. That was particularly evident in the early works of Jacques Derrida and Michel Foucault, though later they changed.

Tu: Toward the end Foucault's life, for example, he became very deeply concerned about the care of the self.

Dallmayr: Precisely. He wrote about this care of the self.

Tu: Right.

Fred: But since that time, I think a change has happened. There's a resurgence of philosophical anthropology or concern about the meaning of what is human, the human being. There are a number of factors that play a role here but especially the resurgence of phenomenology and of humanistic psychology.

Tu: Yes, even like Erik Erikson.

Fred: Erikson, yes.

Tu: Who you studied with.

Dallmayr: Exactly.

Tu: And the whole question of identity.

Dallmayr: Yes.

Tu: And the different stages of human self-realization. Malsow is probably another example.

Fred: Maslow, yeah. So, there's a coming together of some of the humanistic traditions of the 19th and early 20th century, and some of the newer directions in psychology, neuropsychology, and neuroscience. They begin to meet again and to articulate a conception of the human that is no longer purely mentalist nor purely naturalist, but that is truly bifocal. It sees the human through both eyes.

Tu: Yes.

Dallmayr: I find this very fascinating. I myself have been strongly influenced for a long time by Maurice Merleau-Ponty.

Tu: The importance of the body.

Dallmayr: Embodiment. Yes.

Tu: Absolutely.

Fred: Not to neglect the mind or the spirit, but the spirit is always embodied. That is a very important thing. I'm just now working on a major work which Merleau-Ponty wrote just before his death, he passed away early, which include his lectures on nature and human nature. He relies very strongly on the classic tradition of German idealism, Hegel, Schelling, but he moves to the more recent philosophies of Henri Bergson and William James, and then onto very recent developments in neuroscience. This I find absolutely fascinating.

Tu: That's right. I have tried to develop an idea based upon the Chinese notion about the body. The Chinese word can be used as a verb. Embodiment is part of it.

Fred: I see.

Tu: So, the body is not only an object. You don't own your body.

Fred: Precisely.

Tu: You become your body.

Fred: Precisely.

Tu: The body, in a way, is an attainment. As a young person you gradually try to learn how you integrate your body. I think it's not different for the heart and mind; even the soul and spirit are an integral part of the body. The body in this case is holistic. I think we're in the stage where the idea of human has to be rethought and reformulated to go beyond the Cartesian exclusive dichotomy.

Fred: Yes.

Tu: In the *Great Learning*, for example, there are dichotomies, but that they are like the complementary *yin* and *yang*. So, the distinctions between the mental and physical, the sacred and profane, the mind and body all turn out to be outmoded.

Fred: Yes. I fully agree with you. I think the distinctions are not totally eliminated, but there's a new idea of complementarity.

Tu: Yes.

Fred: These things are complimenting each other. They are not contradicting each other, not conflicting with each other, but are supporting each other in a complementary way. So, mind and body, soul, and spirit, all of these are not necessarily the same thing, but they are mutually interrelated and interacting. This is a new way of thinking about the human being.

Tu: My position is probably a bit more radical. In the original conception of the human, the separation itself is problematical, like the basic idea of the vital energy that Bergson talked about. But Bergson is too biological for some of the Chinese philosophers. This idea of the human is by nature the integration of the two. It's almost impossible to imagine you can think pure thought, like the Cartesians, without involving the body, the sentiments, the ideas. It's not a dialectic relationship. It's a dialogical one.

Dallmayr: A dialogical relationship, that's right. That's what I have in mind. It's complementary in the dialogical sense. Of course, the body is presupposed in every act of thinking, in any mental reflection, and yet reflection has to come in to supervene on the body, to make the body reflective.

Tu: Yes. Absolutely.

Dallmayr: So there has to be this mutual relationship. This is the same way we talked about the three dimensions of the cosmos, the divine, and the human. They're not necessarily the same, but they are mutually so closely interrelated that it's very difficult to separate them in any way.

Tu: Yes.

Dallmayr: They only make sense with each other, and so that's how I would see it. Also, the sacred and the secular, all of these things, are so closely related that none of them make sense without the other.

Tu: Fingarette writes in *Confucius: The Secular As Sacred* that the idea of our ordinary experience, of relating, of self-understanding, of even walking and drinking and eating, are not simply "secular" events. They are sacred in the sense that sometimes the ultimate meaning of life ought to be realized in ordinary human existence. If you follow this line of thinking, I would suggest maybe four dimensions, and I'm totally in agreement with you about three. First is the question of the self. I think the failure of some dichotomous thinking is inattention to the question of self-realization.

Fred: That's right.

Tu: The true self, the subjectivity, is radically different from the false self; the exclusive dichotomy is the true self and subjectivism. The true self is not at all in conflict with the objective world or with the transcendent. I think the self, it's already almost embodied itself, has a continuous, hopefully fruitful interaction with many different dimensions of community from the family, to the nation, to even the world. Thus, community is not the Hobbesian idea of contract. Then the cosmos is nature, and lastly Heaven is the transcendent. It's the center of spirituality.

The questions are then: how can the person, as a center of relationships rather than an isolated individual, be able to interact with various ideas of the community? How can the human species maintain a sustainable relationship with nature or Earth? How can the human heart and mind develop, as sometimes in a Chinese case the mutuality or mutual responsiveness, a sort of a harmonious understanding between human and the transcendent?

Fred Dallmayr: I fully agree with you, and I particularly like this emphasis on the self learning about itself in the process of relating to the world and to the divine. Now you also have written about the process of self-transformation, how we are developed from a mundane self into a fully mature self which properly relates to other dimensions of the world. I think that is very crucial. As you know, I recently did this book which is subtitled "A Pedagogy for Troubled Times."

Tu: Yes.

Fred: But it's meant as a learning experience.

Tu: The quest for the good life.

Dallmayr: Yeah. This notion of the good life also resonates with what you're saying about the community, that we should start from the community conception and not from the social contract. The idea of the good life is in opposition to the whole modern philosophy of politics, which is grounded on individual self-interest that leads to a social contract, and then to a political community that is a pure artifact or a machine. It's in opposition to this very self-centered conception of modernity, which is rooted in the social contract. The idea of the community, the focus on a political community that is oriented toward achieving a better life, and the goal is the good life not for an individual but for the whole community. This is a conception which derives originally from Aristotle. It's the Aristotelian tradition and not the Hobbesian tradition.

Tu: Sure. I think the idea of the good life as a continuous process of learning, which means self-realization, evokes a sense of the transcendent. It other words, it's not the secular age which Charles Taylor talks about, but is beyond the secular age. That's the reason you probably—is it a Heideggerian notion or not? —suggest that the idea that the human is not anthropological because the anthropological world is too restricted. The fully human has to go beyond anthropocentricity to include both the anthropological and the cosmological. This is the anthropocosmic vision. You use a comparable term?

Dallmayr: Yes. Heidegger speaks of human being or *Dasein* as an ecstatic creature. Ecstatic means to really stand out from the self, from the anthropological, to stand out into the world, nature, but also to the divine. So, it's an ecstatic relation with all the other dimensions of which the human being is only one part, one particle. It is an important part, but only one part. For me, Heidegger articulates precisely this kind of multidimensional conception of the world in which the sacred and the secular and the imminent and the transcendent are closely related together without being totally fused with each other, closely related and mutually dependant on each other, as you say, in a dialogical way.

All of it involves a constant process of learning, a pedagogy of self-transformation. Now this is where I'm a little bit hesitant to embrace the phrase, Fingarette's phrase, "The secular as sacred." I very much appreciate Fingarette's idea, and I'd like to agree with it. However, there is in our present-day world, so many things which by no stretch of the imagination can be considered as sacred. For instance, genocide, Holocaust, killings, war. So, there's so much in the secular world, which is so hideous, which is so obscene that it cannot possibly be considered sacred. So, in order for the secular and the sacred to come together, the secular has to be transformed. There has to be a learning experience.

Tu: Transformed by the sacred.

Dallmayr: Precisely. It has to be a learning experience. It has to be a transformative experience, so that we can really see the secular world as a sacred ritual.

Tu: This reminds me of the whole conception of Heaven or the transcendent. I think in the Confucian point of view, the highest manifestation of self-realization is the unity between the human and Heaven, which means the transcendent dimension separates the human from the negative features of the secular world. Yet, this idea of Heaven is omnipresent, omniscient, but it's unlikely to be omnipotent. Part of the reason is because of the human element, not just in terms of the freedom that many philosophers talk about, but also in terms of responsibility.

Earlier there was the notion that Heaven engenders or creates but humans complete. It's almost like a partnership. A human being is an observer, an appreciator, but also a participant, and, of course difficult for people who are in the monotheistic tradition to accept, a co-creator.

By implication this creature, who is so powerful or can become powerful, is also potentially a destroyer. So, this is a notion that all these atrocities are not necessarily related to evil in the ontological sense. It is the failure of the human. Since you're also deeply concerned about political philosophy, how do you link this process of socialization with politics? Under the influence of the liberal tradition there's so much emphasis on procedure and process that religion and concern for spirituality are normally relegated to the background as the matter of the heart, whereas politics, ever since Machiavelli, is a different kind.

Dallmayr: I have been very greatly influenced also, by your writings and very much attracted to the Confucian tradition. It resonates with many of the things that I have learned but that Western modernity has forgotten to a very large extent. My basic tradition comes from Aristotle's teaching in the *Nicomachean Ethics* and his *Politics*.

Tu: Virtue ethics.

Fred: It's virtuous ethics. Politics is basically a virtuous activity oriented to the good life, for Aristotle. In the Middle Ages, this was reformulated in a more theological way. In modernity, it was pushed aside by this idea of individuality and the social contract, especially Thomas Hobbes' philosophy which was enormously destructive.

But then, from Aristotle I built a link or a bridge to Hegel, whom I consider the great modern philosopher, who rescued or salvaged some of the ideas of the Greeks, of Aristotle especially, with his idea that the political community is governed by *sittlichkeit*. That means an ethical life. Ethical life is at the core of political life for Hegel.

So, from Aristotle to Hegel and then to modern and contemporary philosophy I find a linkage again to Heidegger, Gadamer, and Merleau-Ponti, who also recapitulate this idea of politics and political life as an ethical life, an ethical community. For me, this resonates very much with the Confucian tradition.

All of this has also led me to a certain questioning of some of the premises of the Abrahamic religious traditions. I myself come from a Christian background, Catholic-Protestant, but still I've come to question some of the premises. I especially question the ideas of a creator God who is initially totally divorced from the world, that the world is purely an act of will by this creator God, and that the creator God could also exist without the world. This vision lacks the relationship between God and world, which I would prefer to see.

Tu: That's called the mutual responsiveness.

Dallmayr: Yes. I prefer to think that God only becomes God through the world and the world also becomes only world, properly speaking, through the divine. So, this interrelation leads me to a certain criticism of an extreme conception of transcendence, the transcendence that is totally outside...

Tu: The wholly other.

Fred: The wholly other, totally outside of all relationships. I have become critical of that notion. I think one can reformulate the Christian tradition in a different way.

Tu: I think with the emergence of our concern for the Earth any tradition, whether Buddhist or Christian, has to develop two very different conceptions of their role. First, there is the need for a specific language within their faith community. Second, there is also the need for global citizenship.

Dallmayr: Right.

Tu: Now, some Buddhists call themselves engaged Buddhists.

Fred: Ah yes.

Tu: I think that two challenges are received. The one from the liberal tradition is that politics is so different from morality, from religion and private matters or matters of the heart. The other one is from Foucault and others who are so obsessed with the question of power, with the question of influence, and with the question of symbolic control. These confront not only subjectivity but a true relationship with the virtue ethics of Aristotle or the idea of self-realization in the Confucian tradition. Of course, you mentioned the whole question about subjectivity now relegated to the back. I gathered the return of philosophical anthropology is an attempt to retrieve some of the great humanist traditions in the West with a view toward the future. I'm very much in agreement with this approach. I learned a lot from your linkage. You've actually been practicing philosophical anthropology for a long time, along with the linkage of that to the idea of the political order. In the Confucian tradition, self-realization, regulation of the family, and peace in the world are all interconnected as a major enterprise. Related to this philosophical anthropology, which has to transcend anthropocentrism, is a new kind of humanism that the Indian scholar R. Balasubramanian would consider as spiritual humanism. This is a humanism, which is spiritualistic and spiritual, not denatured of the spirit.

Dallmayr: Yes, yes. I've been very much influenced by the Indian tradition, by Indian thought, because I've spent a lot of time in India. One of my mentors has always been Gandhi and his kind of spiritual humanism, ethical humanism, and non-violent politics.

Tu: Absolutely.

Dallmayr: I've become very critical over the last ten or twenty years of what is called liberalism, and what you've described as this emphasis on individual self-interest and human freedom. Now there's great value in human freedom, but the problem with liberalism is they have misconstrued the idea of freedom.

Tu: Yes.

Dallmayr: Freedom is very valuable, of course, but there is a misconception of human freedom that it just means that I can do what I please. Freedom really means to do what is right, the ability to do what is right. This is the intrinsic conception of freedom and the great tradition of German idealism, Kant and Hegel especially were still fully aware of this fact. Freedom, yes, but freedom has to be rooted in a conception of goodness, of what is right. So, yes to liberalism if it is not misinterpreted, if it is seen that freedom is really a freedom of rightness. The other thing I have become very critical of is the Foucault you mentioned, not the late Foucault of the care for the self, but the Foucault only concerned with power.

I have recently written some very strong articles against one of the major proponents of the identification of politics with power, a German legal theorist Karl Schmidt. Karl Schmidt has become so popular in recent times, especially among young people, young political philosophers who think everything is power. There are the powerful people in government, and the only thing we can do is to have a revolution and have ourselves in power. This is just changing one power for another power.

That identification of politics with power is completely wrong because politics, and this is the Aristotelian tradition, means the surge in a community for a good ethical life. How can we live together? That's the issue of politics for me. That's the political issue. How can we live together decently, caring for one another? That is the issue of politics. But the Schmidtians completely eliminate this. It's all a struggle for power. Friend/enemy, that's their mantra.

Tu: Yes. Politics, *zheng* 政, in the Confucian tradition is glossed with another word with the same pronunciation, *zheng* 正, which means rectification. In other words, it's a way of finding niche in a society; however, the niche is not fixed, it's fluid. You share part of your responsibility, what Henry Rosemont and others talk about this as role ethics, and in that sense it is to provide the minimum condition, security, and food for human flourishment. That's the purpose of rectification, rectification of the names of father, son, friend, siblings, even ruler and ministers. This process of rectification is the process of searching for the good life not rooted in individuality but rooted in the communal participation. However, one point where I don't agree with the role ethics argument is that Confucianism definitely has the idea of subjectivity. In other words, you realize yourself for the sake of yourself, not for the sake of anyone else.

Fred: Precisely.

Tu: The dignity of the person and human rights are part of this discourse once you become rooted in yourself as a kind of lived concreteness. It's not privacy, but a profound sense of personal investment, and personal means being experientially committed.

Dallmayr: And responsible.

Tu: Yeah. Responsibility and sense of civility all enter into the picture. In this sense, I can now see politics as an integral part of not only the human community, but the Cosmos on the one hand and Heaven on the other. I mentioned and was happily surprised that someone in Switzerland, in his dissertation, would talk about my work as a form of political philosophy. First, I was surprised. I thought I never did it, but I knew you'd been always involved in philosophical anthropology, and now in a very articulate and conscious sense you want to bring it back.

Dallmayr: Well, I have always seen your work both as a form of Confucian philosophy and as political philosophy. It is politically eminent and relevant for our time because it can correct, it can rectify, some of the mistakes that Western politics…

Tu: That's the basic Confucian premise.

Dallmayr: Yes. It can rectify the mistakes that we have made in Western politics from overemphasizing something that is completely misleading us, and not emphasizing things that ought to be emphasized. So, I've always found the rectification in your work very relevant for contemporary political philosophy. One thing I want to add is I fully agree with you that the self remains important, along with an emphasis on community. However, the community only has a meaning if the self is meaningfully involved in this community and freely involved in this community.

Tu: Yes.

Dallmayr: So, it's not just, as you say, a role conception, that I play a role because this role is assigned to me. No. I freely, from my own self, participate in this community and this is a shared freedom. Community is a sharing of freedom. I fully agree with you because otherwise it becomes just a sociological concept. Ethics is reduced to sociology and this I…

Tu: That's not good enough.

Dallmayr: Yes. I was very much impressed once when I listened to the Dalai Lama, and he was asked about political life. He travels so much, and he gives speeches so much. He says, "Well, the best kind of life is that where you are actively involved in communities and political life, but then at least for a month or two months of your year you should retreat into a monastery or some kind of retreat."

Tu: Self-reflection.

Fred: Self-reflection, right. I thought, that's just right, that's just right. One has to care for the self but also for the community, and I cannot properly care for the community if I have not cared for myself.

Tu: I think Richard Rorty's sharp distinction between self-realization and social service is basically unworkable. It suffers from a kind of schizophrenia.

Fred: Yes.

Tu: I'm reminded of William James' idea that "The community stagnates without the impulse of the individual. The impulse dies away without the sympathy of the community." I think this mutuality is absolutely critical.

Fred: Yes.

Tu: Well, we talked more than half an hour.

Dallmayr: That's enough for me. It was a great pleasure talking with you.

Tu: We'll continue.

Fred: I hope so.

https://www.youtube.com/watch?v=WW7G3Ja9Nws

Dialogue With Jerome Kagan 2010-04-09

Professor **Jerome Kagan** (February 25, 1929 – May 10, 2021) was a prominent developmental psychologist renowned for his groundbreaking research on infant temperament, particularly the concept of "behavioral inhibition," where he identified a subset of children who exhibit heightened anxiety in unfamiliar situations. He started at Harvard in 1964. He was the Daniel and Amy Starch Research Professor of Psychology at Harvard University until his retirement in 2005. Kagan's work significantly contributed to our understanding of how early childhood experiences influence later personality development, establishing him as a leading figure in child psychology. He is recognized for his extensive longitudinal studies, which demonstrated the stability of temperament traits over time, linking early infant behaviors to later personality characteristics. Kagan has received numerous accolades throughout his career, including the prestigious G. Stanley Hall Award from the American Psychological Association.

Tu: Jerry, I've been very much influenced by your ideas, and I think your idea about moral development is not simply about an individual, but I think your idea applies to the human species. Therefore, there's a general idea about not just the human condition. Learning to be human has always inspired me, and I find many points of convergence and some very compatible ideas. So, this is a rare opportunity for me to have a chance to talk to you, to learn from you, and also to offer some of my personal opinions on this vitally important subject.

Kagan: Well, thank you. I think we agree that a moral sense is one of the many unique processes that emerge with humans. Remember, we have language. We have opposable fingers and thumbs. We've got no hair on our bodies. A lot of unique things happened when Homo Sapiens evolved 150,000 years ago. Morality was one of them. My view is that human morality, which I'm about to describe, is just not present in any ape. It's impossible because of the complex cognitive and emotional processes that define morality. So, let me try to say concisely what my view is.

Tu: Yes.

Kagan: First, I think we have to differentiate between two related ideas that the ancients understood. One is the community's decision, the majority's decision as to which actions, primarily, but also thoughts are good for the community, which would emphasize Asian values of kindness, cooperation, nurture, and honesty because that's what the community is concerned about. They're less concerned with your thoughts. You can have your private emotions as long as you retain harmony in the community. So, I think it's a useful idea to think about morality as lying in the community's opinion, which all members understand. That is different from the word *conscience* because conscience refers to each person's intention to do good and be moral, and it's obvious that sometimes good intentions don't end up in good actions. For example, a mother who has moral intentions for her child may actually do the wrong thing with her child and hurt her child even though her intentions were benevolent. Take the most obvious example: a person sees a child drowning in a lake. And so, the person jumps in to save the child. His intention is moral, but because he is incompetent, they both drown. So, his moral intention didn't end up with a good outcome. I think that's a useful distinction. The second point is that morality consists of many processes, and they emerge on a timetable in development. And so here is my view of the five stages.

Kagan: The first stage is in the first year, where the child responds to punishments or chastisements by the parent when the child does something that the parent disapproves of, makes dirt, or breaks something. That is conditioning, and that is the least relevant for morality. That's how you train a puppy. But in the second year, unique things occur because of the maturation of the human brain, which do not occur in apes. And now we get to the second stage. In the second stage, the child is now able to infer what the thoughts and feelings of another person might be. No ape can do that. And because it is relevant for morality, you could infer that the other person is hurting, feels distressed, and is in pain because you, in the past, have experienced pain. You are now capable of empathy, and there are many experiments to show that two-year-olds will, but one-year-olds will not. If an adult or the mother makes believe that she's hurt herself, she says, "Oh, my fingers hurt," the one-year-old will do nothing. The two-year-old will go over and show concern or try to help the person in pain. Many experiments show that two-year-olds can infer and, therefore, be empathic, and in my view, that is so critical to both conscience and human morality. That is not the only basis, but it is a fundamental foundation for human morality because it means humans are biased by their biology to NOT want to hurt. Now, they end up hurting, as we all know, but their initial biological preparedness is not to hurt because of empathy.

Tu: Before you go on to the third stage. This reminds me of a very important statement by a major Chinese thinker, maybe in the third century BC. He talked about human evolution. He said, "Everything is made of vital energy." The Chinese word is 气 qì[1], which is both materialistic and spiritual, and only plants have life. Only animals have consciousness and awareness. But only humans have this sense of rightness, which means only humans have a sense of morality, a moral sense. Yet, his position, a scholar by the name of 荀子 Xúnzǐ position, is that morality has to be learned and has to be internalized from the outside. However, an earlier thinker, and perhaps the most important follower of Confucius by the name of Mencius, argued that intrinsic to human nature, there's some disposition or some tendency — he uses the term sprouts. These sprouts are defining characteristics of being human, and the most primary sprout is commiseration, which means sympathy and empathy. I'm sorry to interject this idea.

Kagan: That's right. There's no question that empathy is innate in our species. Now, you raise an interesting point. Anything else? Or does the content of your morality have to be learned? Now, here's the point. By the time you're three years old, every child in the world, every child who has ever lived, has the concepts of good and bad, whatever those concepts are in the language of their community. You can guarantee that it's like every child has language, so the capacity for language is an empty vessel. There it is. Then, the society fills it in with either Mandarin, French, or English. Now, let's go to morality. I'm saying that the vessel begins with empathy. That's there, and what's controversial is: does the rest have to be learned? Do you fill the vessel with the other contents of morality by your culture, the way you do for language? And we might talk about that this afternoon because that's an interesting issue. How much does the child begin with? We know they start with empathy by age two. Does it begin with anything else? And that is controversial.

Tu: Let's say if that's the case, I think it's arguable that empathy or commiseration is something so intrinsic to being human. Human beings are not simply rational beings or

---

[1] Traditional Chinese Medicine philosophy considers 气 qì as the fundamental building block of existence

rational animals, or true users, or, for that matter, endowed with linguistic proficiency or capacity, but human beings are sensitive beings, beings with a basic feeling for the other, and that we normally call sympathy. And that has profound implications for any ethics or moral reasoning we develop. I hope we have a chance to explore that because we have many systems of thought that are all very closely related to this absolutely critical human condition.

Kagan: But later we have to explain, since we agree that this is fundamental, then later in this discussion, we have to explain why it was so easy for Hutus to kill Tutsis and Serbs to kill Bosniaks, and so on; for Sunnis to kill Shia. Because they all have this competence, so, why can you turn it off so easily? Let's go back to the stages, and then we can [discuss]. So, in the second year, you also get your first consciousness of self. One-year-olds aren't aware they have intentions. Two-year-olds are. So, in the second phase, we have empathy, inference, and an awareness that I have intentions. Now, we are in the third year. In the third year, you learn the semantic concepts: right, wrong, good, and bad. And you apply them not just to actions and to people but to yourself. You label yourself, good or bad, depending upon your own behavior. A mother in one of my studies caught her three-year-old pinching himself. And the mother said, "Why are you doing that?" He says, "I don't like myself." And that's because he had bullied a child the previous day. So, that's a very important phase in that third phase. Good, bad. And in the next phase, by four, we return to your prior comment.

Kagan: Now you're capable of guilt. You're capable of shame in the second phase. Through an inference, you can infer. I can infer what you're thinking. And if I infer that you're thinking critically about me, I'm embarrassed. I'm ashamed. I'm not guilty because guilt can only occur after the fourth or fifth year. Why? Because you have to be capable of doing the following thing: relating the past to the present. I did it. I spilled this. I've got to remember that I did it, and I could have inhibited it. A two-year-old does not appreciate that they could have done otherwise if they spilled this cup. A four-year-old knows he or she could have done otherwise. Those are the two ingredients: I was the responsible agent and could have inhibited that act. Now we have guilt, and now there's self-blame and remorse. So, by age five, we have most of the essential elements of consciousness. Then, we add morality. After that, we add one more thing: the categories to which I belong. When you're five, six, or seven, you are now aware of the categories to which you belong. Are you a boy or a girl? Are you Chinese, German, or Finnish?

Tu: Self-identity.

Kagan: These are your social categories. Are you poor or rich? Are you Catholic or Muslim? Now, in each of these categories, by the time you're seven, you know what the features are there if you want to be an ideal Muslim or an ideal Catholic. If that's your category, then you try to match those if you can. Then you experience a kind of category guilt, an identity guilt. And that sort of completes the fundamental phases of moral development.

Tu: One fascinating thing for me is returning to what I refer to as Mencius' theory. It's often misunderstood that he's too much of an optimist. He talks about human nature as good, but that's a total misconception of what he's trying to say. First, he observes that the difference between a human being and other members of the animal kingdom is infinitesimal. It's tiny. That difference is minute. And we say many of our features, our appetites, our desire to multiply, to express ourselves, quite a number of things are shared with other animals, but that which differentiates humans from other animals and that infinitesimal, that little bit, is the defining characteristic of being human. And he identifies four of them. And that, of course, people began to expand that theory. The first one is the sprout of commiseration, which means human beings have this sympathetic understanding of the other, and we'll be able to extend their sympathy, but that has to be cultivated. It's given, but if it's not cultivated, it can be either overcome or even distorted. And the other one is the sense of right and wrong. It's the sense of rightness, not just righteousness. This sense of right and wrong is related to the notion of what is appropriate and is in some way linked to shame and discomfort. Suppose I know right and wrong and fail to do what I think is right. In that case, I have a sense of shame because I can make the distinction, to be aware of my empathetic nature at the same time, to be aware of my ability to make things proper or to distinguish right and wrong, in that sense, good and bad.

Tu: One thing that's particularly troubling to people is, I think, very close to your notion about category self-identification. It's what we call the ritual or the ways people are seasoned or cultivated to become a particular person, and that varies from culture to culture, but that is also an essential ability for a person to have to cultivate morality. So, these four features are the feeling of commiseration, the feeling of shame, knowing right and wrong, and the sense of what is most appropriate to me and what is part of my culture. These are the four very basic elements of being human. Of course, this is very much defined in terms of human morality precisely because each and every human being has these capacities. So, we say human nature, in that sense, is good, and not that human nature is factually good. It's not good in an empirical sense. It's so basic to human beings. You have to recognize it as a distinctive feature of being human. So, I think that sense of human nature has probably never been used in any other philosophical system. The [human] nature is good. It doesn't mean that human beings are normally, or practically, or empirically good, but that they are capable of these four capacities. These four capacities help a person become fully moral; therefore, every human being is potentially a good person. This, I think, in a way, is quite compatible with your observation.

Kagan: Very. I agree with you. However, you know, there are those in the past who said perhaps nature played a dirty trick on humans by giving them the notion of right and wrong because if they didn't, they would be guilt-free half-animals like bonobo chimps who look so happy and joyful. In other words, remember, as you know in Genesis, what is God's punishment? God's punishment to Adam and Eve is to give them right and wrong. The very thing that Mencius says is good. God, the Christian God. So, it has it. So, it has a punishment.

Tu: That's the source of the fall. Then, the reason for original sin, and then, of course, led to the idea of the human being incapable of being fully united with God. It doesn't mean something evil, like a devil who has an independent status, but something that they depart from the loving care of God.

Kagan: No. That's right. You know, I've thought long and hard about the meaning of good. And I think you'll agree with me; it's so abstract that we must decide whether it is a feeling, an intention, or an action. Because it'll vary depending, and now you should smile because this is so Asian, on the context. That is, what is good in one context is not good in another: the same action, as a matter of fact. So *good* is a slippery word, almost like *beauty*, and not like *broccoli,* and we might even get into that later; I think that the Asians understood something the West did not. The West seems to regard good as an absolute. You'll always know what is good and bad. The Chinese philosophers were closer to the truth when they said, "Wait a minute. This action might be good with that person, but not necessarily with a different person."

Tu: Yeah. Many Western scholars are also quite aware of the importance of contextualizing the situation in which one acts according to some concrete environment and trying to remove themselves from abstract, universal principles. There are quite a number of examples of this nature. But let's revisit this very important story about the genesis, at least on the surface. Apparently, you feel uneasy about the notion that the ability to know good and bad turns out to be the fall of the human rather than the other way around. It's an enabling capacity for humans to know.

Kagan: Well, let's stay on this because this issue is really important. There's nothing more benevolent than a baby. A baby harms nothing. It has no concept of good and bad, right and wrong. Zero. Later on, by age three or four, it has that notion. And now it is capable of hurting because it's stronger now. Every four-year-old who has just seen his or her mother bring home a new baby is jealous of that baby and would like to hurt it. It doesn't because of what you said, it has a sense of shame and right and wrong. So, that protects a new baby from anger, envy, and jealousy. So, I think this was very adaptive when humans evolved. They'd better know the difference between right and wrong because they're very strong, and they can hurt. And this is most important; unlike apes, they can harbor grudges for a long time. An animal forgets that they were angry. A human can hold envy and anger for a very long time. Therefore, isn't it protective to have a moral sense? I think so.

Tu: In that sense, the big question for me then is the first year, before even the idea of empathy and sympathy expresses itself, and we know that a baby is totally innocent, not going to hurt. Any of their feeling of attachment, for example, attachment to the mother, may be universal. It's true with many other animals. Is there any difference between a newborn baby and a human in the human community that relates to his or her mother in a way that is different ...

Kagan: Different from an animal?

Tu: Different from other animals, or you have to wait until the second year to have some sense of sympathy if, indeed, your observation shows that the first-year baby is not capable of thinking about someone else's feelings and thoughts and then responding to them., The question is whether there are distinctive features of any kind that may differentiate a human from an animal in the first year.

Kagan: I think the research up to now, new research could always prove me wrong, but research up to now says that in the first eight months. Notice, it's not 12 months. For eight months, a human infant is like a chimp infant.

Tu: Totally.

Kagan: 99% of the time. It's tough to tell from their perceptual abilities, whatever cognitive skills they had. Chimps are actually, from a motor perspective, more agile. What happens in 8 to 9 months is the first time humans begin to spin off. Humans are much better at retrieving. Human infants at nine months are better at retrieving what happened 15 seconds ago than apes. That's it. Notice how important that is for guilt later on to be able to retrieve the past and say, "How does this relate to the present?" It first appears at about 8 to 9 months. Also, around ten months, babies will imitate a lot more than chimps, even spontaneously. They'll imitate something. They'll pick up a doll because they saw their mother pick up a baby or pick them up. So, we're beginning to get the first differentiation early. Eight months is early, sure, but I think it's hard to see any differences in the first six or seven, or eight [months].

Tu: Is it in behavioral terms?

Kagan: Or perception.

Tu: Yeah. Perception.

Kagan: What else can we study?

Tu: Right, of course, that's the case. Suppose we believe human uniqueness manifests in these qualities that began in the second year, third, fourth, and fifth, and probably by the seventh. In that case, many of the basic ingredients of a fully mature and moral person are already present. And so, the question is from an evolutionary perspective, and I think we discussed this before, that there's a difference between emergence and origins.

Kagan: Right.

Tu: For many, many traditions, people are deeply worried about origins: the origin of the universe and the origin of human beings from either a creationist or an evolutionist perspective. However, I think Chinese philosophers are particularly interested in the other question of the human being, as we understand it here and now: "How did he come about and evolve into such a state?" All these are significant and important for us to understand.

Still, we should understand a human being in front of us structurally, not simply in terms of the evolutionary process. The assumption is that if something emerges, let's say if life emerges, there's no question that life, from the evolutionary perspective, is linked to all kinds of other processes, from inanimate beings gradually evolving through life. But once that exists, then it's no longer reducible back to those kinds of processes. That's true with consciousness and undoubtedly true with the idea of morality, let's say, the idea of rightness. And if that's the case, then it's probably an imagination. How do we understand the uniqueness of being human as emergence or emergent? Will you accept that because everything is reducible to the human brain, the human brain, in a way, is so different from the others that ...

Kagan: Never thought you would say that. Not everything – the Supreme Court as an institution is not reducible to the human brain.

Tu: That's precisely what I'm trying to argue against. If you assume ...

Kagan: If you assume, yes.

Tu: The question is: If you assume that the emergence of humans, let's say, as the emerging quality, it cannot be reduced to any of the things that preceded it. That's something unique. Hypothetically, someone would say the difference between humans and all the other things is because of the brain. And I feel very uneasy about that position.

Kagan: But the human brain, Weiming, is different from the ape brain, so that shouldn't threaten you. The human brain is qualitatively different from the brain of the ape from which we sprang. It's very different.

Tu: Right. But the question is: if other animals have consciousness...

Kagan: If...

Tu: And let's say, animals have consciousness according to that earlier position, which may be outmoded. Then, humans have a sense of rightness, meaning they have a sense of morality. One way of doing this is to say that the human brain is so different from the brain of an ape and others, that the differentiating factor of being human is located in the brain.

Kagan: Only the origin. The origin of what you and I accept as human morality, commiseration, and sympathy. That wouldn't be possible without the human and the unique structure of the human brain. But all the brain can do is say, "I'm going to give you sympathy. I'm going to give you right and wrong." But that's as far as I [a brain] can go. You, the society, have to tell me, "For whom will you feel sympathy? What will you consider right and wrong?" In other words, the brain is like a relay race. The brain says, "I stop here because I can't tell you the content of your morality."

Tu: This is something, I think, fascinating, and that's something that I don't think I understand fully. Our brain is, maybe, a structure or a frame, but the content has to come from somewhere else, right? The question is, are the structure and frame so different from those of the chimpanzee and others? So, there must be some intrinsic difference in this frame.

Kagan: There is.

Tu: And that can be studied and analyzed by neurophysiologists eventually in the future. Will they probably be able to tell us exactly what happens?

Kagan: They'll be able to tell us more, but we know that the human brain differs qualitatively from the ape brain. No question.

Tu: And the relationship between that and morality?

Kagan: That we don't know because that would win a Nobel Prize if anybody could say, you see why we have human morality, it's because of this structure in the brain. You would be on the cover of every magazine. We don't know that yet.

Tu: Yeah. I know that, but that's the question.

Kagan: Well, that's one important question.

Tu: Yeah. But I think there are many ways of framing this question. One way of framing this question is to try to locate the feeling of commiseration, for example, in a two-year-old. How is it located in the brain? Your observation is that capacity [of commiseration] is there, but the content is yet to be filled. We know the capacity, the content. Can the two be clearly differentiated? Maybe this is not an argument, but an exchange. If the frame and the content are differentiable, we have the frame without content, and the content would necessarily come from some kind of social conditioning. If that's the case, then the ability of humans to be moral in our terms is dependent upon the approval or disapproval of a community.

Kagan: Well, it depends on the community and what the community celebrates.

Tu: And the standards of the community, let's say, the standards of the community are so crucial that even at the age of two, our senses of morality are shaped by them.

Kagan: Yes. I remind you of something you know. There are tiny communities of criminals where the community views as the right thing to do is to steal from people. That is their morality. John D Rockefeller, the grandfather, once told a reporter, "I make money because that's what God wants me to do.[2]" So, that's why I say the content. I'm sure some of the Serbs who killed Bosniaks thought they were doing the right thing, or the crusaders of the 11th century who were murdering in Jerusalem. So, we've got to watch it here. You can do violent acts and think you're behaving morally.

Tu: Now, then, I don't know. We cannot avoid a form of relativism in terms of social styles of formation. In other words, it's the nature of society, whether it's violent, whether it's benevolent, whether it's pro-life, or whether it's against nature, that determines what the people will eventually become.

Kagan: Yes. What they will regard as moral. Do we agree that when Chinese parents bound the feet of their young girls for five centuries, both the girl and the parents thought they were doing a moral act?

Tu: Yes. It was like, I think, maybe the Elizabethan notion about corsets. The idea about corsets is that they try to destroy their bodies for that particular custom.

Kagan: Right... and Mayan priests in the sixth century AD would throw young virgins down a well; that was a moral sacrifice for them to bring rain. I mean, humans have done some things that, in our eyes, in the 21st century, we say, "Why would you do that?" But in those days, they were moral acts in that context.

Tu: The question is hypothetical. If there is human progress in terms of morals, is there a possibility of broadening the sensitivity initially available to a young boy or a young girl? Various kinds of social conditions themselves have some kind of inertia, but they came into being through a very long process of accumulation.

Kagan: I know. You may disagree with me, but I think the 18th century was more moral around the world than the 21st century, than today. There is less morality in the sense that you and I understand it today than in the 18th century. I think we cycle both the Greeks and the Chinese. It's the West that likes linear progress. I don't believe in linear progress. I believe in cycles. So, there are cycles when morality is generally high across many societies, and then you have dark ages. We're in a dark age that would take us too far. I don't think that we are more moral than any other century. I don't believe that at all. Oh, no.

Tu: I agree, but the question is the interplay between a person and social conditioning. I don't believe, I don't think you believe that the social conditioning is the only input in shaping the moral characters of people, but what, in your view, is this kind of interactive model, and how? First of all, let's assume that the frame of the brain is such that it's capable of sympathetic understanding and capable of some sense of developing morality, and that

[2] [editor] possibly a paraphrase of statements attributable to John D Rockefeller: "God gave me my money." or "I believe the power to make money is a gift from God."

various kinds of societies shape the content. We've given all sorts of examples. Some societies may turn out to be extremely cruel from our point of view, but the people who are subjected to that conditioning believe they are doing not only moral things, but they may be obligated to do that. And one way out is to say that's the situation; let's accept it. The other way of looking at it is to see a much more complicated interaction between the development of persons and the social mores that condition the development of persons. We may consider the persons not powerful enough to overcome some of the acts of a society that, from our point of view, are considered very inhumane, immoral, or cruel.

Kagan: Right. I think it's a speculation. I think the last 50 years, which permitted the internet, CNN, and cell phones to penetrate almost all parts of the globe, have changed everything. Let's go back to the 18th century. In the 18th century, here you are. You're born in a village in Borneo or a village in Tibet. You know your community. You didn't leave that community. 80% stayed there. And so, what determined the morality of that community and its citizens was how much mutual trust there was between community members. What is the disparity in property and power? Is it large or is it small? Is there justice? Those two things. Well, that makes it simple, because if I have a community where the difference between the wealthiest 10% and the poorest is small, and we know each other, that's a pretty moral community. But suddenly, today, in this village in Borneo, this 20-year-old knows about Los Angeles and Paris. And he or she says, "Wait a minute. I thought things were just, but those people have too much. They've got too much." And suddenly, I have an envy that my grandfather was prevented from having. I believe that the community, the fact that everyone can know what's happening worldwide within two minutes of it happening, has changed the game. And we have new sources of envy, new sources of jealousy, new sources of anger that we did not have. Those are corrosive to human morality.

Tu: That's probably your sense that the 21st century turned out to be worse.

Kagan: ... that and everything we know about the two world wars and everything else.

Tu: If we then return to the earlier observation, we cannot, I don't know whether we should, take a relativistic position in the sense that the different societies, especially in traditional world with the mores of that particular society then the persons who were conditioned in that kind of environment had minimal possibility of doing anything. Is that deterministic or not?

Kagan: No, it's not deterministic because there will always be some people who disagree. You'll never find a community with homogeneous moral beliefs or values. They're always going to be rebels in the community. But the point is, we used to be able to deal with autonomous societies, and we can't do that anymore. The narrative we call history is a book that never ends, and we're in a unique chapter. I believe the state of the world today is unlike anything that has ever occurred before, partly because of the global interconnection of everything. And so, we have to see what happens now. We'll cycle out of this. I believe that there are cycles of good and cycles of bad. This is a bad time, but a generation will come that will repair it. Let me just say one more thing. This is the first time in history that humans are making a contribution to the integrity of the planet. They never did that before. And so suddenly, a new moral concern must penetrate humans that they were indifferent to for 150,000 years. That is what is my contribution to environmental pollution, air pollution, and global warming because they're going to threaten the sea. The sea levels are going to rise, and millions of people are going to either lose their homes or die because of this. Even if humans do not contribute to it, this is going to happen like an earthquake. So, I think humans have to be aware, "Wait a minute. Maybe, I should take as one of my moral imperatives: am I contributing anything to hasten this calamity?" Humans never had to worry about that. I believe a generation is going to occur in every society, not just the West, where the youth are going to say, "Yes, that is a moral imperative. I'm not going to make a serious contribution to make the planet worse." That could happen. That would be fascinating.

Tu: You know, this is a fascinating thought and I think that's the reason why we're involved last year in the whole project of rethinking the human, which is also related to the human both in terms of the species and in terms of individuals will have to be embarked on a the rethinking of our condition and our relationship to the planet, of human relationships themselves, our self-understanding, and also our relationship to the transcendent, whether there's a God or not. There are two questions I want to raise. One is that I think you suggested a hopeful sign. That is the new generation with all this clear knowledge about what we ought to do. Otherwise, the viability of the human species will not only be problematic but will no longer be sustainable. Let's say that new awareness will hopefully occur. This relates to the question about human beings being in the world for a long time. And so, what is in a broad sense the cumulative wisdom or experience, or the cumulative concern and consciousness that allowed us here to have this, not necessarily a fate, to have this strong conviction that something will emerge?

Kagan: You're not going to like my answer. And this is not that original, but it's not a common belief, I think. The historical narrative has taught many humans, especially those with a modicum of education, that the poet Wallace Stevens had it right. I think Athenians wouldn't have thought this. Mencius wouldn't have thought this. Montaigne wouldn't have said this. Kant wouldn't have said it. Stevens says that we have to make it up that humans have no choice because of their nature. They have to invent ethical goals. Otherwise, they become depressed, and depression is a painful state. Everyone knows that if I have no ethical goals, then I have no reason to get up in the morning. You must have some, and you must believe that the ones you choose are worthy. Voltaire's mistress, 18th-century Émilie du Châtelet, said, "Illusions are everything. Without illusions, you're lost." A very wise woman. And what did Wallace Stevens say in the 20th century? He said you've got to invent something. You see, that's mine. But recognizing it's your invention, and someone else can invent something else, you must commit to your invention with emotion, and the exquisite joy you will experience is that you're pursuing your ethical goal, knowing it's your invention. Now, if you can manage that, you've made it. And that's what Émilie du Châtelet is saying.

Kagan: "Without illusions, there's nothing," I used to tell my daughter when she was ten. I said, "You've got to get a lot of bubbles inside of you. Each bubble is an illusion, so you can either work toward them or burst them if they're wrong. And you've got to get to 90 years of age with some bubbles left. If there are no bubbles left, you're lost." So, that's what du Châtelet was saying. I think that idea, which Stevens says so beautifully, is new. And so, when you ask me what progress we have made, it's a funny kind of progress because it says nature didn't intend any particularly moral purpose for us. All nature cared about was to survive and beget the next generation. After that, it's up to you. Well, that is deadly. I mean, that is tough on humans. And so, it's a funny kind of progress, but at least we know the truth. Do you remember the last lines of Beckett's wonderful exchange between the two tramps waiting for Godot? One tramp says, "Say you're happy." He says, "I'm happy." And the other says, "I'm happy too. We're both happy." And then the other says, "So what do we do now?" And then the tramp says, "We wait for Godot." Oh, now that's a brilliant line. See, that's what Wallace Stevens said.

Tu: But the new invention or the imagination or illusion, and in confronting a desperate situation, we certainly impute no real human value to nature because it is as it is.

Kagan: Exactly.

Tu: That's exactly something out there. Now, if we try to go back, let's say no other philosophers ever encountered a situation like we do today. So, this provides the possibility of something radically new or even revolutionary. The earlier question I mentioned is that human beings have struggled with these questions for centuries, and there are differences in the broadly defined human project. Now, one position is to say that until now, human beings have been unable to think about the human species holistically because they are separate communities. However, very early in human history, all the major historical or ethical religious traditions seem to have developed a certain universal conception about being human. And even though we know some social forces or cultural forces condition each of them, and yet, you know, last time we also mentioned the Axial Age in this period from probably 1000 BC to the sixth century BC, some great civilizations occurred obviously with no direct connections.

Tu: Of course, they communicated among themselves continuously, but each developed a specific vision of being human or learning to be human. And as late as 1949, I guess the German philosopher Karl Jaspers still mentioned that these major forces may have significantly shaped the human condition. Some societies occurred and eventually faded away. Some societies develop certain moral mores that are totally unworkable from our point of view. You're talking about the inmates or even Rockefeller's notion of greed. Other kinds of ethical standards or ideas not only survived but also flourished and contributed to our self-understanding, no matter how limited that is. Indeed, compared to what's happening now, all these pale by comparison to the magnitude of the human condition as we confront it today because the species' viability is at stake. But the question I have is that there must have been a great deal of resources that human beings have accumulated.

Kagan: What kind of resources?

Tu: Moral or spiritual resources humans have accumulated to confront past situations. Let's assume that the world goes through different cycles, and the idea of progress is certainly not very plausible in that particular scenario. But now, the big question is: probably for the first time in human history, we're not simply the outcome of the evolutionary process but also negative contributors. This was unknown before, but we became aware of the problem. Now, this is a personal question for me: whether all that happened in the various kinds of traditions or in various kinds of people's observations and ways of communicating among themselves, and any cumulative wisdom, did not prepare us. Human cumulative wisdom is absolutely critical for our ability to think right now when confronting this grave threat.

Kagan: Yeah. I understand. I think that the most important insight goes back to hunter-gatherers. Those humans, 100,000 years ago, recognized that they were part of a group and that they couldn't survive alone. Certainly, hunter-gatherers, those groups of 30, couldn't survive alone. They would die. So, you need to be in the group, and therefore, as a human, you recognize that the integrity and health of the group are very important for you and your welfare. Consequently, I've got to keep harmony. I've got to watch my selfishness and everything we call moral. Well, we believe that today.

I don't think that we changed very much. What's changed is the complexity of the context. We don't live in a band of 30 people anymore, but the fundamental property, the fundamental spiritual resource, I don't think that's changed. It is: "I recognize that if I live in a community, I've got to make sure this community is not unpredictably violent, unpredictably selfish, unpredictably malevolent. Otherwise, I will be tense all the time and won't be able to enjoy my life." That insight we recognize, and I think we've always recognized. I don't think we have a greater insight into that now than we did. It's just that the community we live in – we live in too many communities. You and I live in this university community, the community we live in, our nation, and the world. So, we're trying to balance all these communities, and they don't balance well. It's not like being one of 30 people.

Tu: But if we return to the so-called civilizations, they're different and have different ways of organizing their communities. I think what you mentioned about the society a hundred thousand years ago, with a group of 30, was a minimum condition for any society or community's survivability. But then, survivability is only part of the story. Humans strive and have aspirations way beyond survival, right? Otherwise, we wouldn't have anything we have today. So, there are many ways. I wouldn't use the word actualization in a limited sense, but flourishing. I think the Greek word for flourishing[3] is probably a good one. The wisdom or the survival instinct is one thing; maybe that's what we need to deal with the kind of crisis we're confronted with. But there's another side of the story about not just the meaning of life, but human flourishing and how we account for these different styles of human flourishing.

Kagan: Because the living context was different. In 18th-century England, Adam Smith said this is how you flourish: "Put self-interest first, and your society will flourish." That won't work today. So, I will turn the question back to you. Given our knowledge, you and I have the same knowledge of the state of the world today, but I'm not sure of the answer. What is it? What moral imperatives would help humans flourish? I ask you.

Tu: A genuine question. Even in the time of Adam Smith, the nation's wealth depended upon self-interest, and the accumulative self-interest may lead to the interest of the society at large. But he didn't quite consider that as his major contribution. He considered himself a moral philosopher because he was the author of *The Theory of Moral Sentiments*. Obviously, the father of economics did not consider economic issues the most fundamental for human flourishing. He did it for human survival. Maybe you must have that instinct to survive, but that's the minimum condition. We need to have something much more than that. Therefore, the meaning of life is not simply reducible to the survivability of the species, even though that's a big question. There are all kinds of acts people perform that may, on the surface, be against their survivability, but these are great sacrifices that we all celebrate as great contributions. So, in this particular situation, we know that survivability is at stake. There are two ways of looking at it. One is a very thin, superficial description.

The thin description is to say, let's find out those possibilities that will help us to survive. You mentioned that if a new generation begins to think seriously, either as an individual or a group, we will not contribute negatively to the sustainability of human life. So, there's a life change. That's the thin description. But there's also a thick, more comprehensive description. What is a good life? What is a meaningful way of doing it? It's predicated on the realization of our survivability. But that's only a minimum condition. That's not it. That's not good enough.

Kagan: My answer to your question is a good life. A person who says at the end, "I've had a good life," is one who has set up a set of ethical goals (this is Wallace Stevens) and was allowed to pursue them. That's a problem today, not for you and me, because you and I set up ethical goals and were allowed to pursue them; you and I feel very good about our lives. But in today's younger generation, many of them haven't set up these ethical goals, these bubbles. Therefore, they're unhappy because they're not on the train pursuing some ideal that they think is very useful. That's a real problem for this generation. I think generations will come when this will be repaired. Let me remind you what Adam Smith

[3] eudaimonia

said and was wrong; that's what's universal. In the book, he said that humans will always be ashamed of what their neighbors might say. That's over in modern America.

Bernie Madoff didn't care what people were saying. The bankers who sold mortgages, they didn't care. Shame is so fundamental to the two-year-old. It was also critical to Mencius in his earlier writings. Shame has been ill. It has become diluted because we've crowded people together who don't know each other. What Adam Smith didn't understand was that there would come a time in 250 years when people, a lot of people, wouldn't feel shame. He couldn't imagine such a society. Shame is, as you said earlier, a very important component of human morality. Not the only one, but if you lose it, you lose an important foundation.

Tu: Now, if the young generation realizes the need for their survival and the survival of the human species, they will decide not to contribute negatively to that process. Is this the reconstitution of a sense of shame culture?

Kagan: A beginning. We won't do that alone, but it would be a beginning. You have to invent something. You asked the right question, Weiming. You said, "So, what is a good life?" And I think we agree. A good life is: I have set up these moral ideals, and I'm getting closer. I don't have to get there, but I'm getting closer." If you can do that all your life, you'll be happy. It's a great life. Wittgenstein, as you know, was, from a temperamental point of view, a morose depressive. He was always anxious when he was 30. He writes in his diary, "I will never have any joy. Ever." His three brothers committed suicide. I mean, he was melancholic, but he knew he was one of the great philosophers of the 20th century. I read last month that on his deathbed with his friend there, he says to his friend hours before he dies, "Tell them I've had a good life." That's because, if he meant it, he said, "I set up the ethical ideal of knowledge and thought, and I was allowed to pursue it." You couldn't ask for anything more, even though his basic feeling tone was melancholic all his life.

Tu: If, say, an individual decides to set up these ethical goals for him or her to aspire to and try to struggle to achieve them, if that's the idea of the new invention...

Kagan: Not new. Remember, the Greeks had eudaimonia. So, this is not a new idea.

Tu: No, but the interplay between a personal aspiration, you set a goal, and, as we talked earlier, the content of that frame continuously comes from society. So, these goals we set must be integral to certain social approval or at least be sanctioned by society.

Kagan: Absolutely and absolutely.

Tu: But the problem we face when we're confronted with this incredible situation seems to suggest there must be something so new, so different, from what inertia of the human community has led us to this particular point. And I have an even broader question. I think perhaps one of the most tragic situations we may face is that, as you already pointed out, the more we become aware of what we ought to do to get out of this incredible situation, the more we are acutely alert to the institutional, social, and habitual constraints, to all these forces to observe what's going on in the world. Those who are powerful and influential have access to information, ideas, and the mindset that has been exhibited. The more we know it, the more we are acutely aware of it, the more we feel incapable of changing it, at least from one point of view. And so with rational clarity and insight into the precariousness of the human situation. And yet, the whole process continues.

Kagan: That's right. You see, here's the problem, and you see it in the problems in Europe. Most humans find it very hard to say that my category is all humans. I am a brother of all humans. Very hard. Usually, your primary category is smaller, and that's what hurts things. Last week, I gave a seminar to a small group of Graduate students in international affairs at Tufts, and in the audience was a very smart, 40-year-old, moderately wealthy Zambian who wants Zambia to go forward. And we were talking, and I was talking about, look, we have to be concerned with the planet. And then he said, appropriately, "Now look, I'm concerned with Zambia. You guys in the West, you had your chance. You created all this pollution. You had factories pouring out smoke. It's our turn now." He wasn't saying that out of anger. He was saying, I'm concerned with Zambia. That's my category. And I want Zambia to have more hospitals, industry, and wealth. And so, I will build industries and have cars because I care more about Zambians than anybody. But America cares more about Americans. And look at the problem the European Union is having; they are more argumentative now than ever in the European Union. They can't get together, and this is a very small part of the world. The problem is that these categories we discussed divide us, and each group has a primary loyalty to its category. That is from a moral point of view, if we could give the world a moral score, what hurts us.

Tu: This touches upon one of the major problems I've been deeply concerned about. The Zambian response is very much the Chinese response. That's right. And not in terms that are so blunt. The idea is now it's our turn to pollute the air. It's our turn to maximize profit. This is a mentality I call the scientistic mentality, a kind of modernism, materialism, commercialism, and economism. The idea is that being modern is measured in quantitative terms, in terms of material wealth, and so forth. By comparison, even though the economy of China as a whole is large, per capita income is extremely small. It's probably below 140, with 192 countries below 140, and so forth. So, it is our right to develop. It is our right to become modern. And we can never emulate the standards of the United States. However, we should strive to match some East Asian countries, not necessarily Japan, but others. And so, this is an incredible commitment to a process that is, from your earlier point of view, totally detrimental to the survivability of the human species. So, one question I have is that there is a human capacity. This is what I believe: a human capacity to think beyond the categories that define who we are.

Tu: This developed very early in human history. Well, not 10,000 years ago, but at least during the so-called Axial Age civilizations, people began to think not only of a particular tribe, a particular society, or even a particular nation. I believe nation-states probably didn't exist then. But when Christians talk about Christians, they talk about how every person could become a Christian. So, there is universal love. When Buddhists talk about being a Buddhist, there's also this notion that every human being can become a Buddhist, which is the highest manifestation of self-actualization. Let's say, in the Confucian tradition, there is unity between humans and Heaven. And there's a beautiful statement by an 11th-century thinker by the name of Zhāng Zài 张载. In his *Western Inscription*, he says, "Heaven is my father, Earth is my mother, and even such a small creature, as I, finds a small place in their midst. Therefore, that which fills the universe I regard as my body, and that which directs the universe I consider as my nature. All people are my brothers and sisters, and all things are my companions." And you can say, you know, this is the 11th century. You can tell this is a vision that is not only beyond Familialism, beyond the family, beyond the locality of parochialism, or beyond race, beyond the nation, even beyond anthropocentrism, because you talk about all things as your companion or companions.

Tu: Now, I'm not saying that it is widely accepted. That's certainly not the case, but the human capacity to think beyond your own categories, those social categories that define who you are, is something that is significant for us when facing this new crisis. And so, how can this vision be shared in a differentiated, therefore discriminatory, world with the haves and have-nots? In other words, we are all different. Some countries are much more powerful. However, when confronted with a new situation, one should consider human uniqueness. And that's a very serious, key question for me. Some people say, from either a biological or other point of view, our survivability is so tiny compared to many different species, like insects and viruses. So, it's only natural that human beings will not be able to save themselves. But if we're still thinking along the lines that you suggested earlier, concerning the sort of new thinking for the new human, then there must be many listeners or ideas that are still relevant and important.

Kagan: I don't think we can get close to your ideal until the differences in the basic necessities of life are more equal. You know, potable water, sanitation, good medical treatment, schools for everybody. So, we're so far from satisfying necessities that there's no way you can approach this ideal. So, now let's fantasize. Humans are capable of having the thought. Namely, wouldn't it be nice if all humans said, "I am a member of humanity"? John Donne: "Do not ask for whom the bell tolls. It tolls for thee." Now let's have a two-minute conversation. It is now a thousand years from now, and what I just said has been accomplished: all people of the world have homes with sanitation and clean water, all kids go to school, everybody has a high school graduation, everybody's got electricity, everybody lives to at least 75. Okay, that's a thousand years from now. Do you think it would be? Is it possible for people to say yes first, "I am a human being," rather than first, "I'm Norwegian," or first, "I'm a Muslim"? I don't know. See, that's what I don't know. Humans have a strong tendency to say, "My group is different." What are your thoughts here? What do you think? Don't be too idealistic. We've now got this new state of the world. Everybody's got everything they need materially to have a physically comfortable life. Do you think that at that point humans will say, "My primary identity is I'm a human being"? I don't know.

Tu: That's my view, which is probably quite different from yours. We don't have a thousand years to wait for that. Even if we can imagine it, we may not even have 100 or 200 years.

Kagan: But we won't get there in 100 years, right?

Tu: Yeah. Okay. There are two ways of looking at it. One is that it would probably take as long as a thousand years or something of that nature. And we know we don't have that much time to reach that state. The situation will deteriorate quickly if the Zambians, the Chinese, and others do not share this idea. So, I assume we don't have a thousand years, and we will know within 100 years, we're not going to achieve it. Also, we have to think that the horizon cannot be that long, like 50 years, or it becomes unrealistic. We only have 50 years to think about those kinds of issues. Let's say the world is still very widely divided, and maybe 1 billion people will not have the clean air or clean water we take for granted – the situation remains roughly the same. And so, the United Nations Millennium Project, which aimed to reduce poverty in the poverty-stricken countries by 2020 or so, will not be realized, and the situation will worsen. And all this is, right now, common knowledge. What are some of the things the new generation, presumably our children, have to do? What brilliant idea do they need? What would they have to do now? I see several interesting developments. First of all, it's not possible for any religious leader.

Tu: I mean, with respect, for example, in the Christian tradition, to say that we wait for the kingdom of God to come, and the world here is the world of the Caesars. So, let it be profane and polluted. So, don't mind what our world is like. A Buddhist leader can't say, "We are looking for a Pure Land yet to come, look for the other shore. Let this land collect dust to become polluted again." So, whether they like it or not, each has developed two very different conceptions of categorization. One is that a Christian wants to be a Christian because of several great ideas they cherish when defining themselves. And that's true with the Buddhists, but the Buddhist and Christian ideas in some ways are not commensurable. You cannot be a Christian and a Buddhist at the same time. They're very different. So, identification will continue to be strong for the new generation. But this new identity will have to emerge. That is the question of global citizenship. In other words, I am a Christian, to be sure, but also a human being in the 21st century. So, it's my obligation not to pollute, even though the kingdom of God is probably more precious to me as a Christian than the world here. That's also true for Buddhists and other people. You know that sense, if not categorical imperative, that sense of moral obligation, I think, is emerging.

Kagan: I hope you're right.

Tu: I think I'm right in responding to your broader question. And I agree that without an equitable economic situation, the possibility of an international effort to change the global crisis is limited. But we don't have that much time, and changes must be made. And yet we, in our way of rethinking the human or for the next, say, 50 years, really have to be bold enough to imagine something that is required of every person.

Kagan: But I see no signs in this privileged generation of 25-year-olds, even in America. I see very little encouragement that they're using their car less or, you know, minimizing their carbon imprint or whatever that is. I don't see enough in their behavior that this generation will make a major contribution. I don't think it's caught on yet. I don't think they're committed yet to it. We may have to wait for another generation. Look, in 100 years, the sea will rise. We don't know how much. Let's say it rises a foot. Humans are going to survive. It'll just impact the coastal communities. People will either leave or die. They'll probably leave. So, we're still going to have 6.5 billion humans. You're not going to wipe out the species, but you're going to cause pain and distress to many people. But when the plague hit Europe in the 14th century.

Tu: 30%-50% perished.

Kagan: Yeah, but the plague didn't hit Indonesia. So, you know, things happen, and some people get hurt. Climate change will hurt some people, but the species will survive. You and I are worried about not surviving. We're going to survive. Well, you and I are concerned about those who do survive. Can we make their lives fuller? How do we make their lives morally fuller? So, in the end, they can say, like Wittgenstein, that it's a good life. "Tell them I've had a wonderful life." That's what we're talking about. Not survival.

Tu: Yes, but way beyond survival. How is that sense of a good life related to the very beginning of our discussion of the emergence of the human species?

Kagan: It is because we agreed an hour ago that you can't help but erect these ethical ideals by the time you're 5 or 6 years of age. You do that. It emerges. It's universal, like language, singing, and climbing trees. These are all emergent properties of our species.

Tu: ... but these emerging properties, as we noted, are an integral part of the particular environment, especially the social environment, in which we are. And many of these social environments are counterproductive for human flourishing.

Kagan: Well, now we go back to what we said moments ago. But if parts of the world are unequal... If children in the Madras are learning as an ethical ideal that there is the one true religion and every anybody who's not Muslim is less than human, then this is not a very good ethical ideal for children to learn in, if we're living in a global place where we all must be tolerant of and try to help one another. It's not just that – for Benjamin Netanyahu's statement, he will put up more houses in Jerusalem, which doesn't help things. That doesn't help bring peace. So, everyone is capable of being blamed. Everybody is selfish. This is Garrett Hardin's "*Tragedy of the Commons*," right? And, in the end, everybody's cow eats the common, and then there's no more grass left. We're having a hard time getting humans to rise above their family and their immediate group, religion, ethnicity, or nationality, to the next level. It's like you're fighting gravity, and we can't get to that next level so that everyone realizes, wait a minute, I've got to come up one step on the ladder, because the only way life's going to be full if we all recognize we are part of the same family, the human family. And we're not there. There's a resistance. There's a force that is making that leap difficult.

Tu: One question I think related to this is that if economic globalization or globalization, in terms of science and science and technology, has helped to develop a more homogenized World, and therefore, the possibility of a sense of interconnectedness or togetherness might be widely appreciated. However, cultural globalization, the term people use, indicates that localization, or even indigenization, has become very powerful in the 21st century. They are, I call them, the primordial ties such as ethnicity, race, gender, age, cohort, place of birth, language, and not to mention religion. Each one of them becomes very powerful. Identity politics becomes pervasive. Religious conflict and tension rise. You mentioned quite a few of them, and now you have again, returning to your earlier observation concerning a new ethic. A newly invented ethic for not just human survival, but also for the quest for a good life. That is predicated on the emergence of a sense of identity, but not with the particular groups of communities, but with humanity as a whole, primarily as a member of the human community. So, these two forces are: one is the universalization of our categories, and the other is particularization. And there's such tension between the two.

Tu: And I sense that the either-or choice will not work. One would be abstract universalism, where we should follow specific general rules of behavior. And then immediately, your friend from Zambia will have a radically different view, but based upon what? What is needed? That's also the Chinese problem. On the other hand, if we allow particularistic concerns to dominate, then the kind of closed particularism, which may even be highly aggressive, would be powerful. So, there would be no negotiation. I'd like to ask for your opinion on this. Probably, there's a certain kind of interchange. We cannot abandon our primordial ties, the categories that shape us as concrete, living human beings. But at the same time, we know that we have to go beyond ourselves, our family, our community, even simply beyond the human world. What is your view on this? I don't know whether I'm reading you correctly or not. You are much more concerned about breaking all these categories to reach a higher sense of being human than recognizing the richness or fruitfulness of these categories in shaping the concrete, living human being.

Kagan: Well, that's the tension. I think you described it well. Humans have to have a basis for reassuring themselves that they are good (moral).

Tu: Just as a conviction or what?

Kagan: Remember, I said in the third stage, where you learn good and bad, and you apply it to the self. So, you say, am I a good person? Humans cannot avoid asking that question; they just can't avoid it. It starts at age three. Now, for most of history, most humans have used it. They compare themselves with others. The beautiful thing about Buddhist philosophy is that you don't do that. But that hasn't been popular with most humans, unfortunately. So, if citizens of poor countries are aware of rich countries, say, wait a minute, my country's got to be as good as your country, or I can't feel good about myself. How do we move people away from using external properties to judge goodness? To what? To internal property? Am I moving toward wisdom? Am I moving toward knowledge? Am I fine? Am I following my ethics? And if I can say yes at the end of the day, that day was well done, independent of what you do, because you might be doing the same thing. You might even be doing it more than I. But I don't care about that. Can we do that? I don't know because humans are so addicted to comparing their group with another group, rather than each person themselves deciding, as Wittgenstein did tell them, I had a good life. The Buddhists thought it was possible. Theoretically, it should be possible. But we're having a hard time doing that. We're having a tough time moving people away from external comparisons to just judging. Am I moving toward greater understanding and wisdom? Pursuing my ethical ideals, am I? Did I do better today than I did yesterday?

Tu: That idea of intrinsic criteria rather than extrinsic? Precisely that idea. I think, you know, I assume that it's rooted in human capacity.

Kagan: It is, but it's delicate and fragile. It's opposed by the strong tendency to compare yourself with others. Those are two human capacities. And they fight with each other.

Tu: And how? Let's get back to the age of two. How is that sympathetic and empathetic capacity of the aged two? Let's say, sympathy is a kind of intrinsically generated force in negotiating these two tendencies of intrinsic self-realization on the one hand and comparing with others on the other hand.

Kagan: I know, but the Zambian would say, "Now look, if I develop Zambia's economy, I'm not hurting you." So, he doesn't have to feel guilty because of his empathy. He's not hurting me. He's just trying to develop Zambia. But that's external. He wants Zambia to be as good as the West.

Tu: So, sympathy or empathy at that level doesn't help. Is it possible to imagine identifying myself as a member of the human community? That idea is rooted in empathy and sympathy. Can the conscientious cultivation of empathy and sympathy be a way of reaching that particular state of mind?

Kagan: Theoretically, yes. But economists have a lot of theories, too.

Tu: You know, one is theoretical, the other is some kind of moral imperative that we. Given that we agree with the problem, the dilemma in which we find ourselves, and how to get out of it, is extremely difficult. And we're not too optimistic that our new generation will be able to do that. But instead of saying it's a theoretical question, let's say it's a pedagogical one; it's also a question about human flourishing in the best sense of the term. Cultivating empathy and sympathy as the point of departure is the starting point. It's not an endpoint. Any kind of extension is going to be helpful.

Kagan: I think we need a catastrophe to actualize what you and I want. I don't think humans will do it unless they have to. In other words, we need something like the following in the next hundred years. Vast areas of the world have droughts, crops fail, and people die. Typhoons and hurricanes are increasing in frequency. A catastrophe where people say, "Oh, my God, we must do something now." I think there has to be a demand that says an external threat, which says if you don't change your ethical priorities, you're in deep trouble. We're going to punish you more. I don't think it will happen until there are some severe catastrophes. In the war, when the Germans bombed Britain, people became friendly with each other, and they united. It took the threat to bring them together. And for a few weeks after 9-11, Americans were putting up flags. There was patriotism, you remember? It's shameful that humans have to be threatened before they will do something. But I'm afraid the goals you and I want will not happen unless something catastrophic happens.

Tu: Then the whole question about internal criteria, in fact, will become not fictitious but probably cannot be fully realized. At an individual level, there's no question it can be realized. You talk about Einstein. So, in terms of the development of a person, and I am a good person, I try to develop myself according to some of the standards I set up for myself. It's always available to every human being and can be a totally intrinsic value. However, in the broader picture, in terms of societal conflicts or, not to mention, cultural conflicts, these are issues that cannot be quickly resolved unless some incredibly dangerous situation occurs.

Kagan: Yeah. For example, here's a something you and I know that the generation after the defeat of the Nazis, that younger generation is so egalitarian, so sympathetic. Every time I visit Germany, I'm just impressed with that. But they needed that trauma to say no, sir. As a matter of fact, if you talk about patriotism, that's a bad thing to do because of what your country did. And universities sprouted. The Max Planck Institutes were established. It's like the war was a cleansing, but that was a catastrophe. They had to do it. Germany would never have moved in the direction its younger generation did without that catastrophe. That's what I mean; that's what catastrophes do. Now we're talking about warming, drought, and typhoons. I think it's going to be something like that.

Kagan: [In our dialogue,] we've covered a lot, though. Actually, it's gone better than I thought. I thought this was good, didn't you?

Tu: Yes. I enjoyed it very much.

Kagan: Is this what you had in mind?

Tu: Well, a lot of surprises, but it turned out to be happy surprises.

Kagan: Happy surprises are good. Yeah.

Tu: I thought especially of the last part when you described the human condition and catastrophes. Of course, it's depressing to understand what the human condition is. Still, I'll describe what the ideal form of life is. I already mentioned a little bit about the possibility of unity between humans and Heaven, so to speak. But. What we are envisioning now is the, um. Despite all the realistic assessments of the situation, we're still, I think both of us are hopeful that a new kind of mindset, even though it may not be powerful enough to be universal, but a new mindset will develop.

Kagan: We agree on that.

Tu: Yeah, that is.

Kagan: There's no question that the way the story goes, a new mindset will be created. No question in my mind. 6.5 billion humans.

Tu: We can begin now. I think this vision, which I still cherish a great deal in my thinking about the human condition here and now, is very much in line with your very vivid and highly challenging and also, to me, extremely penetrating description of where we are and the danger we face. It's really precarious, and the precariousness is so evident. The emergence of a new, broadly defined humanistic vision is necessary for the human community to deal with this major crisis. It is absolutely necessary. And I think one of the things we should be able to imagine as one of your bubbles. I wouldn't use the word illusion in that particular sense, but imagination. But the imagination is not just illusory. There are four extremely important issues confronting every human being. One is the self – hopefully, this is an integration harmony of the body and mind. One is the person with society and community, and variously understood family, the neighborhood, nation, race, culture, and the global community as a whole. The question of the human species with nature and the final one is which some traditions consider necessary and some traditions, especially secular humanist traditions, consider irrelevant. That's the question of the person or the human heart and mind and the way of Heaven, which means the ultimate meaning of life. In the Christian tradition, it is God. For other traditions, it is Allah, Brahman, or Logos.

A humanistic vision that fails to consider all four dimensions may be somewhat impoverished in dealing with the crisis we face. Then the question is, what does it mean to be human in the 21st century? Following this line of thinking, even if we consider Heaven omnipresent and omniscient, we cannot imagine Heaven or God as omnipotent because the emergence of the human has made the whole situation different. What we do, even in the privacy of our home, would have consequences not only in society and culture but even in the cosmos. In this particular situation, what does it mean to be able to reach the unity between Heaven, Earth, and human? Earth will be our Earth. Now, Heaven is the source of meaning for some traditions (may not be true for secular humanists). Human will have to be responsible member, not only to themself, to their community, or the human world at large, but to the cosmic process as well, because we are now so powerful, so influential, and we're capable of so much. Because we are empowered to do so much, to go to the Moon, and to develop an incredibly destructive force, the Earth may be highly vulnerable to this incredible human capacity to change, to shape, and to destroy. We began with the birth of the human who becomes a sympathetic being at age two. Gradually, by seven, we have all the major ingredients of a fully developed modern human present while facing this severe problem in light of the vision about not only human survival but also human flourishing. You also mentioned the catastrophe that may be a required condition to force the Human to think deeper about our situation. Given all these discussions, I wonder if you have any reaction to my observation about developing an integrated, comprehensive, humanistic vision about how to learn to be human in the 21st century.

Kagan: I think your first comparison, the relationship of self to community, is realizable. We're not there, but people can understand it, and if the conditions are right, it can be actualized. On the other hand, the relationship to nature seems to be backward. I mean, we're destroying the animals of the African continent. There appears to be an indifference to that. And we've spent the last 40 minutes discussing how we raise that consciousness. I think that's doable, but that seems more resistant. The one that you'll have to elaborate on is how to get people to think about their relationship to what you call Heaven. I think the times are very antithetical, and forces are opposed to that now. So, you have to come down the ladder of abstraction a bit and say more. What do you mean? What does a human being have to do to relate himself or herself to what you call Heaven?

Tu: First, I would define a human being as a rational animal or endowed with linguistic capacity. Each one of them is right but somewhat partial. A human being is aesthetic, historical, social, political, and metaphysical in the sense of a quest for meaning. Therefore, human beings are very complex, and we are observers of the idea of Heaven. We are observers: we observe nature. We observe ourselves, our society, and our communities. We are also appreciators. I think that may be distinctively human—this aesthetic sense of nature, of mountains or rivers. If we use the Christian language, we appreciate the world as being created and unfolding before us, but we are also participants right now. We are participants in the so-called cosmic process, in the evolutionary process. So, we are more or less co-creators of the environment in which we are. That leads to the question about human responsibility. We're not only responsible for ourselves but for the community. Also, now, we are responsible not only for our own survival but also for the survival of our environment.

Kagan: Right, but we don't need the concept of Heaven for all that. That's all. I agree with everything you said, but the concept of Heaven doesn't seem necessary in that description.

We humans invent meaning. If by Heaven you mean meaning, then we agree. We are meaning-creating creatures. That's what we do. Bees make honey. We make meaning. I don't think we need the concept of Heaven. We can invent the idea of Heaven, but that's an invention.

Tu: Self, community, and nature will be sufficient to handle the current situation.

Kagan: As long as we have some ethical ideals, ethics that say, "You better deal with it," right? Which we don't have right now.

Tu: Right. But these ethical ideas will have to be universalizable. In other words, these are not ethical ideas restricted to a community and are different from what has happened before.

Kagan: Correct. They have to be.

Tu: Right. Let's assume that the frame you discussed is distinctively human, which is related to the human brain, and the content must come from society. This new invention is to imagine a kind of content that society has never supplied. This is something drastically new because of the threat to the overall environment, partly because of the threat to the Earth, and, of course, the notion that the Earth is our home, and we can even suggest Earth is sacred. And it's not a collection of objects out there, but it's part of our own communion. Therefore, the notion is that not only all people are my brothers and sisters, but all things are my companions – that sense of a new relationship between human beings and nature. There must be a certain kind of imagined core of human self-realization, totally intrinsic to our human nature. It's not dependent upon conditions from the outside. That's a difficult question, I know. Nature is not totally neutral to the extent that it's devoid of values. For a while, we understood nature as it is – it had no purpose, there was no other possibility, and so forth. But right now, in this situation in which we humans are responsible not only for our own lives but for the lives of the Earth and so forth, we need to take nature radically differently. Earlier, we tried to deal with natural disasters. We wanted to control them; we tried to manipulate them. Eventually, we tried to subdue.

But now we know a new relationship will have to be established. With all our great inventions and our ingenuity, we know something is missing. That something missing is the ability to develop a sustainable and harmonious relationship with nature. And this is the context in which the idea of Heaven comes into being in the following sense. Our identity as being human is not simply our nature; it is not merely neutral. It just happened because of the evolutionary process. I'm not saying there's a teleology or intelligent design. I'm not talking about that at all. I'm talking about a force, let's say a force of the universe, maybe nature. The emergence of humans makes a fundamental difference in the cosmic process because human beings are conscious not only of themselves but are capable of creating values, giving names to everything, and are capable of self-actualization. That self-actualization is socially and politically significant. This is the meaning given, but the meaning is also enduring. The meaning is not simply contingent on a particular environment because now we know that the situation is so threatening that we have to be able to think, I would say, a kind of communal but critical self-consciousness of what the real problem is. In that context, I would like to ask you whether the three components we've been dealing with, the question of self, community, and nature, would be sufficient.

Kagan: Well, I think they are. I certainly acknowledge that some people are helped in their actualization and ethical journey by adding your concept of Heaven, but I think it is possible to accomplish what you and I want without that concept. That's my own personal view. Each species has its own set of traits. Bees make honey, you know.

Tu: Humans make meaning.

Kagan: That's right. Humans make meaning. It's not that one is better than the other. That's what happened. Some mutations occurred, and humans make meaning.

Tu: And I think a major difference between making honey and making meaning is that when you get into the question of meaning, it is unavoidable. That's why I believe some description of the good life, the question about ultimate meaning, actually means the real intrinsic meaning. The intrinsic meaning of life is different from the forces that shape a human being into a certain kind. In other words, that's the difference between Immanuel Kant's autonomous morality and heteronomous morality. A child will be shaped, and society will fill the content. And yet, we continuously struggle with this idea that the value I consider truly meaningful is intrinsic; it is not conditioned.

Kagan: What would be the intrinsic meaning of a human life?

Tu: One of the intrinsic values of human life is the unity between humans and Heaven. But now, let's say the idea of Heaven is problematic. This means not simply the human capacity to do things, but to create and fully realize humans as observers, appreciators, or participants and co-creators of the cosmic process.

Kagan: I understand. And that's right. But that's no more intrinsic than nursing a baby, caring for a child, or worrying about your old grandmother. I mean, there are a lot of things we do: painting, composing. These are all uniquely human things, but I don't want to give them privilege. I don't give privilege to the fact that we can imagine ourselves as part of nature and Heaven. That's one of our properties.

Tu: Well, Jerry, I want to challenge you on this. We have different tastes. We have different values. Many of these are intrinsic; they're not imposed on us from the outside. But you gave such a vivid and powerful description of the human condition in which we are. So, this is not a question of choice, right? Of saying, well, you may want to do this. You like Chinese food. I like German food. You like sports or basketball. This is a kind of, I want to use the word, destiny. I think you probably accept human destiny. There's a question of human destiny at stake, which is weighty. There is a tremendous magnitude to that particular question.

Kagan: I agree.

Tu: And you cannot avoid that question. You cannot avoid the question of who we are. But also, the question, why are we here? Regarding the second question, I think you may consider that a trick, as a trick or something. The German president, the current one, organized the conference...

Kagan: Merkel?

Tu: No. The president, not the Premier. I forgot the name. Anyway, he organized a meeting at home. These are the two questions he wanted to address. What does it mean to be human? Why are we here? "Why are we here?" may turn out to be simply a theological question. We just came into being because of this evolutionary process. Let's assume that's the case. I'm not doubting; I'm not committed to creationism at all. Let's assume that's the case. And let's assume that we are now at this particular juncture of human life. If the question arises, why should we continue to survive, or why the continual existence of the human species of any kind may or may not have any value from the naturalistic point of view, but it could have an extremely powerful value from our humanistic point of view. So, then, the question...

Kagan: I would say my answer is that when we say the purpose of being human is, I think it changes with millennia. And we have agreed over the last hour that the purpose today, but not the purpose for hunter-gatherers, not the purpose for Renaissance citizens, is to save the planet, a new purpose. History created a new purpose because we polluted our home, the Earth. But 2000 years ago, the Greeks didn't have to worry about this. The Greeks had to worry about something else. We invent. I don't know if we agree or not. I'm back to Wallace Stevens – you invent a purpose.

There's no intrinsic value in my view. I'm speaking only for myself. There are many people who will disagree with me, whether they hear or read this. This is my view that there is no special purpose to being human, as there is no special purpose to being a mosquito. We evolved. I'm glad we evolved. You and I are having a wonderful conversation. I'm really enjoying this. We evolved, and we're here. But I don't believe nature has any special purpose for us. But we demand it because of our unique genes and the brain we developed. So, we demand meaning. And I would say that there's a core meaning that comes from our moral sense. And then the rest comes from history. And history says you better attend to this. That better be an ethical goal.

Tu: No, no, no. I think you may contradict yourself a bit; you departed from your original basic idea. Let's say we are the meaning-creating animals. And let's say we are faced with a totally unprecedented situation. Therefore, history may give us all kinds of cumulative wisdom, but history cannot give us this ability to rethink and invent. So, this is something that we have to do. And you call it the spirit of the time or the challenge of the time. The meaning creation for us today fundamentally differs from the meaning creation for people in the Renaissance or the Axial civilizations. However, as humans, we are not only socio-political-economic beings but also historical beings with memory. We are also metaphysical beings in the sense that we quest for meaning. We are aesthetic. And so, in this particular context, we are confronted with this new situation, our mission is to save the planet. And that sense of mission in saving the planet is enriched not only by our history but also by our sociality, political sense, and all these other things that become particularly relevant, right? Now, if we agree that's the case, how can we talk about the meaninglessness of being human from the naturalistic point of view? Now, don't you see a contradiction between these two positions? Well, explain a little bit more because humans make meaning.

Kagan: You said it so beautifully that history is the scriptwriter for a television drama in which the actors are us now in this world and history says, "I'm going to give you a problem, and that is going to give you a lot of meaning right now, because you better solve that problem." And that's your meaning for that period. You've got to deal with it. You make up because if history is throwing you boulders, then for that moment, one of your meanings, one of your purposes is to deal with that boulder. And we agree that the state of the planet happens to be a boulder that suddenly occurred in the last century, a new one, a new problem.

Tu: But history means continuity. So, when we think about this question, this new boulder, this new condition, we have all our collective memory to bear it upon. That's distinctly human. And we have all our other senses. Each one is created by a human as a meaning given. So, we invent and create history, we invent and create social communities, and all these other things. It's not a privileged position. I'm not saying my position is that the ultimate meaning of life is different from the human world here and now. That it's dictated by some mysterious force from the outside – that's not my position at all. My position is what I call the *continuity of being*. You know, all these things are interconnected, giving humans the capacity to imagine a common destiny. It especially becomes increasingly apparent with the current situation because we do otherwise, this common destiny, and we invent this new invention. I would say, we have invented the purposefulness for solving this incredibly challenging problem. And from my point of view, this invention, just like history, has all kinds of other contributions from the past. And this invention itself also has rich resources in the human community. Yes, that's my position.

Kagan: We agree. I agree completely.

Tu: Well, how would you square that with the meaninglessness of being human?

Kagan: No, no, but we agree. We mean we agree. We make meaning. And you just described so gracefully the meaning of an important concept we invented at this point in history. I mean.

Tu: And you agree?

Kagan: Sorry.

Tu: You agree that it is...

Kagan: ...that it is a meaning we invented, and Renaissance citizens didn't.

Tu: And in a sense, one thing may be a slight difference is that this meaningfulness that we created, even though it's confronted with radically different new situation, but the creation, our ability to create this particular form of meaning is deeply rooted in history, in all the other situations that contribute to the human condition.

Kagan: Well, the origin is in that. I wish today's 20-year-olds had half the appreciation of history you have. You talk to some 20-year-olds, even Harvard undergraduates, and many have no sense of what happened over the last 8000 years.

Tu: What in the last 80 years?

Kagan: Right. So this is a serious problem. You and I, to a lesser extent, in our minds right now, can see the historical narrative continuously from when man first emerged. But they don't. And that's a serious problem. But otherwise, we do agree. And I think I agree with you that we have conceptions of the ideal. I think Homer's Odyssey is wonderful. Odysseus had a deal. He knew where he wanted to go. He wanted to go home to Penelope of Ithaca. But he had problems - he had to deal with Scylla, Charybdis, and Circe. These were the problems that humans faced during a particular historical era. Odyssey with Odysseus has a particular population, and they have issues. They think there exists some ideal, if you want to call that Heaven. If you want to call that conception of the ideal world Heaven, that's fine with me. Odysseus wanted to get home to Penelope, and he got home. Whether we get to our ideal state, that's less certain.

Tu: I think the final question is that China is in a different situation, maybe closer to the student who raised the question from Zambia, while in Cambridge. Given the complexity of the problem, while facing the challenge, if not saving the planet, at least we should try to do something to lessen the danger that threatens the viability of the human species. Any thought that using our capacity of sympathetic understanding, putting in thoughts and ideas of other people, and what would be the best way that their own self-interest and the interests of the world would be enhanced. What...

Kagan: What should we do?

Tu: What should they do? The Chinese or the Zambians...? But let's say the Chinese. Well, let's say probably we don't know enough about what's going on, so we cannot say anything about it. But now we have such a vast population, very much committed, at least superficially, to the idea of development, modernization, and modernity, precisely as described by this Zambian.

Kagan: I think it's unfair to ask them, who made a smaller contribution to the current problem than the West did, to sacrifice suddenly. And so, it has to be that the wealthy nations have to say, if we share some of our resources to help you meet this new challenge, that will help a lot. But, you know, the West is not about to do this because of the current set of ethical understandings that are so self-interested. You see, the fields of economics and evolutionary biology are fighting us because they say it's natural for humans to be self-interested. You look out for yourself first. That pervades every meeting, every academy, every hall. And that is murdering us. That's killing us because they are saying it as if it were a discovered scientific truth, talk to economists. When in fact it's an ethical position. It's not a discovered scientific truth, because how come humans are so cooperative and altruistic with non-kin who are not genetically related? That gives them a problem. So, they have persuaded the citizenry and those in power that self-interest is a natural law. If you look at nature programs on public television, it's 90% animals killing animals. It's never animals cooperating with animals, but animals cooperate with animals, too. On TV, they never do that. It's always animals killing animals. So, the whole mindset is to look out for yourself and your family, and then for your nation. So, this fight that you and I feel has to be waged, this goal you and I believe in, but the forces acting against it are very powerful.

Tu: Assuming this is also the mindset, which is ingrained in China's political and intellectual elite. So, there's no way out if this becomes ingrained. That's the question. And of course, it's probably unfair to them. But if, let's say, we were in that situation, we were Chinese or Zambians, and we knew for sure this was not just, we're being punished for the wrong reason, and we're asked to assume obligations for things that we have not yet done, and so forth. And yet the global situation is such that if we don't do something, this whole world will not be able to survive.

Kagan: The world...

Tu: Yeah. The world.

Kagan: The world will survive. But we don't know who's going to be hurt. And so, this is a dice game in which the Chinese and the Zambian say, it might not be us.

Tu: I know. Let me try to get this right. One is what is very likely to happen. I think the position you described and what is happening now are what is expected to occur. The other one is, let's say, a moral stand. We're fighting for this moral stand, which is against the other kind of dominant discourses focused on social Darwinian competition or economic choice, and so forth. Now let's assume this "moral stand" has its own intrinsic value. It needs to be not only promoted, but it also needs to be argued. My idea, maybe an illusion, is to say we are willing to converse about the core values, no matter how you define them; say, the core values are self-interest, justice, or sympathy. We would be involved in this discussion with a view towards the survivability of the human species or the protection of the planet. But first of all, I wonder whether such a conversation is meaningful. I don't know what forum it would take place on, but it's a conversation of that nature. If not at all meaningful or in the sense we've been talking about.

Kagan: Yes. As you spoke, I had a thought for the first time, George Bernard Shaw would write a play like *Man and Superman*, in which there was a conversation in which the leaders of China, Zambia, the US, and England were talking, just like you. How do we do this? A brilliant. It would be a brilliant play, six people on the stage trying to resolve the differences between my society's and the larger group's interests. I mean, that's the issue.

Tu: That's not enough, because that's precisely what happened, and I think we failed in Copenhagen.

Kagan: Yes, it did.

Tu: They got together and argued a bargain. It's not a question of bargaining.

Kagan: So, what is it?

Tu: It's a question more profound than that. If human beings are meaning-creating beings, the meanings we create shape our lives, order our societies, and strengthen us. Right now, it is used by many people as justification for all kinds of actions. But just at that level, we can talk. For example, how important is self-interest in understanding the world? There are a lot of very powerful arguments in favor of that. Our arguments questioning that may turn out to be very feeble. In other words, overwhelmed by the dominant discussion. But, maybe it's wishful thinking, if a conversation begins with some of the best philosophers or those people who are responsible for developing the vision about human community, are willing to discuss it with the people with a radically different view. I think you and I probably agree that the conversation will not likely occur. But if it takes place, it will be overwhelmingly dominated by the pervasive mindset. The question is, is it worth doing it?

Kagan: Oh, I'm sure it's worth doing it. I think it's worth doing. As I said earlier, I think having that conversation this year will be most effective. But I think it will be very effective when the first catastrophe occurs. We have to wait. There's something about humans; God didn't finish the job, and long-term worries don't arouse most people. And it's the present. Only patients who are obsessive-compulsive worry about the long-term future, and that's a real problem. That's why the youth don't worry about their mortality when they eat wrong or smoke or whatever. What do you say to a 20-year-old to worry they might get cancer at age 70? Forget it. We also know from research that when a long-term calamity is too far away, you don't worry about it. So, we have to fight. We must fight our nature to arrive at the ideal goal we want. We have to fight our fate. But we are capable of that. We are, because we're an unusual animal. We're the only animal that can put down our nature. For example, infant babies hate the bitter taste. Humans love martinis. Infant babies hate spicy foods. Mexicans love spicy foods. We can put down our nature. Human babies hate dissonant music. Millions of people love Stravinsky. So, we are powerful. No animal can put down its biological nature. We are the only species capable of doing that. This should give you hope that, if we try and have the will, we can say we can worry about the distant future for all, for humans. I don't even know if we are capable of that, whether we do it or not.

Tu: Well, let me just add one thing. I don't know whether you accept it or not. It's not simply a question of transforming nature or putting down nature. It is also, in a very deep sense, the realization of something so deeply rooted in our nature as the human species that allowed it to flourish. For example, if the sympathy of the two-year-old at the beginning of morality is no longer being distorted, wiped out, and relegated to the background, but allows it to flow through education, through all kinds of other mechanisms. This, of course, is the dream of many ethical systems to allow that. So, what you just talked about - the ability of the human to deal with this crisis, and before the crisis, before the disaster happens, requires a powerful, sympathetic, and compassionate appreciation of the human condition here and now. And I think the human capacity to understand, to project into the future, say, 100 years or even 50 years from now, is linked to a sympathetic or empathetic appreciation of something else. So, I sense that your idea of spicy food or martini is one way of cultivating certain human capacities, which are normally not intrinsic to our nature. Still, empathy and sympathy are not only a way to face challenges but also to fully develop something intrinsic in humans.

Kagan: I hope you're right. I pray you're right.

Tu: Well, this one statement is very interesting. It states, "I know that it cannot be done yet. I cannot but do it."

Kagan: Correct. That's lovely.

Tu: That's very interesting. Maybe it's very much like Cervantes.

Kagan: That's right. I like that.

Tu: Well, thanks a lot.

Kagan: This was great. Wonderful. You were good.

DIALOGUE WITH HOMI BHABHA 2010-05-20

Bio: Homi K. Bhabha (born 1949) is the Anne F. Rothenberg Professor of English and American Literature and Language, and the Director of the Mahindra Humanities Center at Harvard University. Born in Mumbai, India to a Parsi family, Bhabha graduated with a B.A. from Elphinstone College at the University of Mumbai and an M.A., M.Phil., and D.Phil. in English Literature from Christ Church, Oxford University. He is one of the most important figures in contemporary post-colonial studies and has developed a number of the field's neologisms and key concepts, such as hybridity, mimicry, difference, and ambivalence. He was awarded the Padma Bhushan award by the Government of India in 2012. Some of his works include *Nation and* Narration (1990), The *Location of Culture* (1994), *On Cultural Choice* (2000), and *Making Difference: The Legacy of the Culture Wars* (2003).

Professor Tu Weiming: I am very pleased and honored to have this rare opportunity to share a series of concerns regarding postmodernism, intellectual developments in our understanding of modernity, and a number of other issues. Homi is one of my close friends and we have been discussing these issues for some time. I would like to begin with a comment Edward Said made about Homi Bhabha. Said says, "Bhabha is that rare thing, a reader of enormous subtlety and wit, a theorist of uncommon power. His work is a landmark in exchange between ages, genders, and cultures; the colonial and post-colonial, modernist and postmodern." Homi, I understand in recent years, you have gone beyond some of the early issues you explored, especially in *The Location of Culture* that was published in the 1994.

Professor Homi Bhabha: There is a 2004 new edition.

Tu: Yes, there are many new editions. You raised some of the themes and questions you are still exploring, and one of the fascinating questions you've been exploring is the question of transition.

Bhabha: Yes.

Tu: Rather than investigating transformation, you focus on the idea of transition. This relates to the themes that Said pointed out that you're interested in, but my sense is that you've gone beyond these dichotomies. Some people characterize you as a postmodernist, but I think you want to go beyond simple postmodernism. I think your work impresses me as not only a reflection on the past, especially the Enlightenment legacy of the West, but also a view toward the future. When we try to retrieve some spiritual values in the past, it is not only to try to understand the past, but also to understand the modern and the future.

Bhabha: First, I want to thank very deeply Professor Tu Weiming. You know, amongst friends we can make many public signs of affection, but what's so important is to be able to say in the presence of a friend something that you appreciate about him, even if you didn't know him. One of the things that I greatly admire about Professor Tu Weiming, which gives such an honor for me today to be in a conversation with him, is that despite his great eminence, knowledge, and scholarship, he has a remarkable modesty and openness before the world. It does not happen very often, because to be open before the world is to actually take the world into your life, to take the world and to find a position by displacing yourself, by not seeing yourself as the center of the world, by putting yourself in another position and looking back on who you are and what you know. I said this with great sincerity, this is not something that happens. People as they grow in lives and their careers want to preserve what they've done. In your case, you have not conserved it, you have revised it and you handed it on to others to transform, and you have allowed others to find their voice in your words. So, I want to thank you very deeply and sincerely for being in that sense for me a mentor and an example. Thank you.

Tu: I very much appreciate your comment, but I think one of the fascinating things for the audience as a whole is your own autobiographical reflection. We all know your eminence in terms of all forms of scholarship. Homi is, as you know, one of the most flexible, open, and pluralistic thinkers in the world today. After Derrida and Said, he is now characterized as a great successor of these traditions, but also, he is indebted to Fanon, to the analytical tradition, the psycho-analytical tradition, not to mention his deep involvement in colonialism and post-colonialism. I think it will be very nice if you can share with us, in just five to ten minutes, your autobiographic reflection.

Bhabha: Thank you very much. You know, to answer very quickly your original question, I very much agree with you that the time was come to go both beyond postmodernism and to go back to the original moments of the modernity in the 18th or 19th century and to see a link between those moments and the moments of globalization. I lectured about this a couple of days ago, when I said that at the moment before colonialism and the moment of colonialism, there were no nations or very few nations. It was a proto-nationalist world. We were looking forward to nations. Now in the way that nations exist, their power exists, and their sovereignty and authority is compromised, we are to some extent in the transnational world. These two moments fit together very well. We learn from the past because we reshape the past, and I think modernity is extremely important from that perspective because while the world was being modernized in the West, while theories of liberalism, nationalism, citizenship, and freedom were being constructed in the West, those were the very same years in which in many parts of the world, people were losing their freedom, people were being subjected to empire, people were losing the sense of modernity.

So, I think what we need to do is to revise that, not simply as going beyond modernity, but questioning the very basis of modernity and seeing where we are now, and how we are to take forward the project of freedom, the project of equality, the project of universality. To go back to this afternoon when we discussed this dialogue, I was asked by Weiming if I would say something about my life and my work, and actually I wrote a few pages, five or six pages, which I would like to share with you and if it becomes too long, please ask me a question and I will stop.

Now, as many of you know, India got its freedom in 1947 at midnight and Prime Minister Nehru gave a very famous speech about receiving your freedom at midnight on August 15th and that's why Salman Rushdie called his book *Midnight's Children*. So, that's where I start. I was not one of midnight's children, as I was born some years after the

Indian independence. My belated birth, a few years after the midnight hour that marked India's tryst with freedom in 1947, absented me from that moment. I was not there to witness the emergence of India and Pakistan, born together from a cleft womb still today as restless in relation to each other as they were then. But growing up in Bombay, as a member of the Parsi community, a small Zoroastrian minority neither a Hindu nor Muslim, was to inhabit a kind of middle-class Hindu-English world. My everyday life provided quite a different inheritance. I lived that rich cultural mix of languages and life styles that most cosmopolitan Indian cities celebrate in their everyday vernacular existence, and it is by appreciating the very mixed, plural, diverse nature of Bombay as I grew up that I decided later on to work on a concept which I have called "vernacular cosmopolitism," a cosmopolitanism that has the desire to be a citizen of the world, but at the same time a desire to understand that the world is made up of partial, specific localities. There isn't some kind of same colored brush that paints the landscape of the world. The landscape of the world is diverse. It is local and yet at the same time it has a scenery which is much more connected.

Now it was liberating, if somewhat unnerving, to be neither a Hindu nor a Muslim, but part of a very small Parsi minority today. There are less than a hundred thousand Parsis in the world, and they are shrinking. Even when I was young, I realized that my inheritance would never be a great total culture. I always realize the way I would relate to the world would be through taking partial elements and traditions from various cultures because that was my position in the world at that time.

Now today my example as a Parsi minority, making a mosaic of cultures or embroidering a tapestry with many different of strings, none of them having a total vision, all of them partial, but all of them very effective, is very much part of the contemporary world picture. Salman Rushdie recently described contemporary world literature as recording, and I quote him, "The culture and political history of the phenomenon of migration, displacement, life in minority groups, a great literature made out the phenomenon of cultural transplantation, and indeed of cultural translation."

Our great desire now, our great project is able to be translate the cultures of others into our own language. When we translate the culture of others, we know that as important as it is to translate other people's cultures, which means to let other cultures speak in and through your own language, is to make another culture part of your own life world. Yet, we also know that there are certain things that cannot be translated. Human civilization, human civility depends on how we deal with the things that cannot be translated. Those things that cannot be translated, if we treat them with aggressivity, treat them with anxiety, then we create tension between cultures. If for those things that cannot be translated, we slowly learn to live with them and overtime to get what they mean, then we grow together in much greater harmony. Much of the world today depends on having faith in human beings and having faith for the things we feel that we cannot immediately understand. For the things that we immediately understand there is no problem, but our moral and ethical strength lines in having faith in human beings, that for the things we don't immediately understand overtime with generosity, with love, and with curiosity we will learn to interpret them.

I want to just end my opening comments by talking a little bit about the India when I grew up in the country and the India today. When I grew up in India, we were always referred to as a third world country; we were always referred to as a developing society. Much of this was true. We were in a project of development, but when people said we were a member of the third-world or a developing society, very often they said that not to describe of our condition, but they said that with a cultural superiority and moral superiority in their voice. They said it to show that somehow, we had not reached the history of the present, that we would have to wait in the antechambers of authority until we emerged.

Today, of course, India is in a different condition, but most importantly the perception of India has greatly changed. Yes, there are great changes in India. In the level of certain educational institutions of the very elite nature, India produces intellectuals that are competitive with those from anywhere else in the world. Yes, at the level of technology, or the level of certain kind of financial markets, India can compete with anybody in the world. Yes, there is a great advantage in India today because Indians believe fundamentally that the past cannot be jettisoned, that the past has to work together with the present, if we want to go in the future. These are the very positive elements and there are others.

But India still has major infrastructural work to be done. India—in terms of public education, in terms of water, in terms of electricity, transport, sewage, human security, in all these important matters, which absolutely defined the way in which people live their everyday life and survive—has a great deal of work to do. It is because of that, because we love our country which is in the process of development, that we must, when we hear the great narratives of Indian development, also maintain the right to question and the right to doubt.

So, when people always tell me, "Oh, your country has got 8% growth for the last 15 years," I say, "That is only one statistic, but please tell me what has been happening to government support of primary education." When you realized the literacy level has not improved a great deal, then you will begin to understand that when you question the progress of your country, you do that because you love your country and not because you are disloyal to it. I think that is one of the most important issues that our colleague, the Nobel Prize winning economist, Professor Amartya Sen has proposed. He says, "Global doubt is absolutely crucial."

Finally, let me say that the Indian Prime Minister Manmohan Singh, in a lecture given a few years ago at the Asia Society in Bombay, himself gave support to such an idea. He said that we can create a lot of special economic zones in India, and I support that, I support globalization and I support many of its market initiatives, but there are two important things that we need to do. One, we cannot fail to understand that until we get this infrastructure, which gives opportunity across the country, we cannot simply be satisfied with having small islands of progress or islands of success. We must lift the country to provide opportunity and freedom, or what Professor Amartya Sen has called "the capabilities," the abilities for everyone to develop their own capacity and capabilities to extend what they want. The Prime Minister said that unless that is satisfied, global development is only a very partial thing. The second issue that he raised, with which I will end, is his belief in what he called "A Look East Policy."

He said many of us in the East have suffered the problems of poverty, many of us share the great differences between cities and the countryside, and we are a largely rural country. Many of us had the yoke of domination, either economical domination or political domination. In thinking of the cosmopolitical or global world, the global world that will produce citizens who when they think of their own nations also think of international responsibilities. He says that we must understand that we cannot only to look to the West and to its notions of progress or universalism, but we have to define these things for ourselves in the company of those in the world of development who have shared our fate and who will share our future. Thank you very much.

Tu: With your remarkably biographic note, I am tempted to ask you to go on. You should continue this eloquent statement. I think you have mentioned a few words that are very suggestive, and very important, like the term "vernacular cosmopolitans." On the surface, we think the "vernacular" is very local and "cosmopolitism" is very universal. This vernacular cosmopolitism reminds me of the idea that local knowledge can be globally significant, especially if the local knowledge is lived, and is an experience of our ordinary existence.

The second word you used is "partiality" or "partial." This is a rejection of an inclusive holistic view that is a kind of universal or universalization as abstract universalism. Abstract universalism should be rejected, but we should also reject closed particularlism and negotiate between the two. I think the idea of vernacular cosmopolitism applies to the

Chinese situation today, but I think it also applies to the Latin American countries, to the Islamic world, and to Africa.

The third word you used is "minority" or "marginality." I think the idea of being a minority is not something that you should consider lamentable. It can provide a strength of self-extending, of self-reflection. You talked about the Parsi as a small minority, and I understand that there are only about 13 million Jews in the world. The population of Taiwan is about twice all the Jewish people put together, and Taiwan is a small province in China. My situation is we Chinese belong to a majority, and so we sometimes fail to understand the strength and the creativity of being a minority. So, I think your term of "marginality" and the verb you used as "minoritization" is a fascinating idea for most of us to understand, because importantly we need to understand not only ourselves, but also all the other 55 minorities in China. A great anthropologist at Peking University, Fei Xiaotong, talked about one unity with a plurality of ethical groups, and how important it is for the majority to study and understand the minorities.

You also mentioned the question of translation. Translation not in terms of translating English into Chinese, but as an intellectual endeavor, spiritual exercise, or even a process of living. When we go through translation a lot is lost to the translation, but at the same time we have new possibilities that open up, and in your view, translation becomes a creative act rather than translation as a rendering of something that is not original.

At the same time, I think the question of anxiety is very important. The whole question about global doubt is related to the sense of anxiety in terms of a personal sense, a communal sense, and even a global sense. I think the world today is such that even the viability or survivability of the human species is at stake. So, anxiety is a commonly experienced reality, but I think related to this anxiety is also the question of aspiration with the view toward the future. So, I like very much the notion of "retrieving the tradition." My own work has been trying to do that for years, but often it has been characterized and misunderstood as a kind of archaicism, as simply going back to the past in order to find a reference for your present today. Precisely because you feel very nervous about your present, you try to retreat into your past, and try to understand the past as a displacement, as a substitute for your present situation.

However, in your rather remarkable idea of retrieving, the past is not simply a burden that you have to overcome, the past is also a way of helping us to understand our present with a view to the future. So, I think one remarkable thing that I appreciated in your work is this emphasis on time and temporality rather than simply space; it is dynamic process rather than a static structure. That is really fascinating. Also, in response to the last point you made about India, and I think I'd like to share some ideas about China.

I very fortunately ran into our mutual friend Ashis Nandy at Tsinghua, and Ashis Nandi told us a story, which he may have told you again and again, about how he never felt comfortable when he visited Cambridge, Massachusetts or for that matter Cambridge, England, because when he talked to some of his friends—let's assume people like Samuel Huntington—they were very open and very nice, but deep in their heart or in their consciousness, may even in their unconsciousness, there was this feeling that our present is your future and your present is our past.

Now this affects the situation where you are having a dialogue with someone. For example, if Homi believes that the present of China is in the past of the United States, assuming he represents the United States as the director of the Harvard Center for the Humanities, there is this sense that it's not only an asymmetrical dialogue, but also that there is a problematic attitude that you must try to catch up to what we've done, that we've already done everything you're trying to achieve. This problematic scenario is something we want to reject.

Bhabha: Absolutely.

Tu: We want to reject this in order to open up new possibilities, so I'd like to offer my appreciation of what actually happened in the last 50 years or 100 years, especially in the American academy. We all share the notion that we need to reflect upon the Enlightenment from 17th century to 18th century and 19th century. We need to sympathetically understand it, but we also need to critically reflect upon it, and some the most encouraging thought-provoking reflections on the Enlightenment, in fact, have been done by academicians in the United States and in Europe. Feminism, is a very good example, which is a very powerful force at Harvard, especially in the Divinity School, but also there is environmentalism, appreciation of the earth, care for the earth as a home; there is communitarianism—our mutual friend Michael Sandel, doesn't want to be characterized as a communitarian, but he still promotes a sort of communitarianism; there is religious pluralism and cultural diversity. These are great reflections on not just the modern West, but also the Enlightenment. I think this opens a possibility, and postmodernism could be considered as part of that. Yet, we want to do something more. If we just remain at that level, it is not good enough.

This is why more than 20 years ago I advocated the importance for China to take India as a reference. I'm not saying China will have to imitate India. That's not my point. My point is to take India as a reference for mutual learning, for mutual appreciation. Why? First, India is the largest democracy country in the world today. It is just one example of the positive aspects of the democracy. Of course, democracy has many, many negative features. Because it is a democracy, it is transparent. There are more than one million

NGOs (Non-government Organizations) in India, and the Indian mass media is so powerful, it penetrates into every level of society. Now Amartya Sen has pointed out that since 1948 there has never been a major famine or natural disaster in India where say 100,000 or 200,000 or so people died. You know the situation in China. There were the "three years terrible years" when millions of people died of starvation.

Another thing very important about democracy is the continuous critique of not only of your polity, but your society and your culture. Another thing to keep in mind is that India has probably 200 million members that considered themselves part of the middle class. We have in China maybe 50 million or 40 million. So, they have a very large middle class. Also, millions of Indians are fluent in English. Because of this, they are not just vernacular cosmopolitans, but they are cosmopolitan in the best sense of the word. Now with the growth of the hi-tech industry, especially in terms of software, India and China can become economic partners. But to me, the most moving and the most important aspect of Indian culture or Indian spirituality that we can discover is the relationship between the present and the past, and the relationship between the Indian intelligentsia and Indian cultural traditions. Concretely, I mean Indian dance, Indian music, Indian philosophy, Indian literature and, of course, Indian devotion, Indian religion, and so forth.

Because of this tradition, there is an incredible respect for artist, for literary figures and for musicians. I'll give you one example. I don't think I have told you this before. I went to India at the invitation of the Minister of Resources, which is one of the largest ministries in India, while participating in the UNESCO dialogue among civilizations. Near the end of the trip there was a major banquet. The banquet was to say farewell to scholars, to the ambassadors, to the high officials. Seated at the event were all the distinguished guests, the scholars, the ambassadors, and the officials, but the most prominent seat just beside the minister was reserved for the musician who actually played for us that evening. He had just come back from London, played, and then he was asked to sit. All the Indian scholars, Indian intellectuals, Indian officials took it for granted that he should have such an honored place, something which is very unusual. Just try to imagine that situation in other societies, not to mention in China.

I'd like to conclude by suggesting you further explore this whole question about not just translation, but transition. We talk about creative transformation; we like the idea of transformation. China is now being transformed from an agricultural society into an industrial society, from a developing country into a developed country, and from a pre-modern country into a modern country. You put a lot of emphasis on importance of transition, not simply transformation. I think it would be nice to share some your ideas about "transition."

Bhabha: Thank you very much, Weiming. I think my emphasis on "transition" comes from my observation that many sins are committed in the name of transformation. Everybody states that this is our goal, and we are going to do this in ten years, we are going to do this in fifteen years, or we are going to do this in twenty years. But while the promise of transformation is being made, people suffer, communities lose their grounding, and other people make huge sacrifices. So, my use of the word "transition" is chosen to have an ethical, a moral, and a social significance. Let us always have our great aims or great hopes for the future but let us not forget what is happening now to the extent to which we can observe it in the name of that great future.

Too many sins were committed because people had great ideas; too many people died because people told them you are no longer important now, what is important is the future. This has happened too many times in the life of the world, whether in the East, or West, the North or the South, and nobody's hands are clean. I don't think anybody's hands are clean. Too many times these ideas were put about and the people who sacrificed and died in the process of transition are forgotten. That's why I connect the notion of transition as a particular notion of time or history in which we can examine with some moral responsibility what we are doing in the world as we try and shape it towards a greater end.

Tu: Yes.

Bhabha: Now there are a lot of philosophical arguments about the notion of time which I don't want to get into here, but I emphasize the sense of transition because it gives us responsibility. Something may happen in world markets, in resources, in securities that we cannot control, but while our societies are in transformation, if we see our everyday implication in the process of transition, then we can actually take the responsibility for the present, for the lives we lead, and the demand we make upon others to participate in the blue prints for the future that we sketch up. This is one of the reasons why I think an attention to the moment of transition rather than transformation is extremely important.

Tu: Let me try to unpack this a little bit further. I think your argument against transformation may be predicated on this notion of the means and ends. You are having an end, which is an aspiration for the future sometimes determined by the leaders. This is our vision for the future, and we have to do things in order to reach that, and there are no considerations of the unintended negative consequences in the social planning or in the social engineering. So, this means an end of the process may turn out to be a disaster, especially for the common people in general.

Bhabha: Yes. Let me give you one example.

Tu: Sure.

Bhabha: This is something that I have tried to debate with people in the government and with people who are much more knowledgeable than I am. We know that in certain sectors of the Indian economy, and in particular the financial sector, there has been transformative progress. But what is happening to the rural sector? One version is that we first need to work on the industrial level, financial level, and economic level, and then we will return to the agricultural level. This seems to me to be a very shortsighted policy. I still believe it is shortsighted.

We have had in India—and this has been mentioned in every paper and every journal—farmer suicides. We have a large number of farmers who have committed suicide, and you know the Indian press is absolutely open and it has made campaigns of this. I am not adding anything new. It is the Indian press and intellectuals that have identified this problem. We've had farmers' suicide when farmers have failed. The agricultural sector has been largely neglected and they killed themselves. So, mistakes can always be made. Mistakes can be made with great ideas and great aspirations, but if we take the smaller measure, then we can understand what is going to happen. We will be more careful with other people's lives, and other people's communities, and we will also, in that context, take greater ethical responsibility. This is just one very concrete example of what is that.

Tu: OK. I can also share an example, but it may not be quite adequate because my knowledge about this is very limited. China is now considered a major economic power. There is no question about the fact that we not only surpassed Germany in terms of trade and export capacity, but we are set to surpass Japan, and before long will be comparable to the economic power of the United States. If we look at the historical process, even on the eve of the Opium War in the 1839, the Chinese economy, globally speaking, was estimated as comparable to the American economy today with a ratio of 24 percent to 27 percent. The Chinese and British two-way trade was totally in the Chinese favor. England wanted Chinese tea, Chinese silk, Chinese china, Chinese handicrafts, and even some Chinese agricultural products, but China didn't want anything from England. This may have been a key reason why opium was used.

However, China collapsed from its confrontation with England, and reason for that collapse was because China was arrogant and ignorant. China didn't know what happened in the 19th century with the major institutional changes of the West. China didn't know about industrialization, scientific technological innovations, and all these great developments in the West. Not only did China not know this, but the Chinese eventual empire was very arrogant. When Macaulay showed up as a representative of England, they immediately assumed his group of people had come to pay tribute to the Middle

Kingdom and they asked Macaulay to kneel down and pay tribute to the empire. You are familiar with the story. So, that's a big problem.

My worry is that even with the incredible role of the Chinese economy as a whole, the per capita income, which is related to your actual experience, is very low. The Chinese per capita income is probably listed below the 104th within the United Nations group of maybe 195 or 196 countries. This is a situation that means that we have a long march. Therefore, it is related to your notion. It is not a question of transformation, or a kind of preconceived idea of what happens ten years from now or twenty years from now that we just try to march toward. It is a question of understanding the transition which we are experiencing because the transition is related very closely to the common experience here and now. So, we need to understand not just the question of time, but temporality.

Bhabha: Yes.

Tu: Temporality is a consciousness of time. At this moment, what can we do as concrete human beings? What can we do as students at Peking University? What can we do as teachers at universities in China? What can we do as officials? What can we do as an entrepreneurs or as members of mass media in this transition? Because transition means unpredictability, means ambiguity, and even sometimes fruitful ambiguity, in this situation we need to be particularly attentive and mindful of our existential situation.

I think in this sense that we are moving beyond postmodernism, because postmodernism is a critique of what actually happened, especially of what happened in the modern West. This is a very strong reaction against not just imperialism, but colonialism and its hegemonic control. Of course, we should still do that, but we should also be aware the Enlightenment legacy. I think we share this idea.

Bhabha: Yes.

Tu: The Enlightenment legacy is one of the greatest treasures in human history. Enlightenment means we are opened through rational thinking, through science and technology, and have a much better appreciation of the world, but at the same time, we need to look to the future. If we look to the future, we will realize it is not enough to have this arrogant idea of rationality; it is not enough simply to rely upon our technology. Many people say that all the problems including the environmental degradation eventually can be solved by science, but I think we need to also raise questions about ethics and about human self-understanding. In fact, recently Barry Bloom, the Dean of the Harvard School of Public Heath, showed me a relevant short statement. I'll paraphrase it:

> Many things cannot be measured by the role of an economy. What is happiness, friendship, to conserve for ones' children, respect for ones' elders, to have a sense

of communality, to have sense of common direction or common orientation? All these things are not quantified; all these things cannot be measured; and all these things are absolutely critical for human existence or human development in dignity and the whole idea of not only human flourishing, but human survival depends on these public goods that are not quantifiable.

Bhabha: Can I take on some of these issues? I hope you see that we are like a jazz group improvising. You play something, and then I take the echo from what you played, and I play my little tune, and you play yours. I hope you are enjoying this jazz concert.

Tu: A duet.

Bhabha: Yeah, a duet. Let me take the issues you spoke about of how we respect the tradition of the Enlightenment, and yet from our own perspective, just as Manmohan Singh takes the "Look East Policy" in the midst of the globalization process and says, "We don't only look west, but we look east and find out own community and solidarity." Let me talk a little bit about the implications of what we've been saying, as you have very generously presented my own arguments and discussions, we have had in the last two days to this audience. I'd just like to add something to it.

First of all, I think the work you have dedicated yourself to, the concept of dialogue, is one of the most important issues of the day. Dialogue is absolutely central to the idea of democracy. In fact, there are many who feel that if democracy only depends on voting, the very important thing that everybody has a free vote, it's not enough. Democracy and voting depend on the possibility of the free exchange of ideas amongst individuals, families, groups, and political parties. Dialogue is very important because dialogues can exist among very asymmetrical members and a society must create institutions where people who have power and people who don't have power, and people who have authority and people who don't have authority can actually come together and dialogue. This cannot simply be the responsibility of individuals; it has to be the responsibility of institutions.

I am participating now in the World Economic Forum where I am the Vice Chair of the Committee on Global Values, and this is one of the issues that I think is absolutely front and center. Now, universities are such institutions. We are lucky to have in universities admission policies that allow people to come in on merit for the most part. Of course, in America, if you are a 9-foot-tall basketball star, no universities will say "No, thank you." They will say, "Yes, please come here" because they have a very strong sports culture. But what I want to suggest is that the more university syllabi become interdisciplinary with many disciplines contributing to particular kinds of knowledge, the more departments and divisions of universities come together. Then a university becomes a crossroads or a bridge where people go back and forth, in and out. Interdisciplinary study, which is very important in the biological sciences and very important in the humanities, is a great encourager of international, national, and individual dialogues and conversations. So, I think this is a very optimistic time for universities worldwide to be the models of what societies can be, because as studies becomes more interdisciplinary the nature of dialogue becomes more and more important.

Now my next point is about the humanities. People say that in the humanities you don't have many statistics. It is not a quantitative science. How are we to judge the humanities? One person has an interpretation that says something, and another person can interpret the same text in a different way. One of the things that I have said often is that the humanities don't build models the humanities build communities. We create communities of opinion, we create communities of interpretation, and therefore the humanities encourage dialogue both within the humanities and outside of the humanities.

To give you an example: after all the work being done on stem cell research, the scientists now demand a philosophical and ethical reflection on this scientific progress. If scientific progress does not have ethical and moral dialogue, it can turn into a monster that can consume the very people who created it. Therefore, I think that it is extremely important to resist the notion of the quantitative humanities and to begin to think about the humanities as the construction of communities.

But then people say if the humanities are not quantitative, how do you understand objective value in humanities? What is objective value? Are the humanities only subjective so that you can have one opinion I can have another opinion, and there is a kind of crazy anarchistic relativism in the world? My answer to that is that the humanity is neither simply quantitative nor qualitative, but they are integrative. They integrate different perspectives and different knowledges. That's the great strength of the humanities.

Finally, I want to take up Weiming's important point that one of the great contributions of the Enlightenment was to make us think about rationality. It suggested that irrational responses, whether they are individual, institutional, or governmental, will not help you to make your own point, will not help you to further your own project, and that a rational understanding enables you to see more clearly what the conditions are within which you act and within which you speak. This is absolutely crucial.

However, countries that have suffered domination, poverty, inequality, countries that have been seen for many hundreds of years and to be on the periphery of the world stage have an addition to make to rational thought, and this addition to rational thought is not irrationality. The contribution we have to make is to say rationality is extremely important, but what is equally important when we think of social changes and social transformation is for institutions to understand the emotional cost of change and transformation. All of us in the public sphere, in civil society, believe in honor truth, labor, dignity, but governments and institutions should be equally aware of people's fear, the fear of change, people's sense of anxiety, people's sense of face or respect, and people's sense of trust. As the world changes, emotions are as important as rational perspectives. This has become even more crucial after 9/11. After 9/11, the think tanks in Washington and New York and London disagreed on many things and agreed on many things, but one thing that they all said was that those have been humiliated are more likely to become attractive to forms of terrorism. Those who feel they have been shamed.

Now we cannot be responsible for everything, as sometimes people can be humiliated when they were not actually, but the feeling of humiliation or shame can be because you live in the sector of the world where you have large unemployment. It can be that you live in the sector of the world that cannot participate in the advantages of globalization. You feel that the world puts you aside. Nobody speaks to your condition. You have to always address the condition of the successful. In such circumstances, we must realize that when we think about constitutional reform and legal reform, we have to understand that behind every legal reform is a human being, a group of human beings, or communities. As much as we rethink the structure of things, we must not also forget the place of imagination, the place of ethics, and the place of emotions. Emotions are as much a part of the social material world as rationality is, and it is only by putting the emotions with rationality that we can emerge towards a greater ethical and political understanding of the goals we want to meet. I feel these issues are still considerably neglected.

Tu: I'd like to respond to Homi's ideas in a reverse order: first focusing on the question of rationality and emotion, then the humanities, and then dialogue. I remember Robert Bellah once made the observation that one of the human conditions is that there is always an affective surplus and a cognitive deficit. In other words, our emotions always flow beyond our rational understanding of the meaning of the relation. So, in this particular connection, emotion is not only not irrational or non-rational, it can be variously understood as complementary on the one hand, and also as a critical reflection on rationality on the other. We know that Habermas, somewhat overwhelmed by the arrogance of rationality, decided to move beyond instrumental rationality to underscore the importance of communicative rationality. So, I totally agree that we need to be sensitive to the non-rational elements in terms of our own personal experience, and in terms of social-political interactions.

This question of rationality is important, especially if it is manifested in a kind of outmoded scientism. I want to make a clear distinction between scientism and the scientific spirit. The scientific spirit is a spirit of discovery; it is a spirit of the quest for truth; it is a spirit of human self-understanding. But scientism as an ideology is an outmoded notion that you can use social engineering or other means in a manipulative sense of controlling or understanding the world. One manifestation in China today is to announce that Chinese medicine is a pseudo-science. This is an idea of imposing certain outmoded standards—Indian medicine would also be considered pseudo-science. It is to use one simple criterion in a quantitative way to understand all dimensions of human experience, which is highly limited. Therefore, the importance of understanding sympathy, compassion, a sense of fairness, a sense of happiness, all these ideas are not only not irrational, not unscientific, or un-rational, they are all important goods both at the person level and the communal level.

So far as the humanities are concerned, I agree that they offer the possibility of creating community, but they also are involved in creating meaning, the meaning of life. This idea of meaning is not easily quantifiable, and maybe can never be quantified. Yet, you all want to be successful in your career, successful in your ability to generate a great deal of income, and to extend your influence. All these are important for anyone of us. But if we have no sense of the meaning of existence, the meaning of life, the meaning of our career, no sense of meaning of our identity, even if you become extremely successful, you will still not be satisfied. There is a great deal of anxiety about the meaning of life. I think the humanities as disciplines will help to create community, to generate meaning, to integrate various kinds of disciplines, and try to develop humanity in a way to allow a person to fully realize him or herself. The idea of a total person is something that has now been very widely acknowledged in China, the idea to develop a liberal art ideal.

I want to simply note that Homi is the director of the Harvard Center of Humanities. I must say this center has been the most vibrant of all the centers. The center not only has daily lunch meetings with people from all over the university and from all over the world. I was privileged to present my own reflections on the Enlightenment there about a month or so ago. It also hosts many great events, such "20 Questions," in other words the attempt to address a particular issue by raising concrete and challenging questions, and people are all involved in that mode of questioning. The most recent event in which I took part had Michael Sandel speaking on justice. He gave a short exposition of his position, then five commentators from many different disciplines, from law, from political science, from literature, from philosophy reflected on his position. He responded to these positions briefly and then opened it up for discussion, and many people raised challenging questions.

One anxiety I have in joining Peking University is that I hope the conversation can continue and I hope many forms of dialogue can occur. Peking University is not simply a university that is known for its excellence in special knowledge. All our faculty members are specialists in literature, in philosophy, in chemistry, in physics, in engineering, in mass media and so forth, but we are all involved, as members of universities, in what one philosopher characterized as edifying conversation. In other words, a conversation is edifying not only to ourselves, but to our colleagues, and to people who are even remotely connected to our own specialization. If coffee and tea shop conversations occur continuously, the dynamics and the vibrancy of the university community will be greatly enhanced.

The third point is about dialogue, which I consider as a way of life. It is not a technique. It is not simply a process that tries to convert. For example, a dialogue between a Christian and a Muslim, if the Christian side of the dialogical partners want to convert the Muslim and the Muslim wants to convert the Christian, there will be shouting, there will be fighting, and eventually there will be confrontation.

Dialogue is not to convert. Therefore, the basic principle of dialogue is "Do not do to others what you do not want others to do to you," because what I think is the best or what I think is most important for me may not be shared by my dialogical partner. If I believed I've received the Good News, then I have to share the Good News with you and I don't care whether you like to be asked to receive it or not. If you say you don't want me to share, then my sense of responsibility actually becomes even more enhanced. I have to help you to realize what is good for you. That kind of dialogical relationship is actually a false relationship; it is not dialogue. Dialogue is not to convert. It is not simply to make a statement, a monologue rather than an exchange; it's not even an occasion to try to correct the perceived misunderstanding of my position because dialogue begins with tolerance.

Tolerance is the minimum condition. You have to recognize your dialogical partner as not only a reality you have to face up to, but as someone with dignity, with worth, and with an important quest for meaning. Only with tolerance and recognition will you be able to have tremendous respect for your dialogical partner, and there will be the possibility of mutual reference and mutual learning. The most difficult side is what I called celebration of difference, even the celebration of otherness. One of the great humanists is the cultural anthropologist Clifford Geertz. He once remarked on the liberating experience of confronting something that is radically different, the liberating experience of confronting radical otherness.

So, what is the real purpose of dialogue? First, I think it is the importance of cultivating the art of listening. If wanting to engage a dialogue, we have to cultivate the art of listening.

Only then can it help us to broaden our horizon, and finally can it help us to enhance our self-reflexivity. So, I think I appreciate very much the three points you make about rationality, about humanities, and about dialogue.

Bhabha: Thank you very much for your wonderful "dialogue." I know now that the concept of translation we are talking about is at the very root of dialogue. You must be open to the interpretation of another, to the language of another; you must try and somehow make that your own without imposing on it your norms. You must allow it to have its own presence side by side with yourself. I think that the act of dialogue has a temporal aspect back and forth, back and forth in time, and a spatial aspect to it side by side. I've been very honored to be side by side with you.

Tu: So have I.

Bhabha: Thank you very much. I think we are going to have hand it over to the moderator?

Tu: Yeah. I think it's the time right for our moderator to come to open it up for discussion, but may I make a one final point. I think the dialogical mode is even more important than the dialectical mode. The simple reason is that in the dialectical relationship there is some kind of violence, some kind of tension: the thesis, the antithesis, and the synthesis. When you get the thesis, the antithesis is overcome, and you reach a higher level. A dialogue in this sense is a communication between the two individuals or groups and the two individuals or groups will become more enlightened because of this communication. It is not because I overcome Homi, or Homi overcomes me that we reach a certain kind of higher level. Instead, I think horizontal interchange is absolutely critical for the dialogical mode.

Bhabha: Thank you very much.

https://www.youtube.com/watch?v=FTZgH5E7E5U

DIALOGUE WITH JC KAPUR 2010-7-11

Bio: Jagdish Chandra Kapur (1920-2010) was an Indian social scientist and entrepreneur. He did his graduate studies at the Punjab University, secured his master's degree from the Indian Institute of Science in Bangalore, and had higher studies at the Cornell University. He was the founder of Kapur Surya Foundation and Kapur Solar Farms and was also the Editor of World Affairs Journal, a publication aiming at and providing a platform for better interaction between the developed and the developing nations. He was one of the founders of The World Public Forum, which is a consultative body that serves as a platform for various non-governmental organizations (NGO), public, academic, cultural, spiritual, social, and business institutions for exchange of views and ideas on global problems and their resolutions, and has held the Dialogue of Civilizations, also known as the Rhodes Forum. His works include *India in the Year 2000* (1975), *India, An Uncommitted Society* (1982), *The Human Condition Today: Some New Perspectives* (1988), *Our Future: Consumerism Or Humanism* (2005).

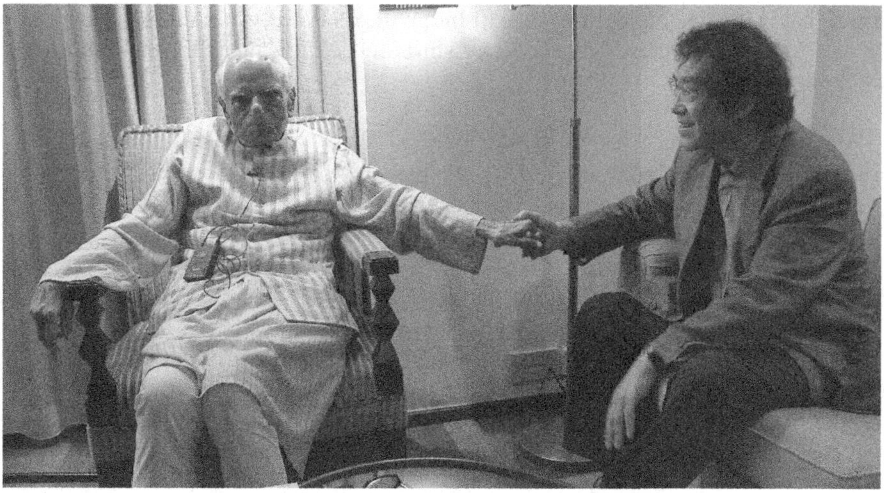

Professor Tu Weiming: I am honored and pleased to meet you.

Jagdish Chandra Kapur: It is a pleasure to talk to you. I always keep talking about you and your work.

Tu: Yes, as a futurist, and also as a scientist.

Kapur: I am looking forward to your work, the story of China, the future of China, and Confucianism, because in my opinion the history of China has been informed by three forces: Daoism, Buddhism and Confucianism. Now the culture of China kept changing after imperial power came, and they preferred one over the others; however then when the republic began, they paid no attention to it, and that is why the youth of China has shifted towards consumerism much faster than the youth of India.

Tu: Right, right.

Kapur: This is what all the people did. This is what has been going on.

Tu: So, one of the major questions you raise is consumerism versus humanism.

Kapur: Indeed. This is what is the problem. Now what I have been trying to understand is, and you will see that in the book I wrote, the difference with India is that India's continuity started 5000 years before, and in temples and in places where there are temples people are reciting the same verses that 2000 year ago their great, great, great grandfather did.

Tu: This is a profound sense of continuity.

Kapur: That is the profound difference of India: the continuity of culture. The only saving grace in China is that there were a lot of shifts in culture, but all the shifts took place between those three…

Tu: Major traditions.

Kapur: That's the only continuity of China. If they were not there, nobody would know where China will go. Somebody emphasizes one, the other emphasizes this, and the third one emphasizes that. Like in India, the continuity for instance when outsiders came. They built their mosques, and the Indian's said, "We have 5,000 gods, probably even more, so what difference does it make?" Christians came, Parsis came, Jews came, and every time, India never interfered. It's affecting, which involves the indicators of India, that India was all the way in history until recently, you see? There was not what we call a "power structure." Their culture was not a continuity of power, as power in any form; it was a continuity of culture. It was called the "cultural republic" because every village and every area of India was a republic with what we call a "ruler republic," and those ruler republics were independent in every way.

How many invasions took place in India? They came, they looted the country, and they went away. India's continuity again grew. Till the 16th century, India was one of the richest countries of the world. At that time, with China together they were 37% of the world's wealth. Even in the 16th century. Now that changes. Because of the continued continuity, India has not created fast consumerism; however, China has succeeded because the

Chinese youth, after the Communist wars, Chiang Kai-Shek, and Sun Yat-Sen, had nothing to look to and went and became part of consumerism. That is why the production increased in China; 40,000-50,000 new factories were built, millions of people were employed, and they produced goods sold to America. For that production they got a lot of cash money, which is now built up into a store of 2 trillion dollars or more. The biggest problem of China today is that of those 2 trillion dollars, 1.5 is invested in American government bonds. As this all is taking place, it is going to affect the stability of China. You get my point? That is the money of China today.

Tu: I think you can put that in context. Ever since the Opium War until the founding of the People's Republic of China, every 10-year period there was a major change, a major rupture. Since the founding of the People's Republic in 1949, until 1979, which we called the period of "Reform and Opening," every 5 years period there was a major change. So, China like India had a very long and continuous history prior to the impact of the West. Yet, in the last 150 years, China went through major ruptures. This was especially true during the cultural revolution, when Chinese culture was not only relegated into the background, but totally disintegrated. As a result, there's a vacuum. The Chinese have tremendous energy, the energy to create, but also the energy to destroy. That kind of energy in the cultural revolutionary period was very much focused on politics, and changing the mindset for the revolutionary spirit, but then afterwards, when people felt that the Chinese economy was very much behind, the energy then was pumped into economic development, into market economy. As a result, as you pointed out, the society was overwhelmed by consumerism.

Kapur: So that's what you're seeing today?

Tu: Yes. In China, because market economy was a dynamic force for creating wealth, the market economy transformed or degenerated into market society, in the sense that every aspect of the society, not only the government, the business community, but the mass media and even the academic and religious communities all became somehow commercialized.

Kapur: All became a part of that consumerism to support the system. But you know what happened to this? One of the most important things to carry the consumer system forward is that all other systems, cultural systems, must be made subservient to the consumer culture.

Tu: Some time ago, maybe twenty years ago, I advocated to my colleagues and intellectuals in China that we must take India as a reference.

Kapur: I saw that.

Tu: It should be a reference society for many reasons. One is India has been the largest democracy, and therefore some people told me that there are more than one million NGOs. There is also a very large middle-class, maybe 20 million. Of course, Indian intellectuals are fluent in English, so they are very cosmopolitan. Now India, and what they call the "BRIC countries: Brazil, India, Russia, and China have emerged. So, economically there is commonality especially in the software area, but the most significant lesson for China is the relationship between the Indian intellectuals or educated people today and the Indian civilization that has existed for a very long period of time. So, you mention not only the temples or the gods, but there is also dance, music, philosophy…

Kapur: Dance, music, all cultural things continued exactly the same for centuries, as they're all spiritual.

Tu: Yes, very, very spiritual.

Kapur: So therefore, India's stability comes from that. Now the most important thing that many people do not know, and I have been stressing for the last about 7 to 10 years, is that there has been a kind of spiritual revolution in India.

Tu: Spiritual revolution?

Kapur: There are 30 million people every day who go and watch spiritual programs.

Tu: 30 million?

Kapur: All kinds of yogis, some fraudulent, but most of them are very good. They are giving lesson after lesson, connecting them to India's culture. Stories on the *Ramayana,* the *Mahabharata,* the *Upanishads* and how India was, what they have done to it, teaching to stop it or otherwise nothing will come to you. Now today my own contention is that India will be obliged to give up the consumer system. I have been warning about this. I also have a feeling that unless India, China and Russia come together, each one separately will be destroyed.

Tu: I sense, if you look at spiritual force and spiritual power, India is one of the great nations that exports all forms of spirituality throughout the world. Russia in recent years retrieved its own spiritual tradition in Orthodox Christianity, which has rich traditions in literature, certainly in art and dance, and many other areas. China needs to revitalize its own spiritual tradition in an extremely urgent manner.

Kapur: I'll give you the reason for that. In my opinion, there are three stages of human development: material, mental and super-mental, and spiritual.

Tu: Oh, you mean 4 stages?

Kapur: You can be up to the mental, the super-mental and the spiritual. These are the forces that are the human development of the future. What is happening is that Europe has stopped at stage 1; they gave up number 2 and that's where they are. America pulled everything towards the material, they have nothing left to think about where we will go. That is when the IT industry came. It was young Indian people who picked it up. In fact, I asked an Indian who is working in America who became a billionaire. I said, what did you do? He said I left India with $100 in my pocket, when I went there, some people helped me to take a job. I went to that job, and there were about 30-40 people there working as computer interns. While everybody was working, I did my work in 1 hour, and I went around to seeing what they were doing. I picked up all that. In a few years, I walked out, borrowed a few thousand dollars from the bank, I started my own business, and that is where I am today. So, what was working? Mental.

Tu: I think in information and communication technologies, and software the mental work becomes particularly pronounced…

Kapur: Therefore, I'm also going to tell you, culture is the software on which civilizations are built. Unless we have solid cultures, there is no chance whatsoever of creating a great civilization. There must be a cultural continuity; there must be a cultural perdition. It must contain all the three elements, material, mental and super-mental, and spiritual. If a country can't do that, can't maintain that culture, and is swept off by the consumerist culture as America is, then you see where that leads.

Tu: I think all over the world one deep worry of mine is this idea of modernization very much has been defined in terms of Westernization.

Kapur: And as material development and nothing else. Modernization in India should take what I call a humanist part, which means the part that increases the potential of man. I want to shift from the money economy to the human economy. That places man in the center of things, not money. When that happens, when man achieves it potential, you will have a different world. Where will it happen in America or Europe? The only hope is India. So, after visiting 96 countries, this is what I feel. Then I said that it should be India and China because they won't let you do it from the inside. They are destroying India from the inside, these external forces. I have been warning, whether they will listen to me or not, but they will. They are coming closer: India's and China's trade, which was $33 billion, is now $50-60 billion in 5 years. So, it happened to China also. What I am trying to say is this, we have to move away from thinking of money as the symbol of power, we have to think of man as the symbol of power. We are not to think about the outer wealth as the greatness of man, we have to consider other spiritual achievements. That's what we have to do. Unless the culture permits that, there is no chance of a culture becoming a great culture, or a great country of the 21st and 22nd century.

Tu: We've been involved in two meetings on the Indian and Chinese philosophical perspectives on knowledge, wisdom and spirituality, once in Delhi and once in Beijing. That was the beginning of a serious exchange of spiritual values and core values, since the border clash in the '60s, and I do hope this will be able to continue. I understand you've been deeply involved in the Dialogue Among Civilizations, and also the importance of harmonious societies all over the world. At Peking University, there is what we call the "Beijing Forum," which is organized by the university together with the municipal government and other organizations. Every year, there's a meeting in November on the question of dialogue among civilizations and harmonious societies. That's the general theme, but there are many different topics. I realized that if you look at the world in terms of linear progression defined in material terms, using what we call instrumental rationality, then we realize there are so many things that GDP cannot measure, such as happiness, friendship, wisdom, knowledge, human communication, human development, and human flourishing. So, I agree with you that this is a central problem of our time.

However, in 1923, one great scholar in China, by the name of Liang Shuming, talked about three different value orientations: the Western, the Chinese and the Indian. The Western approach was very aggressive. It's a Faustian drive not only to understand, but also to conquer and subdue.

Kapur: Even now it is.

Tu: Even now it is. The Chinese one is trying to search for some kind of balance. The Indian tradition puts a great deal of emphasis on spirituality, on what you call the "super-mental." He said at the time, this was 1922, China had no choice but to try and learn from the West in order to survive. It needed science, technology, and all these material things. But he predicted eventually, when this consumerism and materialism became fully developed, people would then begin to realize this is not only emptiness in regard to their own quest for meaning, but also causes serious problems for the world. Of course, at the time, he was not acutely aware of the environmental issues. I think now we can see that the prophetic vision is the environmental issue. My sense is that maybe in the 21st century the prophet is the earth, and the elders in all the traditions, including indigenous traditions, may turn out to be teachers for the new civilization. I think that this may be related to your idea of humanism versus consumerism.

Kapur: I must send you the paper with my last speech from the World Public Forum, where I'm going tomorrow.

Tu: This is a forum that you organized?

Kapur: No, no, I didn't. It was a joint effort with a big role played by Mr. Vladimir Yakunin and that may interest you.

Tu: From Russia?

Kapur: In Russia he is a very important man, very close to power. I had proposed a foundation that would have an effect on solar energy and was making speeches around India in 2000. Somehow when he came to India we met together and he proposed, and I supported the idea of, this World Public Forum as a dialogue of civilizations. So, that was constituted. Since that beginning I have been the co-chairman of the forum.

Tu: This is? How many…

Kapur: About 7 or 8 years ago.

Tu: 7 or 8 years ago, so this is the 7th or 8th meeting, with participants from all over the world?

Kapur: They are from all over the world. In fact, the last meeting was attended by 752 people from 62 countries. And you know why? For a very simple reason that I raised the voice of dissent.

Tu: The voice of dissent?

Kapur: Dissent. There is something wrong. What's going on? I said, "This has to be corrected." I said, "The West and United States are responsible." All over the world, you know 90% is dissent, so all of us are in for the interest for this development. The forum came up by effort, largely by Mr. Yaukunin's effort to where it is today. It is a better place than any other place in the world to fulfill what we are talking about.

Tu: Now we see also the same kind of voice of dissent.

Kapur: As far as I'm concerned, it's the voice of total dissent. However, we cannot know everything; you cannot speak anything you like. Still, ultimately it is the voice of dissent that is the way it will end. You get my point?

Tu: Yes, there's a strong feeling that the viability of the human species is uncertain and how much time we have, we do not know. So, in this particular situation, my sense is that all spiritual traditions, Hindu, Muslim, Judaic, Christian and all the spiritual traditions will have to go through a transformation. The transformation is to recognize the Earth as sacred, or the Earth as invested with spiritual value. There's a new relationship between the human and the earth, and so we cannot say from the Buddhist point of view to wait for the other shore or wait for the Pure land. Or for the Christian, to wait for the Kingdom of God to come. We have to care for the earth. I liked the notion of humanism, but it's very different from the humanism of the enlightenment of the modern West because that humanism is secular humanism.

Kapur: That's right. Why did I raise that voice? Because the whole Western consumerism has become the symbol of money and has become the symbol of power. If you are a good author, how much money are you making? If you are a good artist, what venue are your paintings selling at? In other words, put all the direction of thinking is into consumerism. Go and make money, and that's where you are. They have brought the world to this path and reduced the world to this position as it is today. We have to correct this position, and, in fact, my next move is to speak about the challenges, the major challenges to bring about this transformation. This won't work with small palliatives. It needs complete change. So, what do we need to bring about that change?

Tu: I think at this juncture that one of the great questions is "rethinking the human." You have to rethink, "what does it mean to be human?"

Kapur: That's exactly what I'm doing.

Tu: I think normally, if you follow the Enlightenment of the modern West, the human is a conqueror, the human is the aggressor, the human has power over everything. Knowledge is power.

Kapur: You control it, and the whole thing goes.

Tu: I think the human is an observer, but also an appreciator.

Kapur: And also, a victim.

Tu: A victim too, but at the same time, in a positive sense, the human is a participant in this creative transformation. The human can be a co-creator of our universe.

Kapur: In fact, the whole structure of humanism is built around this.

Tu: Around the idea of participation?

Kapur: Participation. First of all, build every man. I'm saying this is the only way you can bring the world of humanism together.

Tu: In this sense, the human is also the worst destroyer. There's a very old saying in the ancient Chinese tradition that, "Heaven creates, human completes." All natural disasters cannot wipe out the human, except the disasters that are man-made. The man-made disaster is something that we cannot escape. Right now, we are in the situation where the dilemma we face turns out to be man-made. So, one, at least, sliver of hope or optimism is to say that since we got ourselves into this kind of mess, we in a united and integrated way should be able to get out of it. That's the question about humanism. There's one scholar, I don't know if you met him, he is now the chair of the Council of Indian Philosophy by the name of Balasubramanian. Balasubramanian has made the observation, "We need the so-called Confucianism which is a humanism. It's not a secular humanism, it should be a spiritual humanism."

Kapur: That's exactly what I'm saying. It's the humanism that allows complete potential for man, that he can start from material, go to mental and super-mental, and arrive at spiritual. Every human being must have the opportunity to do that. If you make them consumers, they are only fit to be consumers. The whole society will be modernized, and they will lose the strength to do anything in the future. That's exactly what has happened! Now you demonstrated that man and only man can change. This is precisely what I am saying. The humanist movement at the individual level is defined as the potential of man to move up to the spiritual level.

More and more people are become aware of the pressure now. Where is the pressure coming from? Not me or you. The pressure is coming from the people. They are saying, "What the heck is going on?" So, what I mean therefore is this: this is the answer, and we have to find ways and means of implementing it in whatever form we can. In my opinion, the best bet today is that when these three are united (India, China and Russia), no force on the earth can stop them. If tomorrow they get together, you know what will happen? Everyone can be told "stop it," but nobody will dare to challenge this. Everyone separately can't do it, If China did it, they would destroy China. If India did it, they would destroy India. If Russia did it, they would destroy Russia. But once they together…They are doing their best to stop it from getting together intentionally with force, with everything. We have to see that we should all come out of that, and we should be sitting together, solving the problems of the world and saving the world. It can be done.

I'll also tell you, a small story. A young boy went to his father and said, "Father, from tomorrow, I am not going to school." The father said, "You foolish fellow, what are you going to do? If you stop going to school, how are you going to spend your time? How are you going to create your future? Nothing is safe!" He said, "Well, why are you not going to school?" The son said, "There is a boy who failed every time in one class." The father said, "Who is this fellow?" "He has got an inferiority complex. The young boys are moving rapidly up in class, and he is the only one left behind, so they are jeering at him. So, what he does is every once and a while when he has a feeling because they are not supporting him, he goes and beats them up." The father said, "What are your two brothers doing?" He said, "They are afraid." Then the father said, "What are all these young students doing?" He said, "They are afraid." So, then the father went to his room, brought a bundle of sticks, placed them in front, took one, and gave it to his son. The son breaks it. Then he picks up two and gives it to his son, the son tries very hard to break it, did not find it easy. Then he gives him 3 sticks.

Tu: And he cannot break it?

Kapur: The son says, "Papa, I cannot break it." He says, "You understand? If you three brothers stand together, no force in the world can be greater than you."

Tu: But one thought I have is that we shouldn't repeat the psychology of domination, or the mental sense of domination of the other nations. So, this kind of alliance will have to be open. In other words, it's more inviting, not closed. Now in China, I worry that people become so proud that they want to take on some of the great powers alone. This is not going to go well.

Kapur: Everything confirms now, even in the paper and the information in the press, that this is happening. China will be "number one" in a few years, America will be "number two," India will be "number three," and Russia will be "number four." Even in America, they accept this. So, what will happen? They don't want China to be "number one" and leave America behind. They don't want to see India catch up, and because of that all the countries in Europe will become closer to the United States. Also, there is Russia, which has the power, the military and the defense, everything, plus the will and the new backing of the so called "Orthodox Church." This all together is going toward spiritualism; all together being forced.

Tu: The president is a member of the Orthodox Church from Russia.

Kapur: So, you heard my point? This is what is happening, and we should encourage this to happen. I have been doing that; I have done it. They have even published my comments in *The People's Daily*, *The China Daily,* and others. They know my views. In the last delegation of the Chinese to the World Public Forum, there were twenty of them. We had someone in the meeting ask about the Buddha. What did he say and all that. So, after the meeting was over many of them came to me one after the other to take pictures with me. I said, "Why are you doing this?" They said, "We love what you said!" So, there are a large number of Chinese also who are thinking about that. But the bigger question is the bigger pressure at the top is consumerism, and, particularly now, challenging the consumerism, weakening the consumerism, unemployment.

Tu: But, India, China, and Russia at this juncture are going full force towards commercialism.

Kapur: I'll tell you one thing, which is happening. You know I agree with you, but the big problem is that they are going in the direction of what you say, commercialism. India is also going that way. But there is one difference; they have powerful religious, spiritual forces among them, behind the scenes, on the television. This one man he has gone around the world; he has 80 million followers. He is a yoga teacher! And from yoga he has...

Tu: This is also very pervasive, the quest for new forms of spirituality, but I think another thing is your view as a futurist, and if the world is going to be spiritual, then the three powers, we can say spiritual powers, India, China and Russia must be united, and they can have a very strong force in turning the tide around.

Kapur: And protect themselves, they have to protect themselves.

Tu: They have to transform themselves first from commercialism to a form of humanistic spiritualism or spiritual humanism. Now I think the shape of the spiritual humanism in the 21st century involves at least 4 dimensions. One is the question of the self, integration of the self, not just material, but mental, super-mental, and spiritual. But the self is always a central relationship relating to many other selves. So, there is the question about the self and the community. Then there is the question about how human species will be able to re-relate in a sustainable way to the earth and to nature. Finally, there is the whole question, I think India is a paradigmatic example of this, of the relationship between the human heart and mind and the "Way of Heaven" or the source of spirituality. Now the question I have is, there are many many other spiritual traditions, including the Islamic and the Judaic, so how would you from a futuristic point of view relate...

Kapur: The question is very simple. For Judaism, Christianity and Islam, the fundamental problem is in Hindu thought they think man himself is a god. Man himself or herself is a god and he can convert himself to god to mix with that world conscious spirit. What we call God, somebody calls something else. Then the human being has to raise himself to that spiritual level, and then this consciousness spreads to a large number of people. Now, this is not challenging that bigger consciousness. This will be like the river which starts and then goes to the sea. It becomes a part of that consciousness but can't make that consciousness itself. That means they are also saying he will not become god, but they are saying a different thing.

Now, the West and these religions challenge this, they say "no." They are saying there is one God because their whole thing is essentially built on that. Unless they change that with what I call the "challenge of science and religion," that is the conflict. Unless it is resolved, you cannot have peace. Now, they are not willing to accept this. They say they cannot accept what we Indians say. Now, the Indian culture, tradition, Indian spirituality that is emerging, they will never accept this. Then their problem is that Indian philosophy, Indic civilization is the only one which altered with science from Newtonian science to the science of Einstein and Heisenberg and the uncertainty principle. Now this evolution that is taking place is going to, in many ways, define the future. Therefore, I say taht India's and China's future is being defined by these factors. They can approach these challenges of science.

Tu: They can be both appropriate and at the same time be compatible, but I think there is also a major change of the scientific mind. This is because the old positivistic science, anything that you can feel, you can quantify—scientism—is outmoded. We have a much broader vision of what science is because the more we know, the more we know that we do not know. There's a sense of humility, and that sense of humility will help the world to realize the limitations of the human. Maybe I can return to this question, if man is god potentially, that's the relation between say Atman and Brahmin.

Kapur: Total consciousness.

Tu: No matter how hard we individuals or human beings try, there's always a vision that's broader. So, we need to exercise humility and appreciation of something. We are not the conquerors. We are the observers, appreciators, and participants. I think I very much share your vision of futurism with only one caveat: that is, I think the unification of three major spiritual traditions, Indian, Russian, and Chinese ought to be open, pluralistic self reflexive, and self-critical.

Kapur: India adjusts. India has very great flexibility in the matters of religion, culture, and spirituality. If they find tomorrow that the Chinese is better, Confucianism and Daoism are better than Indic traditions, then they'll say that is our tradition, that is a god. Next it becomes god and they make a picture of it for everybody to worship. So, there are 5,000 gods floating around. Some represent intellects, some represent legal powers, some represent protective roles. So, each god represents the power of nature and that consciousness.

Tu: You know, that is both a comprehensive and an integrated vision, and that comprehensiveness and integration will allow humanism to flourish. That may be the great hope for overcoming the incredible power of commercialism.

Kapur: More so is dialogue. Two dialogues. That is my position.

Tu: Two dialogues?

Kapur: Two dialogues. This is what is happening, and there are two dialogues, and we are trying to do that.

Tu: What are the two dialogues again?

Kapur: Number two is consumerism. The armament protecting consumerism is the one, which I haven't accepted. You cannot protect this consumerism without armament. You cannot protect it. Number one is culture. Without the transformation of culture, nothing else will change.

Tu: Yeah, I fully agree with you there.

Kapur: Well, it has been good to speak with each other.

Tu: Thanks a lot for the conversation.

https://www.youtube.com/watch?v=LlyE9QN9WGM

DIALOGUE WITH FRED DALLMAYR 2011-06-10

Bio: Fred Dallmayr is Emeritus Packey J. Dee Professor in the Philosophy Department at Notre Dame University. He is a political theorist specializing in modern and contemporary European thought with an additional interest in comparative or cross-cultural philosophy. He has been a recipient of NEH and Fulbright fellowships and has been a visiting professor at the New School in New York and at Hamburg University (Germany) and a Senior Fellow at Nuffield College in Oxford. Among his recent publications are: *The Other Heidegger* (1993), *Beyond Orientalism: Essays On Cross-Cultural Encounter* (1996), *Achieving Our World: Toward a Global and Plural Democracy* (2001), *Dialogue Among Civilizations: Some Exemplary Voices* (2002); *Hegel: Modernity and Politics* (new ed. 2002), and *In Search of the Good Life: A Pedagogy for Troubled Times* (2007). He is past president of the Society for Asian and Comparative Philosophy (SACP). He is also a member of the International Coordinating Committee of "World Public Forum: Dialogue of Civilizations," and of the Scientific Committee of "RESET: Dialogue on Civilizations."

Professor Tu Weiming: Maybe we should begin with the question of dialogue. I remember that you told me you were very close to Raimon Panikkar. Actually, we did an interview, a dialogue, before the Parliament of Religion in Barcelona. Ewert Cousins, for one, was very much impressed by the distinction that Panikkar made between dialectic dialogue and dialogical dialogue. He envisioned that the new mode of human interaction should be understood in dialogical terms. I understand you also published a book *Dialogue Among Civilizations* in 2002, so your take on dialogue is very important to me.

Professor Fred Dallmayr: Well, this is an idea which has gained increasing prominence in recent times, during the last 50 years or so, because it's an effort to rethink the character of human relationships not just as two egos meeting separately, but really encountering each other, without dominating, without converging, and respecting each other and the integrity of each person. By coming together through dialogical interaction, we come to understand what the other person is trying to say, what the other person represents, to accept this, to understand the other person, and then to respond in such a way that the other person can reciprocate. This is a development that is very crucial in many parts of the world, but especially in the Western world where we have for a very long time forgotten about this kind of dialogical interaction.

As you say, we were dominated to a very large extent by either dialectic or pure logic. This logic of non-contradiction has two elements that cannot meet together because they contradict each other. Similarly, there is the dialectical relationship, which is basically a relationship of opposition, and overcoming the opposition through some form of dialectic. This is the Hegelian position: thesis, antithesis, synthesis. So, that's one way of dealing with oppositions, but it is not yet the kind of method that we require for true encounter, for true mutual understanding. So, in lieu of the dialectic way, we have come to this idea of dialogue, and some of the main thinkers of dialogue in the 20th century were people like the very important Martin Buber.

Tu: Yes. I-Thou relationship.

Dallmayr: I-Thou relationship. But then, very importantly, there is the philosopher Hans-Georg Gadamer, who had great influence on my own thinking. Over the years I became very close to his work, his writings, have commented in many places about his writings, and we developed a kind of a very friendly relationship. So, I came to really understand the importance of dialogue, which in German is called "*Gespräch*," and for Gadamer the basic idea was that we are constantly in a *Gespräch*, we are constantly in a dialogue. We are in dialogue with ourselves. In order to understand myself, I have to also ask myself questions, and I respond to these questions. So, I am in dialogue with myself. I'm in dialogue with other people, with my family, with my friends; I dialogue with them. But we are also dialoguing with texts, with literature, so for Gadamer the reading of a text was to enter into a dialogue with the text. If, for instance, I want to understand a text by Plato, I come to Plato and I ask a question. I ask, "What do you mean?" "What does the text mean?" and the text responds in a certain way by giving me some sentences, but I may not fully understand these sentences. I come to this text from my own background, from my own frame of reference, and the text may not completely correspond to my frame of reference. So, I have to ask questions, and the text responds to my questions, and I have to open up my frame of reference in a broader way, and thereby come closer to the meaning of the text. So, it's a search for the meaning of the text—could also be a poem, could be literature, could be music—that through question and answer I open myself to the meaning of what is presented to me. But Gadamer extended this further, and what particularly excited me was how he extended it to inter-cultural dialogue, inter-cultural relationship.

I think Gadamer was one of the few truly dialogical philosophers, who were also interested in cosmopolitan, global, inter-cultural dialogue. I talked with him many times about India, about Asia, and he was very much interested in that. He was very much opposed to a monological kind of system, which exists in the world when a dominant power dictates the frame of reference and the discourse in the world. He was very much opposed to imperialism, to unilateral domination, and for him, the basic idea was to overcome monologue through dialogue, the dialogical engagement, between cultures, between religions, between traditions. To overcome this unilateralism, which is basically an egocentrism, or ethnocentrism, one must open oneself up. I found this was absolutely crucial in our situation in the Western world because to a very large extend the Western world has become, or has been, a domineering culture that has tried to dominate everything in the world unilaterally, without listening, without engaging the other truly in dialogue.

That has been the curse of Western civilization. There are many good things about Western civilization, but the curse of Western civilization was this impulse to dominate, to dominate other cultures, to dominate other religions and that came to be known under the label of "Orientalism." We orientalize the others, treat them as an object for our benefit. This is also the same kind of domineering impulse that relates to the notion of culture versus nature. We try to dominate nature, control nature, and exploit nature for our own benefit. It's a form of control, which is very destructive. So, this tendency to dominate others, other cultures, we have to overcome through dialogue.

There is also the tendency to dominate nature, which is deeply rooted in modern Western civilization. It is deeply rooted in the whole tradition that comes from the late Middle Ages, from Francis Bacon, Newton, and Descartes. It is that Cartesian idea of the ego standing over against the other world, the outer world. There's this inner ego, and what is the ego is supposed to do? It is to dominate this outer world. That is the seed of unilateral domination, and we see the effects of this in modern technology, and the modern exploitation of nature, which may really lead to a natural disaster because the resources are not renewable, and this whole process is not sustainable in the long run.

So there too the idea of dialogue comes in. Instead of dominating nature, we need to enter into a dialogue with nature, and listen to what nature is telling us. Now, we cannot talk to nature, but nature does speak to us. It does not perhaps speak in a human voice, but nature speaks to us through certain events, through certain phenomena, which we discover, and which are triggered by our form of exploitation of nature. Nature responds with certain catastrophes, with tsunamis, with things which are overwhelming—nature catastrophes. Nature is telling us something. These are its dialogues with us, and we have to respond to these natural catastrophes. Anyway, there's dialogue in many, many directions, and the ultimate dialogue for Gadamer, and for me also, is the dialogue with what is sometimes called "the Divine" or perhaps "Heaven" in Chinese. These are the fundamentals of dialogue, to overcome unilateralism, and to become really part of a cosmos. That's how I see it.

Tu: That's great. Yeah, my sense is that the dialogical mode is predicated on the aspiration that human community, what I call a kind of "fiduciary community," will be able to cultivate a kind of dialogical civilization because dialogue among civilizations is absolutely necessary for the cultivation of the culture of peace. Now many people are very suspicious about whether dialogue is possible between two people who are not on equal footing. For example, the series of so-called dialogues between United States and China on trade, on the evaluation of renminbi, on even military strategy are strictly speaking not true dialogues. They are just bargaining, exerting pressure, and using strategy to maximize one's own profit.

Normally the dialogical mode, even with Martin Buber's "I and Thou," is between two like-minded people committed to the quest for a common way of human flourishing. So, people are very suspicious of whether in the 21st century—with all these conflicts and tensions where globalization actually leads to regionalization and localization—Panikkar's notion about the dialogical dialogue is realizable. I don't know whether a kind of optimism is required in order to appreciate it, or it is so crucial for the human community that it's an art that needs to be cultivated.

Dallmayr: Well, I fully agree with you, and I did not mention previously the name that you now introduce to our discussion, the name of Raimon Panikkar. I referred mainly to Buber and to Gadamer. Now, Panikkar introduces a very important dimension of dialogue, namely a dimension across cultures, across different language games, and across different idioms. Panikkar is deeply rooted both in Western philosophy, but also in the Indian philosophical tradition. In the Indian philosophical tradition, he found a very congenial kind of medium of expressing himself in the tradition that is called the "Advaita Vedanta," the non-dualistic Vedanta that completely opposes the Cartesian bifurcation of mind and body, inner and outer, and mind and matter. Vedanta is precisely the opposite of Cartesianism, and Panikkar developed this very well with the idea of *advaita* (non-dualism): we are all involved in a cosmic unity that cannot be split apart into separate elements.

Now, to what you were saying regarding the difficulties involved in all forms of dialogues, there are many skeptical arguments regarding dialogue. One skeptical argument is that dialogue is simply impossible. If people do not speak precisely the same language, and do not come from the same background, there is basically an incompatibility between different perspectives, between different languages, and you cannot translate them, you cannot dialogue between them. It is frequently called "incommensurability." Language games are incommensurable with each other, so you cannot possibly dialogue. I think this is an important point, but it has been proved to be wrong because to a very large extent it is possible to translate between language games. We have shown it through translations which are never perfect, but at least some of the essence of a statement, of a perspective, of a tradition can be translated approximately, and made clear to other people. Thus, the incommensurability thesis can be refuted and overcome.

Then there's the point that you mentioned questioning if there can be dialogue among people who are not really on the same level, in other words basic "inequality" between the participants. That's a frequent objection made, especially by people who claim to be realistic and not utopian. They say, "Well there is no such thing like dialogue because there are always inequalities, and the stronger always dominates the weaker." That is an argument that the so-called "political realists" always make. But the point is this, there are certain preconditions of dialogue, and so if we want to have real or genuine dialogue, we have to work at removing the inequalities that might prevent a genuine dialogue. So, the first precondition is that we establish a certain commonality between the participants of a dialogue a rough equality, not an absolute or numerical equality, so that neither party feels superior or inferior. Because if one party feels inferior, it immediately feels dominated or exploited. So, there is an important aspect of trying to establish equality between the participants. If you can do this, then you have at least one precondition fulfilled for dialogue.

There is a second precondition that I would also emphasize, and this is that all the parties of a dialogue have to have the good will to dialogue. If there is no good will to dialogue, then you talk to a wall, and cannot advance in a dialogue. For this reason, we have to cultivate the good will to dialogue. This was a very important point that Gadamer made. There is an ethical foundation to dialogue; dialogue doesn't just happen, you have to have an ethical precondition, and this ethical precondition is one of good will. That basically means that I'm willing to learn from you, and I'm willing to engage with you. Of course, there are people who are stubborn, who don't want to engage, who have no good will, and so the problem is how we can overcome bad will, or the absence of good will.

All of this means that dialogue is not easy. There's the problem of incommensurability, not everything can be translated; there is the problem of inequality; there's the problem of the good will to dialogue. In the famous exchange between Gadamer and Derrida, Derrida opposed this idea of dialogue because he said there's no such thing as good will. He said that is too Kantian an idea. Anyway, Gadamer always insisted that any general dialogue requires ethical foundations, and that leads me to think that something like virtue ethics is really a requirement for dialogue. You cannot have dialogue without virtues, and that leads me to have a certain sympathy toward Confucianism and Confucian virtue ethics. I think Confucianism precisely is also a very good basis for a dialogical dialogue. So, that's where we meet, in that domain.

Tu: I think one way of looking at the Confucian tradition is as a certain form of openness; it's not universal or an abstract universalism. and certainly, it's not a closed particularism. It is an openness that presupposes pluralism. Now the question is that there is normally the exclusive approach or the inclusive approach, but neither one is particularly satisfactory. The exclusive approach is a form of closed particularism, which sometimes is even aggressive. It is not only self-imposed isolation, but aggressive and hostile towards the other, the other often misconceived as the enemy. Whereas the abstract kind of universalism is in search of the lowest common denominator in any kind of encounter, so this leads you to the thinnest area and the richness of concrete persons is lost.

For the kind of dialogue that is necessary, I think the most fundamental ethical principle is reciprocity, which is often the Golden Rule stated in the negative: "Do not do to others what you would not want others to do to you." Now, Hans Küng, maybe more than ten years ago now, insisted that the Golden Rule stated in the positive is more or less identical with the Golden Rule stated in the negative. In my view, the "Do not do unto others what you would not want others to do unto you," as a spirit of reciprocity, is probably more basic than the assertion that you have to do to others what you want others to do to you. I don't know whether you have reflected on this kind of difference, and especially in reference to your notion about conversion?

Dallmayr: Yeah, I have thought about this. These different formulations of the Golden Rule to some extent are equivalent, but one can differentiate them in certain ways. I find the negative expression "Do not do to others that which you do not want them to do to you" quite appealing, but also somewhat limiting because it only insists on the not-doing. This notion that "I do not do something to you which you should not be doing to me" could be almost like a total withdrawal from a relationship. "I don't do anything, so you don't have to do anything for me," "I don't do anything for you, you don't do anything for me." It is almost like an abstinence of interaction.

This is why the formula "Do to others as you want them to do to you" is a more positive dimension. It forces me to be engaged. I have to do something, and I cannot just wait and not do anything. It forces me to engage with others in the hope that others would reciprocate, and they will also do for me in the way I did for them. But, of course for me, coming from a Christian background in a very ecumenical sense, I cannot forget the instructions that we find in the Gospel to go beyond even the Golden Rule and to walk the extra mile, even beyond what you could expect through reciprocity. For instance, Jesus demands that if we are slapped on one cheek, we should offer the other cheek. That's going beyond pure reciprocity. This is the idea that we should be always doing more than what is expected, going the extra mile. This is a positive ethics that invites us, or even requires us, to be particularly engaged, and do good works without expecting a return, without necessarily having reciprocity. That is a sort of very pure ethics that may be beyond ordinary human expectations, but it's a good utopian goal to aim for.

Anyway, I favor the more positive expression of the Golden Rule because it requires me to get involved, to do something good, and it can never be a limit to this "good." In many human relationships we find that we have to go the extra mile. Take the example of mother and child, where the mother always does much, much, much, much more than she can expect the child to return. The child cannot return all the goodness, which the mother showers on the child. The same goes for friendship. If you are really a friend to somebody, you want to do much more than what you expect that the friend might do in return. Sometimes they call it the "ethics of giving," and in that respect Emmanuel Levinas was particularly emphatic about the ethics of the gift, the gift without reciprocity. You made the argument that there's a Golden Rule, which combines all cultures; I think in all cultures one can find something like the Golden Rule.

Tu: If we want to be more precise, the Golden Rule stated in the negative is not just Confucian it's also Jewish. I think Rabbi Hillel, at one point, was asked by one of his students to give a summary of the core of the Talmudic tradition as a whole. He said, "Do not do to others what you would not want others to do to you," and so there must be a subtle difference. Let's say, in a dialogical situation the positive way certainly is a way of engagement, of maybe even a sense of responsibility toward the other. Let's assume that I've been blessed with the Good News, and I'm obligated to share it with others. Additionally, if the other refuses to share, I feel more obligated to engage.

Now, if the other turns out to be a Muslim who's committed to a different style of life and a different sense of transcendence, then a clash is almost inevitable. So, we may think about the minimum condition, which is to avoid the conflict of conversion. But then you really also need to have a positive charge, otherwise the minimum condition, as you pointed out, becomes too passive and does not necessarily engage with the other. So, the more positive formulation in the Confucian tradition comparable to the positive Golden Rule states that "In order to establish myself, I have to help others to establish themselves; in order to enlarge myself, I have to help others to enlarge themselves."

Dallmayr: That's a beautiful saying.

Tu: The question of the reciprocity relates to the spirit of tolerance. This is tolerance in the sense that the otherness of the other is not perceived as a threat, and not only is it not perceived as a threat, but I should also welcome it as a positive contribution to my own understanding of the world. If it's not an occasion for conversion, I have to exercise a certain kind of restraint even though I feel obligated to spread the Good News. My sense is that the minimum condition of dialogue is tolerance. It's related to the idea of reciprocity, but tolerance is the minimum condition. Without recognition of the uniqueness of the other (not only the uniqueness of the other, but also the irreducibility of the other in terms of my encountering), without constraining the desire to spread the good news, and without understanding what the others want, the sense of engagement dictated by my own sense of responsibility may turn out to be counterproductive.

So, the respect of the other and the integrity of the other that sometimes believes something radically different from me is necessary for the possibility of mutual referencing and mutual learning. So, dialogue must avoid even the motivation of conversion in the beginning. Of course, we are delighted if our own position is appreciated by the other, but we have to somewhat overcome even the hidden desire to convert. Nor is it the occasion to try to make a statement about our own faith. If we become too forceful in trying to make a statement, the dialogical atmosphere would be somewhat polluted. Also, it's not even the occasion to try to correct a perceived misunderstanding of my position by the other.

So then, you don't convert, you don't make a statement, you don't try to correct some kind of misconception. It seems the dialogue becomes too passive, but I think one great benefit of this kind of attitude towards dialogue is to cultivate the art of listening, and to listen to the other. This listening is not ordinary listening; I think they use the term "deep listening," which is not only attentive, but also open and receptive. This is something, maybe a virtue, to be cultivated. It's also an occasion to broaden our own intellectual horizon, like Clifford Geertz's notion about confronting radical otherness as a way of liberating ourselves. Before we try to impose our own sense of what is reasonable, what is right upon the other, in other words, judgment, we need to ask ourselves whether our own frame of reference is broad enough. I think Gadamer is very realistic and wise to make explicit the bias and the limitation in the background of trying to understand something.

I think another thing that may turn out to be extremely beneficial for the dialogical situation is to enhance one's critical self awareness: the other would not only not be perceived as a threat, but the other may even be considered as a cause for celebration. My own personal experience is very much a confirmation of that attitude. I consider myself very much of a beneficiary of Christian theology, because some of my esteemed friends are theologians who help me to understand my own tradition. One colleague Fritz Mote, actually one of the most respected Sinologist, is deeply concerned about the implicit Christianization of the Confucian position.

I, however, underscore the importance of religiosity. Confucianism may not be a religion, but religiosity is very important. There is a sense of transcendence, even though you can see the form of transcendence as an immanent transcendence. If there's nothing that transcends, it becomes impoverished as a humanism, and so that is the benefit of encountering the various kinds of theological perspectives.

I'm critically aware of the fact that historically the particular question of transcendence, especially radical transcendence, never really occurred to the followers of Confucius as a necessary condition for being able to develop an ultimate concern for human flourishing. They felt we are in the world, and we have to try to transform the world from within, and even though there's no radical otherness or the wholly other, the divinity of spirituality works through our own concreteness. In that particular situation, the transformation has to be done through a dialogical encounter with the other. I think the mutual responsiveness of the two dialogical partners is predicated on some kind of self-restraint in the beginning.

My recommendation is that you have to work at the same time with two very different modes or ways of engagement. One is critically aware of the limitation of my own horizon. I may fail to listen deeply, and I may also not be self-reflexive enough. This is almost like a form of self-cultivation that is not at all in conflict with my sense of responsibility, my sense of positive engagement. But there is also the problem of the point of departure. I would say the point of departure in a dialogical situation might be better described by the negative formulation because the danger of imposing something I cherish, and which may reflect a kind of bias. Any religious tradition in this pluralistic context is a concretization of some great values, but at the same time it is at the expense of others. So, with that self-awareness as a precondition, more positive engagement becomes beneficial. We avoid the danger, and then try to underscore the more positive formulation.

Dallmayr: Yeah, I follow your argument, and I think on the whole we are together in this whole matter. First of all, as you correctly say, we always approach the other, we approach the world, we approach the text with certain preconceptions, or what Gadamer called "prejudgments."

Tu: "Prejudgments," and sometimes just "bias."

Dallmayr: This recognition of prejudgments in his argument was critically directed against a certain kind of Enlightenment rationalism, where we are able to completely cleanse ourselves of any kind of prior assumptions, as if we were entering the world like newborn babies, having no frame of reference with which we approach others. Against this—what he called "the bias against bias" or "the prejudgment against prejudgment"—he critically responded to a certain kind of Enlightenment universalism, which completely ignores that all of us come from a certain background. We are all rooted somewhere. We are finite beings. We are not free-floating intellects. We are finite beings, who come from a certain background. The task is then how to correct prejudgments or biases, if we find them to be untenable, if we find them to be misguided, simply erroneous, or false. How can we overcome them? It's a slow process, as we cannot just jump into this universality of reason. We have to work on our prejudgments, and slowly through dialogue to learn to think better about the other person, or about the text that we encounter.

So, it's this way of proceeding slowly, correcting oneself, listening more and better to the other side, and asking new questions to slowly overcome these kinds of limitations, while never assuming that we have reached a total uniformity of beliefs or of existences. We all come from finite localities, and finite backgrounds, and finite languages, so ultimately there'll always be a plurality of perceptions. The question then is how we can come from our perspective, from our background, from our prejudgments, toward some kind of an agreement with others, or kind of an engagement with others. On that point, you are quite correct that we have to restrain our impulses to dominate the other, to try to manipulate the other, which is sort of deep seeded impulse of egotism that seems to be deeply rooted, at least, in modern Western people. How to restrain this? Ethics is precisely one of the main ways of limiting, of restraining, of curbing these kinds of impulses. Now, one of these impulses might be to convert the other to my point of view, to my frame of reference. Yours is the wrong and mine is the right frame of reference, so I try to convert you.

Now I think that any kind of dialogical position necessarily has to reject conversion. I am thoroughly opposed to any form of conversion, missionary activities, all these things. We had too much of that during the last several centuries. Colonialism was basically tied up with missionary activities, with Christianizing the heathens and natives. The most horrible example of this form of missionary activity happened in Latin America.

Tu: The Crusaders.

Dallmayr: The Crusaders, and the butchering of the natives. In order to Christianize them, they butchered them. There are horrible examples in many places, as this was repeated. So, I don't believe in conversion. Now, can that to be reconciled with the request or commandment that Jesus gave to his disciples to spread the Good News? As he said, "Go into the world, and spread the Good News." But what is the meaning of that? Does that mean conversion? Well, I resist that idea. I think you can spread the Good News without converting anybody. You spread the Good News by being good to everybody whom you meet. You treat them as equals, as human beings with dignity and with respect. That is what is known as spreading the Good News. I spread the Good News not by converting you to become a Christian, but by showing you what it means to act as a Christian should act, namely, to act as a good human being to other human beings. So, absolutely no conversion is necessary or possible with that attitude. That has to be resisted.

It does not mean that one cannot practice one's religion and practice one's faith. If somebody else is interested in asking about what I believe and what rituals I have, I can tell them where I come from. But I always make it clear that I don't want to convert you at all. I spent quite some time in India, for instance, and had young Indian friends. I went to some of the temples, and I worshiped with them at temples. Then they said, "Well, I want to go with you to Christian church." I said, "OK, I will take you on the condition that you realize I'm not trying to convert you. You just look at it, see what you find there, and then you go with that." On that basis, we went to a Christian church, a Catholic church, and we had the service together. It was a learning experience for them just as it was a learning experience for me to go to their temples. But when I went to those temples, they never said, "You must be converted into Hinduism." So, any kind of a truly dialogical relation with another person excludes conversion or even the idea of conversion.

Gandhi, one of my great models, always said, "This is wrong; conversion is wrong. It's always unnecessary because ultimately, we all believe in the same Divine." Whatever we worship are just modalities of honoring that great presence, or that great being that allows us to be. There are different ways of doing that, so there's no need to go from one religion to another religion because this is just like changing one melody for another melody. Anyway, I agree with you on this. There should not be conversion, but there should be an openness to the others. Now I would go a little bit beyond the idea of tolerance or toleration because toleration can mean I really don't like you, but I tolerate you. You could say, "I really can't stand you, but I tolerate you." That's a problem. One would have to say I go beyond toleration; I really go toward appreciation.

Tu: Recognition, appreciation, and respect.

Dallmayr: Recognition and respect, yeah. Also, the great poet Goethe said, "*Toleranz ist nicht genug, Anerkennung ist erfordert,*" which means "Tolerance is not sufficient, recognition is required." This is very important. If I recognize somebody else as an equal human being with integrity and with the divine spark in him or her, as I believe all human beings have that divine spark, then clearly, I cannot try to convert and dominate that person.

Tu: To return to your beginning observation about the relationship between "me" and the text, in a way there is a qualitative difference between the dialogue between the two concrete living persons, and the relationship between the reader and the text. Focusing on that, I agree with you that the presumption of the possibility of emptying out all of your prejudgment—you use word "like a baby"—or holding a totally value neutral, disinterested position to try to arrive at a certain kind of objective condition is not only an unrealizable but may not even be desirable. Some people take a very positivistic view that since the text consists of dead letters you have to breathe in a certain kind of vitality. But my understanding of the dialogical relationship presupposes a kind of prejudgment. Thus, the more I'm critically aware of my prejudgment, even though I'll never be fully aware, the better. The idea that you can approach it from a totally neutral point of view is an assumption that many of the philologists or textual analysts in the so-called "Sinological tradition" hold. They believe that the more you can distance yourself from the text or the more you can neutralize its values, the more you'll be able to understand how objectively the text really presented itself. I don't think that works.

This reminds me of Paul Ricoeur's notion of "ego" as the more negative feature of subjectivism, where self can open itself up to certain kind of texts. This means we don't simply read about it, we read from it. Thus, the reading itself is a dynamic process of doing, in a sense of trying to develop a kind of embodied knowing, or experiential understanding of the meaningfulness or the meaning of the text. The text is alive, and it speaks to us in a way that is not simply imagination; a text is the embodiment of the great spiritual masters or spiritual forces that will enlighten us.

I think the Enlightenment mentality is not only anthropocentric, but it also assumes that the enlightening process is the process by which the light source is going to overcome all the darkness. In other words, the more knowledge and the light source extends, the more this ignorance will be expelled. But I think in the more modern understanding, the more I know, the more I know I don't know, and the more I know I need to know more. The spread of a certain kind of light to the darkness of the world, often has the unintended negative consequence that the veil of ignorance becomes even thicker, so we can never fully overcome it. We have to recognize that there's more than one interpretation, that there is a plurality of interpretation.

Right now, I'm very much engaged with a group doing close readings with undergraduates. We are reading of some of the very fundamental texts, and not in a way of explaining what the most accepted approach to the text is, but allowing the texts to be interpreted by the students who engage themselves in a continuous dialogue with the text. By communally sharing some of their insights there are conflicts and tensions, but there are also points of convergence. We have plurality, but it does not degenerate into relativism. There's also always the continuous encounter between the reader and the text, which is alive and transformative. The reading itself is almost like knowing as a transformative act, rather than knowing as a cognitive reflection of a totally disinterested scientific mind. This situation is, as you pointed out, if not diametrically opposed to, is significantly different from the Enlightenment mentality. In the post-Enlightenment situation in the West, there are feminist interpretations, ecological concerns, religious pluralism, cultural diversity, and all these, even including deconstruction and postmodern ideas, are critical reflections on the limitations, or even the distortions of the Enlightenment mentality.

The irony is that outside of the West in places that haven't yet gone through this critical reflection, they still commit themselves to a modernizing process that is very much the outcome of Westernization, modernization, and globalization dictated by the Enlightenment mentality. If you look at China today, maybe the most powerful ideology is a kind of scientism, as a reflection of the Enlightenment mentality. Whereas the West has already moved beyond the Enlightenment and move into a postmodern ethos or mentality, many people in developing societies, China in particular, are still committed to the modernizing process as progress. It is also based upon the Kuhnian notion that human history progresses from religion to metaphysics and then to science; once you get to science and rationality, then metaphysic and religion can be easily relegated to the background.

This situation both enables and compels me to develop a project that I simply characterize as a Confucian reflection on the Enlightenment mentality that balances both sympathetic understanding and critical analysis. It is not about how the tradition is able to live up to the standards of the Enlightenment, but about reflecting on both the strengths and limitations of the Enlightenment. In order to do that, the first step is simply to understand the world of thought in China at a time when there was contact, maybe 17th or 18th century, between the East and the West. In that period, you could say many of the Eastern ideas or Confucian ideas became influential in the beginning of the Enlightenment movement. People like Voltaire, Leibniz, Rousseau, Montaigne, Diderot, and Quesnay were all under the influence of this tradition.

In his book *Enlightenment Contested*, Jonathan Israel, who is now the history professor at Princeton's Advanced Institute, indicates very strongly that the West was not only influenced by Confucianism, but also became concerned with Hinduism and Islam. So, the claim can be historically or empirically verified that indeed the Enlightenment of the modern West, especially the emergence of rationalism and so forth, was at least inspired, if not totally shaped or influenced, by Confucian humanism. Yet, when China and the West because of the Chinese Rites Controversy were no longer was able to communicate to each other, during the hundred years from the 18th to the 19th century, something very dramatic changed in the West.

The first thing is to understand is Chinese world of ideas, and to say what kind of universe or life of the mind there was at a time; this not only includes Matteo Ricci and his associates, but also some Muslim thinkers, philosophers, people in literature, in art who all existed as part of the richness of this symbolic universe. Then parallel to that are the current modern, including yourself, most forward-looking philosophers reflecting upon the Enlightenment as a legacy of modern philosophers. The third step is to understand why the Enlightenment mentality, which was under the influence of Confucianism in the earlier period, has now become so rooted in modern Chinese consciousness to the extent that even though the West already moved beyond it, the commitment to modernization, to progress, and to what I would call the outmoded positivistic understanding of the Enlightenment continues to persist as a powerful persuasive and explanatory force in China. I think with that background, we can then begin to talk about Confucian humanism in the 21st century. It's a historical narrative, together with a critical, social, political, and philosophical analysis of the current situation where scientism is so powerful in China and opens the possible space for a genuine Confucian reflection on the Enlightenment.

Dallmayr: Yes, I think I fully agree with you on the problem of the Enlightenment and the counter-Enlightenment, and the post-Enlightenment. I have experienced a similar phenomenon in my visit to India, where there's also suddenly a tendency to try to catch up with the West, with modernity, modernization, science, and also the Enlightenment. This frequently leads to a total erosion or neglect, or amnesia of the great Indian traditions. It's just wiped out because the modern Western Enlightenment is superior or assumed to be superior to all of these traditions. So, all of this is wiped out, and in some of the young generation, they go to the West to study; they go to Oxford or Cambridge or Harvard. When they come home, they totally disdain or have contempt for their own tradition, and only repeat what they have heard in the West, especially from analytical philosophers.

This is a very unfortunate situation, because, as you say, in the West there already has been for some time an effort to move beyond this kind of Enlightenment mentality, which is reflected in an absolute or universal rationalism. Steps have been made, but this does not mean that we want to reject Enlightenment, that we want to reject reason or rationalism. The question is just how to position the Enlightenment, and how to reinterpret reason and rationality.

Many important steps have been made in this direction. For me a very crucial influences early on, when I was skeptical or somewhat uncertain about the value of Western modernity and Western Enlightenment, came from phenomenology and hermeneutics. The idea of Enlightenment as a full Enlightenment, that every darkness is excluded and we are totally rational, had already been overcome by people like Heidegger, Merleau-Ponty, and Gadamer. The idea that we are basically finite rooted beings who come from a certain background, that we are not these free-floating intellectuals or absolute universalists, had already been overcome by the very idea that Heidegger puts at the very beginning of his major work *Being and Time* when he says, "Human being, what is that? Das Sein is being in the world."

This means we are rooted somewhere. His emphasis on human finitude, that we can never totally overcome our finitude, leads him to speak of our being-toward-death. Death is not just an accident, but death is what characterizes, what constitutes our human being. We are moving toward death; death constitutes our finitude as human beings. So, that's already way beyond the conception of Enlightenment, where you can do away with all darkness, with all finitudes, with all limitations. That's already a whole new path. For me this was a great revelation, this idea of human finitude, of being in the world, of being-toward-death. Much of it was also existentialism that moved beyond this Enlightenment absolutism.

Now, emphasizing human finitude and limitations does not mean that we reject infinity or the infinite. We are finite, but that doesn't mean we celebrate our finitude or our particularism and neglect totally the idea of infinity and of the absolute. The question is "How we talk about these things?" and that actually leads me back to a discussion we had in our conversation at the conference here in Vienna. There the whole idea of dialogue was first being introduced as a way of dealing with the question of transcendence and immanence. The relation between finitude and infinity corresponds to the relation between immanence and transcendence, so sometimes people say that Heidegger and the existentialists only emphasize finitude, in other words they emphasize that there's nothing but immanence. That's frequently a criticism which is made, that they neglect transcendence or infinity.

The point that was made in our conference, and where this idea of dialogue came up and why it became relevant, was that I tried to indicate that these (finitude and infinity, immanence, and transcendence) are not binary conceptions, not opposites, but that finitude is precisely a precondition of our striving toward infinity. As finite creatures, we are longing for infinity; in our immanence, we are longing for transcendence. But the two are intimately linked together in a dialogical relationship, not a dialectical relationship. This dialogical relationship is what Panikkar calls *advaita*, or a non-dualist relationship.

This is an accusation that is frequently precisely made by Enlightenment philosophers who say, "Well, all these people like Heidegger, Gadamer, and Merleau-Ponty only emphasize human finitude and imminence, and they are totally neglectful of universalism." This is a misreading. They merely show that every light presupposes a shadow, every lightness presupposes darkness, and every rationality presupposes non-reason. So, it's this kind of relationship between immanence and transcendence, or finitude and infinity, that is linked in a dialogical connection. That's what came out in our discussions at the conference, and this is how the idea of dialogical relationship was introduced. I think this is a crucial step beyond Enlightenment rationalism.

Tu: I think the question that looms large in my mind is rethinking the human. That kind of abstract universalism focused on the original state, the generalized self, and the totally disembodied idea of a person, without history, without society, not historicized, not contextualized, I think people are increasingly worried about this particular style of philosophizing. Rather, we should consider concrete humanity, or the concrete living person, as the point of departure. If we take this particular approach, there is the danger of becoming very parochial, very local. But I'm not that worried about it. I think the question is the global significance of local knowledge. Realistically, in the academic community and in the intellectual world in general most of the globally significant forms of local knowledge came from the West: the local knowledge of Paris, the local knowledge of London and New York. Modernization theory, construction, deconstruction, they all came from Europe.

I remember many, many years ago, maybe in the 1960s, I had a conversation with Robert Bellah, and we agreed that the next generation of real global thinkers, or at the time we said "world thinkers," would have to acknowledge at least a willingness to engage the non-Western world. It's not possible to imagine how someone could be considered as a world philosopher, while deliberately confining himself or herself to the Eurocentric world view. In a way, what happened was that some very influential prominent philosophers such as Foucault, Derrida, Habermas, and maybe Merleau-Ponty as well were only focused on the modern West, and somewhat unmindful of the world beyond. In other words, it was almost like the West and rest. If you were able to face the challenges of the West, then the rest would be able to follow the right path. I think this reminds me of Ashis Nandy. He's a very creative mind from India. He said that he never feels comfortable in Cambridge because the close friends who sit beside him seem to assume that "Your present is our remote past, and our present is your distant future." You now have this kind of unilinear progression…

Dallmayr: It's an insult.

Tu: Well, it's an insult, but it's assumed by a lot of people. It's like when Derrida made the remark in China that there's no Chinese philosophy. A major debate in China is whether we have Chinese philosophy, or simply we only do philosophy in China. That to me is very strange. We move from that particular Eurocentrism to a much broader horizon of the world. I think you represent this engagement in India and China. Robert Bellah also did his doctoral thesis on Tokugawa religion. Of course, he became involved with the American scene, the happiness of the heart and the good society. But now his theory of religion is global. Following much broader insights, he returned to that. I think if his book comes out, it will be marvelous. I think to a certain extent Charles Taylor can be included, but in terms of his whole orientation relating to *A Secular Age*. However, I wouldn't speak to him directly, as it's very much focused on the experience of the modern West.

Most forms of local knowledge that are globally significant originated from the West, but now with a view toward the future forms of local knowledge in the East will also increasingly become globally significant. The work that I've been evolving is one of those examples. This is what actually happens to the Confucian tradition rooted in the local knowledge of the Shandong Peninsula in period of Confucius, as it expanded in China, then in East Asia, and now has the possibility of being globally significant. This is a new form, which certainly will challenge our view about what's going on.

To me, the intriguing thing was that after the First World War, with Spengler's *The Decline of the West*, there was the Institute for Chinese Philosophy in Frankfurt, organized by Otto Franker, who was originally the founder of sinological studies in Hamburg. Many important people were affiliated with that center, including Martin Buber and Carl Jung, and younger scholars were thus introduced to Buddhism and Japanese philosophy, and I'm definitely sure that Heidegger was influenced by these. The beginning of his section of "The Letter on Humanism," written toward the end if his life, was almost a different style of writing and reflected this openness.

Yet, after the Second World War and the rise of America as a superpower—the Marshall Plan on the one hand, and the occupation of Japan or turning Japan into a younger brother on the other—America transformed herself from a great learning civilization that had learned from the France in terms of the Enlightenment traditions, from Germany in terms of science and technology, and from England in terms of literature and language into a teaching civilization that was sometimes very arrogant.

In this new situation, if we rethink the human with a view toward the future, my sense is the viability of the human species looms very large in this discussion. In our current discussion about politics and religion, there is a transcendent dimension. But nature seems to drop out of the picture, and yet it is perhaps the primary datum in any reflection on the human. If we want to begin rethinking the human, then earth looms large in this consciousness. Almost all major religious traditions have been transformed because of this new reality, or this new awareness. I think the dialogical mode based upon reciprocal relationships rather the dialectic that always involves violence and overcoming may be the only way for humanity's different civilizations and cultures to cultivate cultural peace.

Dallmayr: Well.

Tu: Your concluding remark.

Dallmayr: It just so happened that the last book I've written—it's not yet published, but it will be published this fall—is on nature. It's called *Return to Nature?* and in that book I developed what I call "an ecological counter history," a counter history to the dominant Western narrative of philosophy. It is a counter history of people who en seriously engaged with nature. In other words, instead of the dominant form of dualism that characterized the modern West, the Cartesian dualism of mind and body, of ego and nature outside to be controlled, they have tried to develop a thought of wholeness, of unity, of cosmos. I begin there with Spinoza, then Leibniz, and from Leibniz to Schelling, from Schelling to the great Romantics, then to John Dewey, and finally to Heidegger. The concluding chapter makes some references to Asian philosophy, and how all these come together.

All of these are attempts to overcome the binaries or dualisms that characterize so much of Western civilization, which is basically a unilateral or monological kind of dualism that imposes something on the rest of the world. Nature may become very crucial as another dialogical partner with whom we have to interact. We have to listen very carefully to nature. What nature tries to tell us about all this violence we do to it, it is that "we don't like this violence." So, we have to be very engaged dialogically with nature in order to restore a sense of wholeness, a wholeness which is also a wholesomeness in the world. This will overcome all these dualisms that pervade modern Western thought, which is the aspect of Western thought that troubles me so much.

With this new direction, I tried to overcome the dualistic framework which characterizes modern Western thought, the Cartesian framework which persists in many contemporary thinkers, including people like Habermas, Richard Rorty in different ways, and Michel Foucault. Regretfully, even though in many ways I've been fully in accord with our friend Charles Taylor, I had to conclude that at least in his most recent writings he was slipping back into these dichotomies which split wholeness apart and make it impossible to restore a unity to the world. This is especially evident in his…

Tu: *A Secular Age* on transcendence.

Dallmayr: …opposition or the dichotomy between immanence and transcendence, claiming that these are two different realms.

Tu: You have to bring the transcendence back to re-enchant or to re-sacralize.

Dallmayr: Yes, we need to show the dialogical relationship between imminence and transcendence, that they interact with each other, that they respond to each other. Immanence responds to transcendence, and transcendence responds to immanence. This is why I gave to Charles Taylor a picture of Dürer showing a mother and child, and asking him very pointedly, "You show me where is the immanence, and where is the transcendence? Where does immanence stop, and transcendence begin?" You cannot do that. You cannot separate them because they are interlinked. They are inescapably connected with each other, influencing each other, and responding to each other in a dialogical way. That was the main point. But in other ways, of course, I feel that Charles Taylor has made enormous efforts to overcome, to some extent, ethnocentrism or Westerncentrism or Eurocentrism. He has now spent some time in India, for instance. So, I fully recognize that, but there's still a remnant of that…

Tu: I think it's painfully difficult to move from the "either-or" mode of thinking, to "both-and."

Dallmayr: Yeah, that's the thing.

Tu: Ai Bei offers a very interesting image, as she's a writer, about the question of the full moon. Right now, it's only half full, so it's a half-moon. But there is the other side, whether you call it in our technical language "the politics of absence" or the idea of "lacks." We don't have democracy; we don't have science; we don't have this critical rationalistic thinking, and so forth. So, now the time is ripe for other side of the moon to reveal itself. So, the wholeness you're talking about in terms of human consciousness has to be a fusion, a healthy fusion of the two. I think the challenge of the earth may provide the last chance for this particular thinking. Even though I'm quite pessimistic about whether we'll work on that, given the constraints of institutions, of habits of the heart, of politics, and so forth, I think everybody is aware of the fact that without this new integration, without this new sense of wholeness, without genuine dialogue—I call it "the emergence of a dialogical civilization"—the possibilities are very limited. In this sense, in the 21st century a kind of spiritual humanism will have to emerge as a point of departure for philosophical and religious reflections from many different kinds of faith communities.

In other words, we have to admit that we are human first before we are Christians, Buddhists, Muslims, Confucians, and so forth. This reflection on the human from the evolutionary perspective suggests the emergence of the human is such an important cosmic event. Something dramatically changed. We're no longer the outcome of evolution; we've now shaped the direction of evolution. The Confucian idea of partnership or co-creator may be distorted, may be totally inverted to be the major destroyer of not only the human community, but nature as well.

We definitely now have in our possession the possibility of doing that, and that's the kind of Faustian spirit, Promethean spirit, the unlimited quest for not just knowledge, but also wealth and power and influence at expense of our own well-being. With this particular situation, I think of Ewert Cousins' notion that maybe in the 21st century the prophet is the earth. Earth is going to tell us what is allowed and what is not. Yet, the teachers who may help us to move out of this mess might turn out to be indigenous elders with the notion about listening to the voice of the earth. The indigenous traditions, either in Hawaii or here, seem to have rich resources that the modern people have inadvertently lost, so…

Dallmayr: Lost mainly because we have separated ourselves completely from nature. We have become exiled from nature. We have to learn again that we are also nature; nature is in us, not just outside of us, not just something we observe. We are part of nature.

Tu: There is a very powerful Neo-Confucian thinker in the 11th century or 12th century named Zhang Zai. His *Western Inscription* begins with a beautiful line, "Heaven is my Father and Earth is my Mother, and even such a small creature, as I, finds intimacy in their midst. So, that which fills the universe is my body, and that which directs the universe is my nature. All human beings are my brothers and sisters, all things are my companions, and I form one body with Heaven and Earth and the myriad things." This notion about nature as part of us is not an imagined possibility, but it's actually lived reality. We can feel it.

Now this is quite different from the Heideggerian position because Heidegger, and maybe the existentialists, assumed we were thrown to this world without being aware of it. To exist is to make choices, to authenticate what we are. This finitude, Kirkegaard's notion of sickness until death, is a profound sense of alienation that especially exists because of the scientific technique that has made us totally autistic towards the voice of being. Now the new humanism, the spiritual humanism, that emerges will have to have a very comprehensive and all-embracing sense of wholeness, and that sense of wholeness is predicated on a form of self cultivation that helps us to move beyond this build-in sense of alienation. So, the finitude, as you pointed out, is infinite possibility. Put another way, the finitude is such that human beings must recognize the limitation of the human project, and the inevitability of moving towards death.

But in the Confucian sense, it's the concretization of the human itself. Unlike the Platonic idea where any concretization is a distortion, for the Confucian any concretization or incarnation is a realization. It is a realization of the potential and actual human as not only an observer and appreciator, but also as a partner and co-creator. This incredible power of humanity, especially as a community, will have to develop a critical sense of not just humbleness, but a critical sense of the proper niche for the human. So, it's almost as though in the 21st century even a high school student is a global thinker, whereas in the time of Hegel some of the most brilliant minds failed to realistically understand the wholeness of the earth.

My sense is that all spiritual traditions are rich resources for us to think through this kind of problem. Both the strengths and limitations of the Confucian tradition seem to suggest that being without radical transcendence at the time of the axial situation may not have been a lack. If it was a conscious choice, it may have been a very significant one. So, the separation of immanence and transcendence, and all the other binaries and exclusive dichotomies you pointed out have not necessarily been overcome but have been deliberately rejected. The new situation then is the possibility for the Confucian tradition to articulate, in this rethinking of human, a very basics stratum of being human. Maybe that's the reason why it's possible to talk about the Confucian Christian, Confucian Jew, and Confucian Muslim, and so forth.

When I first was involved in a Confucian-Christian dialogue in Hong Kong many years ago, I realized my partners representing Confucianism, like Julia Ching, Theodore de Bary, John Berthrong, and Bob Neville were all Christians. It was not only a Confucian-Christian dialogue; it was a Christian-Christian dialogue. It took me a while to discern the difference between a Confucian Christian and a non-Confucian Christian. My answer now is that if you are Confucian, you have to be politically concerned, socially engaged, and culturally sensitive or informed, but it's perfectly alright for a Christian to reject politics, to deny the legitimacy of society as the world of Caesar, and to consider culture as superfluous for one's faith. That's also true with Buddhism and so forth. However, as a Confucian Christian you just cannot afford not to be engaged. This is why is there the power of engaged Buddhism and holistic Buddhism. Even though Confucianism is not a religion, the religiousness, or the spirituality of the Confucian tradition can be easily shared as part of the human project. So, this may be presumption to make that observation, but I do believe that something rather significant is there.

Dallmayr: Could I just make a brief footnote to this? I would say the Christian who does not get engaged in the world, and with neighbors, and helping others, and visiting the orphans and the widows, such a person is not a good Christian.

Tu: This description of the Christian project is a radical departure from the myth of Abraham, where faith is so important. Kirkegaard would say "the night of faith."

Absurdity is an indication, and from the sociological point of view can be a test of, one's faith.

Dallmayr: But still, for a Christian to be totally withdrawn from the world is not a good practice of being a Christian. Just another footnote to make is about Heidegger. The notion that we are orphans, that we are *geworfen* "thrown into the world" is precisely a critique of Enlightenment universality. We are thrown in a place at a time.

Tu: In a specific place at a time, and so we are fated to be a concrete living person.

Dallmayr: Precisely.

Tu: But that fatedness can be very positive.

Dallmayr: Only in this fatedness, in that finitude, can it make project. The relation here is between two terms which are difficult to translate: *geworfen* and *triff*. We are thrown into a certain finite situation, and in that we have our perspective, we have our aspiration, we make project. This is only a thrown project, so it's not an absolute project. There's always this relationship in Heidegger's work. There are some other elements in the later Heidegger that are very close to the Confucian statement that you cited from the 11th century Confucian master, because Heidegger later emphasizes the so called "fourfold": earth, Heaven, mortals, immortals. These are the fourfold that Heidegger talked about. It's very similar. It's not the same, but similar to this idea of wholeness where everything is included: earth with Heaven, mortals (finite beings) with immortals (divinities or divine). Heidegger has a sense of coming closer to the Asian sensibility of the world, and it's not surprising that at one time he even tried to translate the *Daodejing*...

Tu: He's worked with Xiao Shiyi: this Chinese scholar was actually the only one who accompanied him when he was in self-impose exile in the Black Forest in Switzerland. I would say that Heidegger's "fourfold," from my Confucian point of view, is actually just two: Heaven and Earth. My sense of the fourfold is self, community, Earth, and Heaven. Maybe it's better for us to say the self, which is a center of relationships rather than isolated individual, is linked to community, but also linked to Earth and Heaven. This sense of connectedness is very different. It's much more complicated than the Habermasian idea of fixing the individual, fixing its relationship to society and community. Rorty's thinking, first of all, is very "either-or." Either you cultivate and realize yourself or you offer social service. The two are incompatible. Furthermore, since philosophy is edifying conversation, it's better for us to be realistic and cultivate ourselves even though we are not able to serve society. So, the moral obligation sometimes is relegated to the background.

My sense is, in the new humanism in the 21st century, that we have to at least take into serious consideration these four dimensions in a holistic way. You cannot avoid understanding the person not only in terms of the body, but also in terms of the mind and heart, the soul and spirit. Also, there is the community, which has to be highly differentiated and yet totally comprehensive. We can expand this from the person to the family to community and nature, the world, and beyond. The Earth or nature dimension expresses the need to reestablish a harmonious, sustainable relationship. In this conception, Heaven is no longer that ineffable otherness that we know has overall power over us, but we can never understand through rational reason. Because we are partners, Heaven or divinity is immanent in the person. The person is not just immanent, because without that reference to the transcendence, the full development of the person is not possible.

Kirkegaard has three very distinctive domains: aesthetics, ethics, and religion. In this new vision, ethics or morality has to be rooted in basic human feelings. As a result, aesthetics is not at all in conflict with ethics, and ethics is much more than simply rule-governed behavior. Ethics has to be extended beyond not only society, but also the anthropological world to connect with Heaven. So, aesthetics, ethics, and religion are a continuum rather than totally separate. I admit that analysis is absolutely critical as a way of training us, as a heuristic device, but the reality is a holistic unfolding of humans.

Dallmayr: May I just say that this was a beautiful exercise of a dialogical dialogue.

Tu: I don't know, maybe it's premature for us to congratulate ourselves, but I do believe it was dialogical. Certainly, it was not a confrontation. I think we can even use Rorty's notion about edifying conversation.

Dallmayr: It was more than edifying; it was really educational. It was not just edifying but was a pleasure.

Tu: I agree. I think that's probably a limited notion.

Dallmayr: This is an example of how somebody like me, who is basically from a Western background and a European philosophy background, can make contact with somebody coming from a very different background. Although we sometimes use different terminologies, we sense the affinity of these different terminologies. We sense an affinity and a similar striving toward something that we, for better or worse, call wholeness, a form of cosmos.

Tu: Or "embracing fullness," using the idea of the full moon. Well, thanks a lot.

Dallmayr: Thank you.

https://www.youtube.com/watch?v=OJohc_reFwM

DIALOGUE WITH GHOLAMREZA AAVANI 2013-06-17

Bio: Gholamreza Aavani is a Professor Emeritus of Philosophy at Shahid Beheshti University in Tehran, Iran. He is a permanent member of the Iranian Academy of Sciences. He is head of the Iranian Philosophical Society and the International Society of Islamic Philosophy (ISIP). He is a Member of the Steering Committee of the International Federation of Philosophical Societies (FISP). For one semester of each of the last three years, he has served as the Kenan Rifai Distinguished Professor of Islamic Studies at Peking University. He was head of the Iranian Institute of Philosophy from 1984 to 2011. Among his works published in English are *Nasir-I Khusraw: 40 Poems from the Divan* (1998) and *Rumi: A Philosophical Study* (2016).

Professor Tu Weiming: Professor Aavani, it's my great pleasure to welcome you to a rather auspicious place called *Hui xin ge*, a pavilion where hearts meet. I know it's an auspicious day, not only for you and us but for Iran because of the successful election of President Rouhani. You may want to share a few words about this incredible event with us.

Professor Gholamreza Aavani: Of the elections?

Tu: Of the elections. Yes.

Aavani: Thank you very much for inviting me to attend. It is a great honor and pleasure to be with you, Professor Tu. The election that took place in Iran was very, very good, and the results were quite unexpected. Though some people might think that somebody will win or others. We do not have only two parties. We have free nominations.

Tu: You have five or six candidates, right?

Aavani: Six, chosen from among maybe twenty or thirty. Well, there were one or two hundred that were registered, but not all of them were qualified. There are some people, let's say among people from a street, who think that they can run the government, so they register. However, to be president, they should be qualified. But I think these six were the most qualified, having a longer history of political engagements. They had high and important posts, so I think they were very good. But there was a sort of competition between parties. There was only one independent nominee; four were from the right side and two from the left. Of those two on the left side, one was a former Vice President of President Khatami. He resigned, and he was a very well-known professor who was the head of Tehran University for many years.

He graduated from Stanford University, was a very, very brilliant scholar, and was a permanent member of the Iranian Academy of Science. He was the head and director of the budget for many, many years, so he was a very efficient man. But he resigned, so there was only one nominee from the left. He was favored both by Khatami and by Rafsanjani. Rafsanjani was the former parliament speaker and twice the president of Iran. Khatami was also twice president of Iran. The two confirmed him, and people voted for the two, but nobody would think he would win. But on the day when votes were counted, he was always in front. He first had 48 percent, then 49, 50, and finally won with 51 percent. People were very glad because it was very good party work. There was very good collaboration among party members, so he was able to win. Now, his name is Rouhani, and he's not an upstart at all. He was involved since the revolution and even before the revolution. He was a very close friend of Khomeini and Khamenei and was a representative of Khamenei in his atomic effort.

Also, he's a lawyer. He has a PhD in law from London University, he's a cleric, and this combination is very fortunate. To be a cleric and to have a PhD from London University means he has not been confined in a very restricted environment. He knows the world and has been involved in many important functions. So, he's not an upstart at all.

Tu: I think this symbolizes a really brilliant new chapter in Iranian history, both in terms of internal cohesiveness and dealing with the rest of the world.

Aavani: Yes. The rest of the world.

Tu: Especially the so-called industrialized countries. I had a very distinct feeling last time I had the privilege of visiting Tehran that Iran is really a land of philosophy. People do take philosophy absolutely seriously. Also, the Iranian intellectuals, you are an outstanding example of this, are deeply immersed in both historical consciousness and a kind of modern manifestation of human spirituality. Of course, this may be a rather superficial observation on my part. Still, I feel this very strongly, especially after I talked to young people—I spoke to people in many different walks of life, certainly philosophers—that people take ideas absolutely seriously., They are also very deeply involved in what, in the Chinese tradition, we call self-cultivation philosophy.

Aavani: Self-cultivation.

Tu: Self-cultivation philosophy, *xiushen* 修身. The *Great Learning*, one of the *Four Books,* states that from the Emperor to the commoner, each should regard self-cultivation as the root. So, self-cultivation is not simply the privilege of the few. Certainly, if you have an excellent environment like this, where you have music, you have fragrance, you have lovely tea, you have a beautiful environment, you can feel relaxed with the spirit of tranquility, and spirituality can be easily manifested. But I think in classical Chinese ideas, this self-cultivation philosophy is not only the privilege of the few; it's the moral obligation of each and every human being. This is how you learn to be human. If you're not involved in cultivation, it means that you're not critically aware of what you want to do or what you're doing. If you're not trying to refine yourself daily, you're not living meaningfully as a human being. I sense that this is also deeply rooted in Iranian culture, both in the earlier Persian tradition that is still very viable and pressing and in the Islamic tradition, as well.

Aavani: That's quite true. You pointed out very important facts about China and Iran and the similarities between the two cultures. First, there is the status of philosophy in Iran. It's very deep-rooted. Iran has a very, very long and deep-rooted tradition of philosophy. It's perhaps the only place in the Islamic world with a continuous philosophical tradition from ancient times. Nearly all these philosophy laws existed in Iran, and they became a peripatetic tradition. They took from the Greek and elaborated, perfected, and even surpassed it, like how Avicenna surpassed Aristotle on many, many important points. Avicenna even founded a new school of philosophy called Oriental Philosophy, which was not based on Greek philosophy.

Right at the beginning of his masterpiece *al-Shifa,* which is his magnum opus, it says that I've perfected the peripatetic philosophy, which was not in Aristotle. It was pretty scattered. I've axiomatized, I've systematized and perfected it. There were many lacunae and many gaps in Aristotelian philosophy, but those who want to study my philosophy—he was writing when he was less than forty years old—I have another book called *Oriental Philosophy,* which is my true philosophy. He founded a new foundation, which was later developed by Suhrawardi and his Oriental Philosophy, *Philosophy of Illumination,* and also by Modasena. Most of the great scholars and philosophers in the Islamic World came from Iran.

There is a saying attributed to Prophet Mohammed that, "If knowledge were to be found in the Pleiades, some Iranians would reach it." Ibn Khaldun, a famous Muslim scholar and sociologist, has a very, very important book called *Prolegomena.* He has a chapter on this saying, "If knowledge were to be found in the Pleiades, some Persians would reach it." He explains it.

Even in our time, there are many, many great scholars from Iran. I was walking in the bazaar in Egypt and found this book by an Iranian, that book by an Iranian, and so forth. As you said, in China, the idea of self-cultivation is very important. It is very, very important in Confucianism, Eastern cultures in general, and for Iranians. Iranian culture, that is, Persian culture and Chinese culture, are very similar in many ways. Of course, there are differences, but they're very close.

First, there is an idea of government where wisdom and philosophy are not individual. They are social phenomena; they are political phenomena. Justice is not something personal; it's social. So, they were able, both China and Iran, to have very great empires, as they needed a lot of wisdom. It's not just book learning; it's not just pure conceptualization. It's a sort of realized wisdom that should apply. This was again the case with Iranians. Iranians from older times, from the Achaemenids, the Sassanids, and later in the Islamic world, had very great empires. For example, at the time of Darius, Iran expanded from Greece to near India. That's why Hegel said somewhere in the *Philosophy of History* that the first historical consciousness came into being in the Iranian empire.

This wisdom of running a government is also in China, in the philosophy of Confucius, for example. He went from state to state, city to city, ruler to ruler, and governor to governor to teach them. Even if they were accepted or even if they were rejected, they considered it a great responsibility to educate, to cultivate, to show the way how to develop oneself as an individual and, especially, the family life, which is the intermediary between the individual and society. Family life is very, very important both in Islam and Iran and also in China. I mean, filial virtues are very important. Virtues are not only personal; filial virtues are the links between society and are much emphasized. I do not see, for example, as much emphasis on this in some Indian philosophies or Christianity as compared to those in China and in Islam. Again, I mean it is much emphasized.

Tu: You mentioned this great philosopher Avicenna and a kind of ecumenical vision, a comprehensive vision about philosophy. He assigned himself the task of filling in the gaps in Aristotelian philosophy, so he developed his Oriental philosophy in a more comprehensive and integrated version. You also mentioned Ibn Khaldun. When I was at UC Berkeley, a colleague of mine, Ira Lapidus, was one of the leading American scholars of Ibn Khaldun, both as a social thinker and an original philosopher. Even with a very superficial exposure, I was impressed by his comprehensiveness and over-arching vision of the human community. I was impressed not only by his understanding of people but also his understanding of cities, cosmopolitan areas, social life, and every aspect of the lived reality of being human.

You mentioned, in particular, the importance of governance. This relates to the importance of understanding the person not as an isolated individual but as a center of relationships in lived communities: the family, the neighborhood, the nation, and the empire. So, these are not only speculative philosophers; they are action intellectuals. They are very much involved in the process of not only governing themselves in terms of their emotional life but also in terms of society at large. This is very different from the kind of spiritual exercise that often is simply related to the cultivation of the inner heart and mind. I totally agree that the importance of governance is both an art and a science, the ability to organize a large society based upon universalizable rules so everybody…

Aavani: Universal wisdom.

Tu: Universal wisdom. So, right now, for example, the new president, Rouhani, is a legal scholar with a law degree, and these practical matters are absolutely important. As you pointed out, Hegel mentioned in the *Philosophy of History* that the Persian Empire may be the first consciousness of governance in human history. But as you know, Hegel is very much Europe-centered, so he said the sun would eventually set in the West.

Aavani: It helped Europe; otherwise, he wouldn't have said anything. He was very unkind to China and to India.

Tu: Very unkind. The notion that Persia, India, and China in the dawn of history, when the consciousness began, may have made major contributions, but eventually, the sun is going to set in the West, set in Prussia, and, of course, set in his philosophy, is now, from our point of view today, really outmoded.

Aavani: It ended in him, in Hegel himself.

Tu: But I think in this very grandiose vision about the world order, about governance, about social relationships, about a person as a center of relationships rather than an isolated individual, self-cultivation in terms of Iranian or Persian forms of spirituality, is very deeply connected with the ability to tap the inner resources of each and every person. In other words, the importance of governance, the importance of society, and the importance of social order notwithstanding, a person as a spiritual being is constantly in touch with inner life. We can even use the expression of inner subjectivity. You can even say it's deep and can always be deepened. Therefore, it's a deepening subjectivity. Confucius talks about his learning as learning for the sake of the self, not just learning for others. You don't learn for your parents or even for society. You learn to build your character and refine yourself, and that's the core. Once you establish yourself as an independent, autonomous person with dignity, then your ability to extend yourself to others will be genuine. If you don't have that inner core and no inner spirituality, even though you are very influential, the influence may be counter-productive. I think that aspect is also very strong in Persian philosophy.

Aavani: Yes, in traditional philosophy in general.

Tu: Right, and the meaning of philosophy is not only a love of wisdom but a manifestation, a realization…

Aavani: As the manifestation of wisdom itself.

Tu: Yes, I would like you to elaborate a little bit more on this dimension of being human as a spiritual being, drawing on the poetic vision of Rumi and great minds and philosophers. I think this is desperately needed in China today because society has been overwhelmed by market forces. I'm sure this is important not only for China but also for the world at large.

Aavani: It has been the main question for every age, and so far as man lives on this earth, it's among what you call the first questions in philosophy. The first questions should be first because they are the most important, like the problem of self, divine self, and who one is. Of course, you know better than I do that science cannot answer this question because science deals only with the phenomenon of man, not the noumenon, the reality of man. Only philosophy in the ancient sense, only wisdom itself, can address this question, not science. Science deals with phenomena and the appearance of things, not the deeper self within us, which has many dimensions, is very deep, and goes to the origin of things. This self has been a problem of much concern in Eastern philosophy, in Islamic philosophy, among Sufis great Gnostics such as Rumi and Ibn Arabi, by Confucius, by Laozi and Mencius, and also by Zhuangzi and many, many great sages including great Indian sages. But unfortunately, recently, it has gone under a veil, and the question of who I am is lost. The question is, who am I?

Tu: Personal identity.

Aavani: My personal identity, who am I? It is a very deep question. All religions and all traditional wisdom have addressed this question. They have given more or less the same answer that our "I" is heavenly; it's not earthly. We are not just our body; we are, first and foremost, the higher and deeper levels of being what we call our soul. Higher than the soul, our spirit, our heart, our innermost nature, which is even unknown going back to the principle of Being itself. Our self, which is related to the divine self, according to these teachings, according to Rumi, according to Ibn Arabi, is a divine self. God is "I." For example, we have the formula in the world, and God says there is no "I" but I. There is no "thou" but thou. There is no "he" but he. There is no "God" but God. So, the I-ness of the "I" with a capital I goes back to a universal "I," which has reflected itself in everything, even human beings. Even a bird has an "I." If you ponder and contemplate a bird, a cat, or a mosquito, it doesn't depend on the smallness or bigness of its being. An elephant is no different from a mosquito. A mosquito has as much itself in itself as an elephant. I have many times wondered about a mosquito when I'm reading a book; a mosquito sits on my book. I never disturb it. I like it, and I try to ponder it and study it. It has very, very strange behavior. It thinks it stands, and it decides. It decides to move, and it flies. I cannot fly, but it flies, and it decides suddenly to fly away.

So it has a divine "I" in it even when it's the smallest thing. According to the teachings of great sages, there is nothing in this world that doesn't have an I. I would not call this a spiritism or something similar with a different name. However, there isn't a difference between minerals, plants, and animals, though most people think an animal doesn't have an I. It has an I. It suffers, it feels, it thinks, and everything in it goes to an I. This is the case with a plant and every being, even if we don't understand the language. We understand the language of Being as a language. The language of Being is ontological; it needs a sage to read it. Science is not able to do this. Of course, it discovers laws, and it thinks laws only exist in a soul. Something that has regularity and universality has a soul necessarily. It has a function. Everything is endowed with a spirit, especially man. The best spirit belongs to man. Man is unique among all beings and has peculiarities not shared by other beings, which are the comprehensiveness of his being and the universality of his intellect.

More than any other being, man has language; man has reason of the highest nature, including partial reason and universal reason. He is able to communicate and express; he is able to understand everything. Look, for example, at a university. You have different departments: physics, chemistry, biology, anthropology, psychology, sociology, economics, politics. All branches of learning, of being, are the subject of human study, of human knowledge. What does this mean? This means that man is a universal being capable of having a dialogue and discourse with others. He's first able to cultivate himself by understanding things deeper and better and better. This is what we call understanding. Higher than understanding is intellection, which goes deep into what was understood, going still deeper to reach the essence.

Moreover, he can communicate with and share with others because they are all selves. They have the same or similar experiences; they have the same function; they can understand; they can meditate; they can speculate. He shares in a dialogue with others and this is very, very great. This is unique. According to some of the sages and according to what is taught in the Quran, even angels with their highest rank do not have this capability. That's why they say that man is made in the image of God, or in Quranic terms, God gave man and manifested in man all his attributes. He gave not part of his attributes, but his quorum was the totality of his attributes that he had reflected and manifested in man.

So man is an image of the total ideas and total realities and total attributes and names of God. Why, for example, are they what they call in philosophy nomothetic? Why are they givers of names? In this way, man is unlike any other creature. Even angels are not nomothetic. Birds are not nomothetic. Animals are not, but man is. This is because of the universality of his nature. A name is not a word; it's a meaning. He grasps the meanings of words, of everything. After getting and grasping the meaning, he gives them a word, a name. Then he understands and tries to intelligize and see what its nature is, so far as he can, and then communicates this order. These are very great human properties that all other beasts or even angels do not share.

Tu: You began your reflection with a question about the centrality of the question, "Who am I?"

Aavani: Who am I?

Tu: Therefore, the idea of the self. Then, in your discourse on the self, you evoked the idea that a person is the embodiment of virtually all the attributes of God.

Aavani: All the attributes, not some.

Tu: So the ability to assume many, many names, and each name carries a distinct meaning, and the realization of that aspect of meaning helps to demonstrate one aspect of being human. All forms of knowledge—we talked about different departments, natural sciences, social sciences, humanities—can be understood as ways of understanding the complex but also rich processes of being human. The uniqueness of being human in this connection is because man is made in the image of God. This is a prophetic vision, and a human being ought to consider that as the sacred mission of not only realizing himself/herself but realizing all the potentiality endowed by God in being human.

I think that in the 21st century, one of the central questions that we are confronted with is rethinking the human. We try to think, "What does it mean to be human?" Of course, on the surface, there are two radically different approaches. You have the creationist; you have the evolutionist. The two are not necessarily totally incompatible, but certainly, there is tension. Another great Confucian thinker, Xunzi, made an observation that I'll try to paraphrase. Everything is made of the vital energy, *qi*: minerals, plants, trees, animals, and humans. However, only plants have life, only animals have consciousness, and only humans have the ability to use rightness, which can be read as moral sense.

Everything is made of vital energy, and only a subset of all beings that are made of vital energy have life, like plants. The plant's vitality is a manifestation of the vital energy, but it is not reducible to vital energy. It is something new that happens when you have plants. When you have animals, animals have consciousness and therefore animals are alive. Animals are endowed with vital energy, but you cannot reduce the consciousness of the animal simply to the life of the plants or the vital energy of all things. Then there is the emergence of the human. Human has this quality, let's say moral sense, which means that humans are conscious, alive, and full of vital energy. So, the question then is what is that uniqueness of being human? There are two questions. One is the emergence of a new reality. We call it "the emergence. The life emerges…

Aavani: Like evolution and…

Tu: Like evolution, life emerges, consciousness emerges, and human moral sense emerges. The emerging quality of being human is rooted in animal consciousness, life, and vital energy. That's the reason why we can learn a lot about ourselves by studying animals. We learn a lot about animals by studying plants and so forth. Also, we're an integral part of the animal world, an integral part of the life world. Yet, we have to say there's something unique about being human, which is not simply understandable by referring to the rules of the game governing the animal world, governing the role of life, and the world of vital energy. That is the uniqueness of being human. This is shared by all major Confucian thinkers. Confucius didn't talk about it metaphysically, but Mencius already talked about that with a very graphic demonstration of the human ability to feel the suffering of others. You mentioned the dialogical. It is the ability to have commensuration. According to one account, Jerome Kegan who was an eminent psychologist, said "Normally, a young baby at the age of two is capable of responding to the suffering of others." Now some people say it is way beyond two, even a baby of a few months…

Aavani: Even before birth, some people say that.

Tu: All right, so a defining characteristic of being human is this ability to find a sympathetic resonance with other human beings of the world and so forth. So, that's a quality. Mencius makes it more elaborate. He includes this commensuration, but also the sense of shame, the sense of right and wrong, and the sense of willingness to defer to others. Many qualities that we call moral qualities are intrinsic to being human. They are not simply learned; they're invoked. They are part of our nature. It's not drilled from the outside; it's not solely socialized There's something intrinsic in being human, and in one of the classical texts, it explains that human nature is conferred by Heaven. This is like saying human nature is created by God.

Aavani: By God, yes.

Tu: It is *Tianming zhi wei xing* 天命之為性. Now the word *ming* 命 in that context doesn't mean "mandated." It means "ordered." Our nature is intrinsically a gift of Heaven. Our nature, in this sense, is identical to the nature of Heaven, and because it's given by Heaven, the implication is that through self-understanding we can understand other human beings, we can understand things, and we can understand the Will of Heaven. There is a very powerful and very moving statement in one of the Four Books, the *Doctrine of the Mean*. It says, "Only those who are the most sincere are capable of fully realizing themselves. If they can really fully realize themselves, then they can fully realize humanity. If they can fully realize humanity, all human nature, then they can fully realize the nature of things. If they can fully realize the nature of things, then they can take part in the transforming and nourishing process of Heaven and Earth. If they can take part in the transforming and nourishing process of Heaven and Earth, they can form a trinity with Heaven and Earth."

The idea of a human being is as a part of Heaven, but also as a part of nature. Therefore, humans can be conceived as a bridge or as a mediating structure that can link Earth to Heaven. So, the completion of the human project means the reconnection between Earth and Heaven.

Aavani: And man does this function of connecting all levels of things.

Tu: Right. So, man can have many, many names because human beings are endowed with ability. Therefore, human beings are given the privilege, as well as it being commanded by Heaven as an obligation, as a human obligation, as a commitment. Self-realization, in this sense, means the realization of others in the world at large. So, that notion of the self is not an anthropological concept alone. I coined the phrase "anthropocosmic." It's both anthropological and cosmological.

Aavani: That is everything you've said: big I, smaller I, universal I…

Tu: Right, so in the *Book of Mencius* there are two terms. One is *xiaoti*, which means the small body, which is our physical body. The other term is *dati*: the great body. The great body is the body that can embody not only society but also Heaven and Earth. That's the cosmic body, the great body.

Aavani: So you have the same idea in Confucianism?

Tu: Yes.

Aavani: Of microcosm/macrocosm...

Tu: It's a microcosm/macrocosm. That's the question I raised yesterday with Professor Clooney about the body. Rather than looking at the body as separate from the spirit and soul, the body can be considered a site, a location where the heart and mind and the spirit and soul reside.

Aavani: It's spatial-temporal. It's space-body otherwise it's not spatial-temporal. There's no one if there is no body.

Tu: Right, and it's also sacred. So, the sacrality…

Aavani: It embodies the spirit.

Tu: Yeah, so there are four dimensions, four or five. Let's say the body, the heart and mind, the soul, and the spirit. In Chinese, we have the word *shen* 身 which means the body (*shenti* 身體). *Xin* 心 is the awareness of heart and mind. The soul is a subtler, gentler form of being able to connect…

Aavani: That's the intermediary for body and spirit.

Tu: Yeah, but there are four dimensions: the body, the heart and mind, the soul, and the spirit. For example, we can say the soul can spatially be understood as something that's locatable. You can say the soul of a nation; you can say the soul of a university…

Aavani: …of the body, like an example of Plato's. Let's say there's a pilot of a ship. The pilot sometimes is on the ship; sometimes he goes out. He is a normal man. So, it is like there are two functions. It's the same thing. Sometimes it manages the body and sometimes it's outside the body. So, when it manages the body you call it the soul, and when it goes you call it the spirit.

Tu: So the commander, the captain…

Aavani: Yeah, he is not always the captain. Sometimes he goes to the shore and…

Tu: Sometimes he is absent.

Aavani: Yeah, absent, yes.

Tu: Yet, if the body functions in a healthy normal way, the soul has to be inside. The idea of embodiment is an idea I am developing, which is somewhat associated with Merleau-Ponty's notion of the body and some postmodern thinkers as well. The term "embodiment" has now assumed a very significant philosophical importance, I think that's true with Islam as well. It may not be fair to criticize Catholicism, but we know one big problem with the Catholic Church is precisely this question about asceticism and the inability of many Catholic priests to take care of their bodies, especially in terms of uncontrollable sexual drives or something of that nature.

Aavani: Yes, that's very difficult.

Tu: Yeah, it's very difficult and they cause all kinds of problems.

Aavani: Yeah, outrageous acts.

Tu: Outrageous acts. So, now the question is how do we re-examine the body in the 21st century as a spiritual being. Normally we would say asceticism itself may be a spiritual choice, but it's so exceptional. It shouldn't be imposed upon every person or it should not be idealized as the purest form of self-cultivation. This is my position, but I think it's debatable. In other words, the sensuality of the body and the spirituality of the body are not opposites and we know in modern Western philosophy, with the emergence of the Cartesian division, the "I think therefore I am" makes me very different from my body.

Aavani: That is dualism, utter dualism.

Tu: Not only dualism, I call it "exclusive dualism."

Aavani: Exclusive dualism.

Tu: The idea is if it is body, then it's not mine.

Aavani: Very dangerous.

Tu: Yeah, if it's soul, then it's not spirit. If it's a flesh, it's not soul. Dualism is necessary for thinking. For example, in the *Great Learning,* there's a difference between the root and the branch, a difference between the former and the latter.

Aavani: Principle and manifestation.

Tu: Principle and manifestation or substance and function. There are all kinds of ways of looking, like with *yin* and *yang*, at the complexity of the human condition with binary thinking. The polarity of binary thinking is absolutely necessary, but if you take an exclusive dichotomy by separating the body and mind, separating the flesh and the soul, separating matter and spirit, and separating the sacred and profane, then you privilege the importance of soul and you consider body…

Aavani: You forget the body. You set aside the body and abandon your body. That would be dangerous.

Tu: In medieval Christian asceticism, sometimes the body is considered as the prison of the soul. So, you have to get rid of the body.

Aavani: Even the Greeks had a proverb "*soma sema*." *Soma* means body; *sema* means prison.

Tu: Spiritual exercises can turn out to be very brutal; you torture your body. You force your body to suffer to free your soul from the body.

Aavani: Self-flagellation and things like that.

Tu: It's just incredible. I think in the 21st century it would be considered torture.

Aavani: It would be against human rights. It's not only against human rights, it's...

Tu: You're not allowed to torture yourself because...However, cultivating a healthy body, doing exercise, and so forth, is also a spiritual exercise. Like Yoga.

Aavani: Yes, spiritual in the East, in the oriental philosophy.

Tu: A big question here is the link between social service and spiritual self-cultivation.

Aavani: Yeah, how we can combine the two?

Tu: There is a radical position held by Richard Rorty. He is a very close friend, but also quite annoying because he thinks in a totally secular, postmodern way. The term that he has used time and time again is hybridity. Almost everything is a mixture of everything else. Now he would say you have to choose whether you want to cultivate yourself or whether you want to perform some public service to society. You make the choice. If you want to cultivate yourself, forget about society. If you want to serve society, forget about yourself. You just cannot get both.

Aavani: [laughs] Two extremes. He thinks that there's no other way.

Tu: Yeah, I told him that if you are right, then the whole Confucian project fails.

Aavani: Society itself fails because you can have no society because it's based on both.

Tu: Absolutely. So, this negotiation—I hope it's not just a negotiation—the mutuality is based upon some kind of mutual enforcement. The more you cultivate yourself, the more you are prepared to care for others. The more you are able to care for others, the more you're going to have a deepened and deepening self-awareness. These two are so interrelated that if you make a choice prematurely, you choose not only one at the expense of the other, but the one you choose itself is inauthentic because the authentic self is always the center of relationships.

The authentic way of serving society is not at all in conflict with your character building. So, the great idea of being human is a combination of two: one is a question of sincerity or authenticity and the other one is a question of reciprocity and considerateness. The more you're honest with yourself, the more you are in keeping with the reality and truthfulness of your nature, the more you are prepared to express a feeling of reciprocity towards the other. Honesty with oneself and consideration towards others are not two separate forms of exercise. They are so closely linked.

Aavani: They're correlative.

Tu: They're correlative. They're involved in a continuous interaction. It's not a return in terms of a circle. Certainly, it's not a vicious circle. It is a virtuous circle. If we have to imagine it or conceptualize it, it's like a spiral. The more you interact...

Aavani: Complementary, not contradictory.

Tu: Yes. Complementary. Therefore, concerning the question about governance earlier and the question of inner spirituality, right now in the 21st century, we need to consider these two domains as important for each and every human being. This is not just for leaders but for commoners and everybody. Sometimes it's not very satisfactory to use quantitative methods, but if we say humanity as a collective enterprise entails the participation of every human being, any human being who refuses to take part in this great enterprise of realizing humanity is doing some damage to the totality of the humanistic spirit.

The worst is a group of people who hurt themselves and hurt others, because they're stupid, because they're unreasonable, because they're governed by uncontrollable passion. They're very self-centered people; they are willing to hurt others to benefit themselves. Society will not survive if there are a lot of people like that. We do have a lot of people who actually benefit themselves by not hurting others. They're tolerable, but still, they're very isolated.

Aavani: Some of them are very dangerous individuals who are worse than beasts. They do things beasts would never do, even in the name of religion.

Tu: Right. It is extremely important to expand this sense of benefiting oneself as a basis for benefiting others and benefiting others as the basis of benefiting oneself. This is why Mencius criticizes the Mohists. The Mohists are collectivists and universalists.

Aavani: Jurisprudentialists? Yes?

Tu: Not the Mohists, but the Legalists.

Aavani: The Legalists.

Tu: These Maoists are interested in some kind of universalizable abstract principle. For example, you should love everybody equally. The idea is you love the parents of a stranger.

Aavani: Even distribution of love.

Tu: Yes, you should love the parents of the stranger as intensely as you love your parents. Mencius is not happy with that. First of all, it's not practical.

Aavani: Never practical, never.

Tu: If you impose that principle on everybody, then you treat your parents as indifferently as you treat the stranger's. But that's only part of the story. The idea is that you should continue to extend your humanity, and like water flowing the water can only flow if it fills all the holes in front of you. If the water supply is not strong enough, it will not flow.

Aavani: It will stop.

Tu: If the hydraulic level is high, it will flow far. You cultivate your level, and you judge and experience it concretely and honestly. If a person can care for only his parents, that's better than simply to care just for himself. But if he can care for not only his parents but also his other relatives, that's better. The water flow can carry a little bit farther. If we all aim at this particular idea of cultivating ourselves and helping others, then the supply of humanity will be greatly enriched.

Aavani: Yes.

Tu: That notion on the surface is like a remark that Karl Marx made, "The freedom of one person is the basis of the freedom of all people." Or the humanity of all people depends upon the humane acts of every human being or every member of the human community.

Aavani: Yes, you mentioned very, very important points, and I just wanted to talk about some of them because there were so many points you mentioned. I had put down some of them because they were very important. For example, you mentioned the idea of evolution, the idea of energy, the idea of embodiment, the nature of embodiment, the nature of the body, and the virtues. There were and many, many other points, which are very, very important, but I wanted just to say that for certain themes many errors are common. We should discover errors, as there are many errors in thinking. Formerly, there were laws of thought, and the violation of any law of thought was considered if done intentionally, a sophistry. If it was done unintentionally, it would be an error. Nowadays, many errors are made on points of knowledge, ontology, and many things like that.

I wanted to say something about evolution, about scientific concepts. Nowadays, most scientists act as scientists and philosophers, but they have no right in science to do philosophy. Scientists certainly should make their observations, but if they make conclusions, this is philosophy, right? There are many mistakes of this sort. They put questions that necessarily do not belong to science at all. You can have many different answers in philosophy. Some of them are what we call first questions, but the deepest ones philosophy itself cannot answer. The higher levels of wisdom can solve, for example, the question of who I am. It is not a problem of psychology. "I" is not a problem of science at all. They will say it is a matter, but that's not true at all. Or on the problem of evolution, evolution is more than a scientific concept, much more. It's a philosophical problem. However, not every philosophy can solve this problem, only sapiential wisdom can give an answer.

For example, my senses see something, but they cannot interpret it. It is not the function of the senses to interpret things. It's like a camera that shows me things; it shows me the appearance of things. It shows phenomena. It's not able to tell me the nature of a thing at all. Above is imagination. Imagination is about the same thing, but more luminous. Even more than that we have reason. It's the reason which judges. The great mistake of empiricism, all empiricists from Hume on, is that they confuse the function of reason and sensation. Sense does not judge; it cannot judge at all. They say judgment is a function of sensation, Malebranche, Hume, and others, but it's the function of reason when you make a judgment; it's reason at work. Reason has a higher function, the function of interpretation. How do you discover the laws of gravity, the laws of science, physics, chemistry, and all other sciences? It's not a sensation. It's the reason. It's done by reason. Still, you have a higher stage of reason, which is not usually paid attention to. I mean, there's no good discussion about reason. All discussions about reason by Western philosophers are mostly mistaken, from Descartes to Kant and Hume.

For example, you find in Plato a higher level of wisdom, which is able to make another interpretation of the statements of science. Science cannot interpret. The lower partial reason, which we call *ratio*, is able to interpret sensation, as sensation itself is not able. There is a higher reason, which looks up what reason has discovered and is able to give another higher interpretation. In Plato, this is called *noesis*. *Noesis* is very difficult. The sages of medieval philosophy make a distinction between *intellectus* and *ratio*. The r*atio* is a calculated reason. The *noesis* is the spiritual vision, which gives another higher interpretation. According to Plato, dialectic is possible through the higher reason, not the lower reason.

What of the law itself? Are laws mechanical, or is the existence of law, as Heraclitus said, as Laozi said, a manifestation of Dao, a manifestation of divine Logos? When there is law, it can be discovered by reason because it's the manifestation of divine reason. It's not mechanical. Nowadays, they take laws as mechanical material things. This is totally mistaken. I mean, modern science has posed many questions and has tried to give answers through science, but there are those that do not belong to them.

The question "Who am I?" is the deepest question. It cannot be solved either by psychology, or by physics, or chemistry. Only in the highest type of metaphysics, which we call Oriental metaphysics, will you find a good solution. You find it with the sages of India, with the sage of China, with the sage of Sufism, with the sages of Islam. The Persian poet Mahmoud Shabestari, whom I was teaching in this course here, says that when one person sings himself an "I," a particular "I," he starts to contemplate "who am I." From this particular "I," he goes to the origin of the "I," which is the universal "I." He makes a journey from the particular to the universal to the origin. This is not haphazard. This is not by chance. Science should be interpreted through a higher knowledge.

In the Middle Ages, beginning with Aristotle and Plato, *scientia* was linked to the *suprima*, the *suprima* to *sapientia*. *Scientia* is a lower type of knowledge, which we call science. The higher wisdom, *Sapientia,* should interpret this science. But nowadays, *Sapientia* is totally cut off. *Scientia* is cut off from *Sapientia*, the highest wisdom, and it considers itself to have the full authority to interpret the whole universe on the basis of science. It's totally mistaken. As a lower type of knowledge, science has forfeited absolute knowledge. Partial reason, which is *ratio*, has forfeited the right of absolute reason, which is intellect. Nowadays, there is no differentiation between universal intellect and partial intellect, universal knowledge and partial knowledge, and *sapientia* and *scientia*.

This is very important because metaphysics deals with vertical causes, not horizontal causes. All sciences are horizontal. Their causality even is horizontal, but metaphysics is vertical. Moreover, things are symbols and manifestations of principles. From the symbol, you should go to principles. In philosophy, in pure metaphysics, these are not taken as facts but as symbols. In science, everything is taken as facts, and nothing is taken as a symbol. This is a very great difference between true metaphysics and science. If there is an "I," you should take it as a symbol. Why is there an I? If you take it as fact, science tells you there is energy and things like that. This is the case with the existence of energy. This energy is the divine energy. There's no material energy. They attribute everything divine to matter.

It has functions, laws, and the manifestation of qualities. There are many qualities. Power is a quality of Being. Being is power. Nonexistence has no power because everything that is is a power. It has other qualities, too. It's not only a manifestation of power. It is a manifestation of wisdom, too. They do not see the wisdom behind things. More than that, wisdom is a manifestation of knowledge. This is very important in Oriental philosophies, in Islamic philosophy, in Chinese philosophy, in Indian philosophy, and traditional philosophy in general, but much neglected in modern philosophy. This world is a manifestation of total wisdom and total knowledge.

The carpenter who made this table had a deep knowledge of carpentry. You can see this. If an ant is walking, it cannot see the carpenter. It would think that this has come into being by itself. But I know that there is the wisdom of a carpenter behind it, and the more wisdom and knowledge of the carpenter, the more perfect this world is. Every being in this world, whether it is an artifact or natural, is the manifestation of divine knowledge and wisdom to the utmost degree. Without knowledge and wisdom, there would be chaos.

After Descartes, whom you mentioned, his dualism was very destructive. He damaged both philosophy and science. Why? It is because he was, first, the father of philosophy, and second, one of the fathers of modern science. He could bring together the two as a great scientist and a great philosopher, but by his dualism, the body doesn't think, and the mind has no extension. Every substance has one quality, and two substances with opposite and contrary qualities are totally different, so there can be no causality. This dualism is totally false. Matter is not pure extension. It has many, many qualities. It manifests many qualities which are neglected. For the first time, he totally separated the two. The attempts of his followers to make a connection with the two were totally fallacious, whether it was Leibniz, whether it was Malebranch, or occasionalism, or pre-established harmony, or negation of the spirit, or negation of matter by Berkley. These were never solutions.

But in the East, this was not the case. Our philosophers say that two contrary substances should have an intermediary. The function of the intermediary is to be a link between the two. This, to Muslim philosophers, is called the rule of *barzakh* (برزخ), the rule of the intermediary. The intermediary is related because it has the qualities of both, for example, imagination. After Descartes, there is no discussion of imagination. You have mind and body. Imagination is a reality. It links the two. Like an image in the mirror, it is particular like an image. When you are looking in the mirror, it's showing me. It's not man. It's me. Imagination shows things. I see things in my imagination right now like a mirror. It's particular like sensation but numinous like spirit. Everything that comes down from above passes through it. When an architect wants to build, he first conceives it by his intellect, then particularizes it through his imagination, and then builds. It always functions as an intermediary. Always between another world and this world, there is an intermediary. Even between Heaven and Earth, there is an intermediary, which is man, who has qualities and functions as an intermediary.

Another point, which is very important, is embodiment. I should explain. Christianity believes that only Christ was God embodied, but this is not the case. Everything in this world is embodied, is a spirit becoming a body, because everything has descended from the principle of God. There is no leap between worlds. It doesn't leap down here. Everything has an origin, whether an atom, an electron, or a human being. Whatever it is comes down from there. There is no leap. It brings with it everything down from there to the earth—knowledge, power, things like that—even if you do not see it. The strangest phenomenon in our world is the problem of embodiment. Not our embodiment, but the embodiment of this table, the embodiment of everything.

First, it has to become spatial-temporal. There's no spatiality or temporality. The way is not through outward senses. We have another way through internal senses—this is something that man forgets, always. They are not the outward senses, which are eyes, hearing, touch, smelling, and things like that. This is for the external world. However, there are four other windows to other worlds. This is for the other worlds. Imagination is a way to a world, according to Muslim philosophers. As an eye, I do not see my eye alone. It's not imprisoned in itself. It's open to an infinite horizon, infinite things, and so is our internal sense. Our imagination is not closed, is not imprisoned. It's a gate opening to an endless universe much higher than this universe but close to us and accessible only through this aperture.

Reason, again, is an inner aperture to a world of reason in which all things participate, no doubt. We see only the exterior of things with our eyes, but we discover through the inner. How do we discover the law of physics? Not by senses but through our interior. Things have an interior, which are discovered by the interior, by reason. They have that function, too, but it's not visible to the eye. First, things have descended from there. For example, if you read Plato, if you read Plotinus, if you read Heraclitus, if you read Parmenides, or if you read Laozi, things that have no name have become named by descending to become the ten thousand things here. Or, let's say Confucius, he's concerned about how they have come from there. This is known.

People think that there is no there, that everything starts from here from senses and things like that. This is not at all true. The problem is that, first, everything in this world is spatial-temporal. Being is not necessarily spatial-temporal. People think that after Kant, this problem came into being. Kant says that Being is spatial-temporal. There is no Being outside spatial-temporality. Hegel and also Heidegger took this. They were not able to think that there was an existence above spatial temporality. I believe this is completely wrong. Second, this world of spatial temporality is the world of embodiment, not our embodiment, but the embodiment of everything. Embodiment is the nature of this world. A very important thing is that our soul makes our body. Did we make our body? No, we did not make our body, our self. Our soul, both soul and spirit or whatever we call it, is a manifestation of divine I.

It has names at different levels. When my eye sees, I see. My eye is called eye or sight. I feel; it's called feeling. I write; I am a writer. I do this. I say *my* body, but I'm not necessarily *my* body. If I were *my* body, *my* body would be a tautology. It would be a tautology if I said *my* shoes and I were *my* shoes. Whenever I think of myself, I should say *my* shoes. But when I say my body, my shoes, my spirit, they are manifestations at different levels, and at each level it's the same as that function. It creates the body to function according to its different divine attributes. It sees; I see through my eyes. I hear through my ears. I move through my legs. I move my hands through my hands. It's all the soul of *my* I. *My* I descended and made these things in this world. It's part of me so far as I'm in this world. It's part of me. I cannot separate myself.

Islam is like Confucianism. The Prophet said there is no monasticism in Islam. It is much better to be active, to go and act in the way of the good life, to write, to think. There are two multifarious worlds. In this world, we are present, not in the hereafter. In the hereafter, we leave this body, but we survive. Our I survives, but we leave the body in the grave. We leave our body in the grave, but still, we have our I with us because our I is not the body.

Each level of Being has laws. On this level, we have physical laws. They are studied by physics and chemistry. Moreover, right down here, laws are not physical. You have ontological laws, laws of Being as such, because the matter is, the body is, the spirit is, I am. Being itself is subject to universal laws, which are not necessarily physical laws. Sciences are concerned with only visible, sensual manifestations of things we see in this world and explaining them. However, metaphysics even considers these laws. Leibniz said, "Why is there something rather than nothing? Why is there a matter at all? Would it be better not to be?" He is concerned about why there is something. Why is it? How is it? This is not a science concern at all. It's the concern of metaphysics. The theory of evolution is also not a scientific problem alone; it's a metaphysical problem. The very idea of evolution, not devolution, is that something evolves according to a law. Why is there evolution? What do you call evolution at all?

They express it mechanically, but we have another explanation for the same phenomenon. There is right evolution. We have another explanation that is more beautiful or maybe just more correct. Modern science, generally speaking, has forgotten many forms of causality. Because of the connection of contemporary science with mathematics, science was mathematicized. In medieval times, in Aristotelian philosophy, mathematics played no part. After Copernicus, Galileo, and Descartes especially, modern science was mathematicized. Mathematics, according to Descartes, is only quantity, is quantified, and is interpreted not metaphysically but mechanistically. You have mechanic laws operating by themselves, like a watch, without having any reason. Sometimes, they bring in God as a watchmaker. When they have no other solution, they bring in God, but that is not necessarily so.

Look at mathematics in Plato. God is a mathematician; therefore, God had final causality. Final causality means everything exists with an end; otherwise, it is futile. Why did man come at the end of evolution, the last being in evolution? It is because the final cause of creation, the final cause, always comes at the end. It is first in the mind of the maker. In the mind of the maker, it is first, and in being is last. For example, a builder wants to build a building. It is in his mind first. But, in order, it's last, because he has to plan, to bring all the materials, and to build walls. For example, a gardener wants to have fruit. He should buy land. He should till the ground, and also he should plant the seed. It should grow. It should have roots. The final goal comes at the end, the fruit. Man is the fruit of creation and comes when all things are made ready for him, prepared for him to be king. This is not physical but ontological because the end result is because of divine consciousness.

The problem of consciousness is never material. It's divine consciousness because for divine consciousness to be known, as our sages say, is God as the principle to himself. He wanted to be known through the other. He wanted to be found through the other; otherwise, he would know himself. This being recognized by others to the highest degree is realized in man. Man, more than any other creature in the world, is able to know God because he was made in the image of God. This recognition of God is like what Ibn Arabi says: "God saw himself in himself." He wanted to see himself in the other as in a mirror because to see oneself in oneself is not to see oneself in the other as in a mirror.

So, he created the world as a mirror to see himself, and he is known through the other. To know the principle is the ultimate aim. This is very much forgotten. Science cannot solve this problem of knowing the principle. This is the missing message of Eastern wisdom, whether Chinese, Indian, Persian, Islamic, Christian, or ancient Greek. The sages were all concerned with knowing things through their principles. This message is quite forgotten in modern philosophy and is never the business of science. It's no business of science to be concerned with it, so it's forgotten totally. Man, his reality, can only be known through his principle.

There is a saying attributed to the Prophet that God addressed David the prophet. He told David, the Jewish prophet, "Oh, David, look, I created this world for you, but I created you for myself. You are not for the world. You are for me." This is a very profound saying. Man is not made for the world. The world is made for man, in a sense. He is the macrocosm because he knows the world. The world doesn't know him. The article, which I will read next, will explain the function of man in the universe. He is the mirror of divine consciousness. God knows the other through him.

We are here to realize this potentiality. The Muslim philosopher Mulla Sadra says that man is made in the image of God. He is what he makes of himself, of this image, what he does with this image. Man does not change anything. Whether or not I know God, I'm the same. What is the difference between a sage and a person who is not a sage? They are both human beings. They have eyes, ears, and hands. They do things. They have the same functions. But, there is a great difference in consciousness. It's the awareness.

For the person who becomes a sage, nothing changes physically. There is a deep spiritual change in him: the change of consciousness. He becomes a new awareness. This new awareness we call awakening, illumination, and enlightenment. They have different names. This changes the direction of the consciousness. It is what Plato calls an *epistrophe*. It means a return to the origin, which is the beginning of philosophy. What we call, for example, the journey back. Or, as Heraclitus calls, the way up, the way up to reach the origin and to see from there.

The concepts of there and here are repeated in Plato: there and here. It's repeated in Plotinus. It's repeated much in Rumi. There and here. If there is a here, there is a there. We should go there and see what the things there are like. This is something quite missing, especially in modern philosophy. It's a function not of science but philosophy. Philosophy is in denial of metaphysics, but it should deal with these things. This is one of the mistakes of modernity. I don't know how much we'd agree with that.

Tu: I think you give us a very comprehensive, thoughtful, and persuasive statement about the outward meaning that ought to be in the general concern of the scientific enterprise, but because modernization is often understood as secularization, that particular sense is lost. I think most people are aware that the defining characteristic of being human is the unfortunate surplus in the affective aspect of being human and a deficit in cognitive understanding. In other words, our ability to understand always falls short of the emotional need to understand what we call the gap between affective surplus and cognitive deficit. One clear indication of the cognitive deficit is the inability of science, no matter how broadly you define it, to understand dimensions of rationality that have been taken for granted as absolutely essential for any kind of spiritual understanding of the world in China, India, Persia, ancient Greece, or the Judaic world. It is now rejected outright.

Aavani: Including the notion of self.

Tu: Absolutely. We have this problem. In 1923, there was a major debate in China between a Confucian philosopher by the name of Zhang Junmai, who gave a series of lectures at Tsinghua University on the philosophy of life, and a geologist by the name of Ding Wenjiang, whom many other so-called positivistic scientists, such as Hu Shi and Wu Zhihui supported. These pro-scientific thinkers are very shallow.

Aavani: Knowledge itself is the appearance of things.

Tu: They are very positivistic. Anything that cannot be calculated, counted, or quantified is not knowledge. They firmly believe that science will eventually solve the problem of the riddle of life. The philosophy of life, the experience of life, can also be digested, analyzed, and understood by science. Now, we know that the question raised by Zhang Junmai about the meaning of life is still very much of a live question, whereas this kind of blind faith in the omnipotence of science is no longer acceptable. We know that

Wittgenstein talked about two types of riddles. A riddle that can be solved or understood is never a significantly important one. The riddle that cannot be solved...

Aavani: Very deep, very deep ocean.

Tu: The riddle of life is a riddle that is not solvable, but we have to live with it. We have to appreciate it and understand it. The human imagination, the ability of humans to imagine the ultimate meaning of life, is based upon the human ability to appreciate many levels of analysis and the level of senses; you cannot justify or judge the meaning of that at all. At the level of rational calculation, that's instrumental rationality, which is extremely powerful...

Aavani: Very powerful through science, philosophy, and positivism.

Tu: I consider that as a kind of ruling ideology in China.

Aavani: Almost every technology is something like that.

Tu: It's a kind of scientism.

Aavani: Positivism.

Tu: It's not the scientific spirit, as I understand it.

Aavani: Interpretation of science, perhaps.

Tu: It's an ideology.

Aavani: Very good word. Ideology, not based on...

Tu: It's a false consciousness. It's not real consciousness. Sometimes, it's constructed by political means, by a certain kind of ethos that fails to understand...

Aavani: This is against science and philosophy, this ideology.

Tu: So we need to have a mode of thinking that not only goes beyond senses or instrumental rationality but also goes beyond communicative rationality, as Habermas talks about it. Habermas is interested in this question about the communication of the best possible situation in which human beings can live together peacefully, from liberal...

Aavani: Secular and liberal...

Tu: A kind of political liberalism of John Rawls and others. We know it's an idea that is now very seriously challenged or even rejected in America. That's one of the reasons why there is a number of people who call themselves communitarianists, who challenge the idea of the public sphere as defined exclusively in terms of the political procedure in which...

Aavani: Like Habermas.

Tu: ...the question of religion is totally irrelevant. It's a matter of the heart. The interesting thing about Habermas is that, I'm told, he's just written a book on religion. He now takes religion seriously, though it's a little bit too late. We know that not only should you rise above the senses to have an appreciation of how reason works, but you also have to rise above instrumental rationality to appreciate communicative rationality.

Aavani: Also, the nature of reason itself has been forgotten. For example, Kant, the greatest philosopher of the age, was really confounded about reason.

Tu: Of course, Kantian rationality is way beyond instrumental rationality. After all, he's deeply concerned about the limits of rational discourse, and one of the reasons for that is the strong desire to leave room for faith. Even in Kantian philosophy, the idea of rationality…

Aavani: This is, again, a dualism. Faith cannot be without reason.

Tu: Right. In the Western tradition, you have the Greek focus on rationality and the Judaic focus…

Aavani: And Muslim. There is a long history of reason in Islam, which is very profound.

Tu: There is a very profound tradition of scientific inquiry, incredibly broadly defined, in the Islamic world. Anyway, we want to go beyond not only instrumental rationality but even communicative rationality, even the Kantian notion of limits of epistemology or his idea of *The Metaphysics of Morals,* to address…

Aavani: It has some metaphysical foundations. Kant denies speculative reason but opens the way for praxis. It's very strange. This is a paradox. How does this work in its own sphere but works in the sphere of volition?

Tu: In a profound sense, it doesn't work. Part of the reason is that in Kantian philosophy, there's nothing comparable to what we call self-cultivation philosophy or the question of spiritual exercise, as Hadot and others talked about. He wants to develop a mode of thinking that denies any philosophical significance of passion or the philosophical significance of the inquiry into human nature. For him, human nature is understood in terms of passion and not in terms of intrinsic value endowed by God. I think we all agree on that. We need to have wisdom in the classical Platonic sense. I may have mentioned that over the years, I've organized a series of discussions between Indian and Chinese philosophers entitled "Indian and Chinese Philosophical Perspectives on Knowledge, Wisdom, and Spirituality."

Aavani: Very important, very close.

Tu: Very close.

Aavani: I wish there had also been a discussion of Islamic, Indian, and Chinese philosophy. It could be very interesting. They are very close.

Tu: It's very important to invite you to participate in the conversation. The first one was in Delhi, and the second one was in Beijing; we may go back to India, but anyway, I want to broaden that. The question then is, as you pointed out very beautifully, if we say embodiment is the incarnation, the Christian idea that the only incarnation in history is of Jesus' incarnation doesn't work. Jesus is only one of many exemplars in the Islamic and Confucian worlds.

Aavani: Many exemplars of this world.

Tu: Numerous exemplifications, not only just the humans. How a human being is able, using your vocabulary, to live up to the divine mission of embodying all the attributes of the creator is to incarnate…

Aavani: Is already incarnated, already incarnation.

Tu: Allow all these attributes to be embodied and incarnated.

Aavani: And realized.

Tu: In a sense, fully realized…

Aavani: Fully.

Tu: …in ordinary human existence. That's both a great challenge and also a great privilege. So, that is the idea of incarnation. The major problem for me then is the idea of Heaven as a creator.

Aavani: *Tian*.

Tu: Yes. Let's assume the following. There are various deep-rooted traditions in China…

Aavani: Not physical heaven, but a symbol of that Heaven. By Heaven, they mean spiritual Heaven.

Tu: Absolutely.

Aavani: It's symbolic, not factual.

Tu: Not factual at all.

Aavani: We see this Heaven is a symbol of that Heaven.

Tu: But it's not symbolic in the sense that it's not real. It's very real.

Aavani: Yes, it's very real, but it symbolizes that very real Heaven.

Tu: There's a strong notion about, what I call, mutuality or mutual responsiveness. Heaven creates, and humans complete. In other words, the creativity of Heaven is to be realized in the concrete creativity of the human. So, human beings ought to…

Aavani: All attributes of God are manifested.

Tu: All right. Human beings, first of all, are observers. Of course, dogs and cats are all observers, but humans cannot…

Aavani: It's a total manifestation.

Tu: Holistic observation.

Aavani: Holistic.

Tu: It's impossible to imagine anything in the world that is not a potential object of human observation. So, the human ability to observe is comprehensive. However, human beings are not simply observers; they are also appreciators in the sense that they do not necessarily observe with the intention of utilitarianism. They don't just observe to use it. Of course, the hunters, the fishermen, and so forth observe, but our observation sometimes is totally disinterested. When we look at the mountain, we just want to look at it because it's beautiful. That is the idea of appreciation.

Aavani: It is the truth of the thing, but not the use of it as an instrument. It is to read the reality that is already reflected in us.

Tu: Right. So, this idea of humans...

Aavani: We would be realized by this reflection, realized because knowledge, according to the ancients, is the same as Being. It's not accidental that it comes out. It's the real Being when we realize that knowledge. We ourselves are realized because of the equivalence of knowledge and Being. Substance is not an accident of knowledge that comes from outside. We are realized through true theoretical reason and knowledge.

Tu: It is because that cognitive act is, by definition, transformative.

Aavani: A transformative act.

Tu: It's not just observation; it's a transformative act.

Aavani: Yes, the transformation is very great.

Tu: That's the reason why, as an observer and appreciator, a human being is involved in self-transformation and, therefore, self-realization. In this sense, human beings also actively participate in the creative process. That's why I cite that quote, "If you realize yourself, you realize human nature. Realizing the nature of things, you take part in the transforming and nourishing process of Heaven and Earth." Then the big term, which is not allowable in Christian theology but I think in Islamic theology is probably permissible, is the idea of co-creators. In other words, human beings are...

Aavani: Participants.

Tu: Human beings are observers; human beings are appreciators.

Aavani: Co-creators of what?

Tu: Human beings are participants; human beings are co-creators, almost partners.

Aavani: That's important in another sense. I will explain.

Tu: This is very important now. If you take this, you have different conceptions of what Heaven is, or in other cases, God, Yahweh, or Allah. There's no question that *Tian*

(Heaven) is omnipresent, so everywhere. You cannot imagine anywhere Heaven is absent nor can you imagine Heaven as not omniscient. Heaven is totally aware of everything, everywhere.

Aavani: Everything, otherwise it wouldn't be present. Its very presence is Being.

Tu: However, there is a major theoretical or theological problem. Heaven is most likely not omnipotent.

Aavani: Omnipotent, in what sense?

Tu: Let me finish this point. This is critical.

Aavani: Yes, Heaven is not omnipotent.

Tu: No, I think the notion of the myth of Adam, who was tempted and therefore sinned. Adam is flawed, but in the Chinese sense, there's nothing that is evil. The idea is a positive rejection of evil that has ontological status. You don't have a devil or evil that is independent, has its status, and can do evil things to humans.

Aavani: There is the idea, you see, that…

Tu: The rejection of the ontological status of evil.

Aavani: Why is there evil in this world? Why is there Satan?

Tu: Evil is understood in the following sense. If the creative process is somehow stopped and there is no creativity, that's the beginning of evil. Just like if the water doesn't flow, there will be stagnation, and the water will then get sour. That's the first thing. Second, evil occurs when there's a premature self-imposed limitation. For example, someone told Confucius, "I like your ideas, but I don't have the energy to put them into practice." You see, that's not true. The people who don't have the energy to put it into practice failed to do that after they tried. You haven't even tried. You say you don't have the energy, which means you draw a line before you've tried.

Aavani: Because you have not tried to do that.

Tu: Yeah. Self-imposed limitation. Then, there is self-deception. Self-deception is believing that you can do this or that. You think science is omnipotent. In fact, it's a delusion. It's a human delusion based on ignorance, arrogance, and all kinds of things. There are many, many reasons why the world has evil and why there are a lot of limitations. It's not because there's a Satan who has ontological status and is trying to do evil things.

For example, if you say a Nazi or Hitler is evil, you can understand the phenomenon by analyzing what happened. You can give a good explanation. Many Jewish thinkers and German thinkers have accomplished their understanding of the negative features of that example.

Aavani: You mean that there is dualism here?

Tu: Not dualism. Not yet. Human beings will definitely be able to survive and overcome any natural disaster that happens that is not willed by humans. You can have a big earthquake, flood, and other things. However, the only disasters that human beings are not able to survive are man-made, such as the nuclear holocaust, pollution, and so forth. In this situation, the ethic of responsibility is absolutely critical.

Aavani: Very, very critical.

Tu: There's no problem of theodicy. If it happens, don't blame God.

Aavani: Yeah. We should also blame ourselves.

Tu: God is not responsible. Confucius made a fascinating remark. "I don't blame Heaven. I don't complain about humans. I make the utmost of what I am able to do, and I allow the objective situation." By that, he means my fate, and fate implies destiny. Each and every human being is the embodiment of incarnation, of creativity.

Aavani: And responsible for it.

Tu: Right. Each and every human being is constrained by time and space and by all the forces beyond human control, like ethnicity, gender, language, socialization, and place of birth—you never choose your parents—sometimes even your basic value orientation. These are constraints. The interesting thing is that learning to be human from a Confucian point of view, like self-cultivation, is how to creatively transform the constraints or perceived constraints into a vehicle for human self-realization. We have a term that many people in complex systems like. The term is enabling constraint.

Aavani: Enabling constraint? Very good.

Tu: Right. The constraint is almost like a paradox; the constraint is incarnation. If it is incarnated…

Aavani: You have no choice.

Tu: …it means concrete humanity.

Aavani: You have no choice.

Tu: Yes. All these forces over which we have no choice, each one of them turns out to be an enabling constraint. For example, you're constrained in Arabic, I'm constrained in Chinese, but you realize yourself in Arabic.

Aavani: It's enabling. It's a potentiality.

Tu: Your gender, your ethnicity, your language, your birthplace, and so forth.

Aavani: Because it is there.

Tu: It is there. In that sense, there is diversity but never closed particularism. It is not closed particularism, not abstract universalism. It's dialogical.

Aavani: That's true. You mentioned a very, very important point. The first idea is we are made in the image of God. More particularly, as the Holy Quran says, "God taught man all his names that are manifested in man." If He had not manifested all names, God would not be known because he should have shared something of his attributes to know that. The fact that we say "God" and think of God means that we are made in the image of God.

Tu: Also, I like the idea that God created many people so that they can get to know each other. Right?

Aavani: Yeah.

Tu: The idea of the Tower of Babel.

Aavani: And babbling of the languages. It is the confusion which came in reason and language, too.

Tu: There's one compelling image in the Confucian tradition. It's called the oneness or singularity of principle and the multiplicity of its manifestations.

Aavani: That is oneness and many-ness.

Tu: The oneness of principle and the multiplicity of its manifestations. Each case of the many languages or cultural diversity gives us a sense of the infinite variety and richness of the human experience.

Aavani: That's true.

Tu: At the same time, pluralism is welcomed, but not relativism.

Aavani: Yes. Pluralism in the true sense.

Tu: But not relativism.

Aavani: It is divine pluralism, not secular pluralism. There is a divine pluralism.

Tu: The divinity implicit in this quest for self-realization is the oneness of principle, which, in the highest philosophy, in any tradition, one always has access to. If you don't have that…

Aavani: One principle. Unity.

Tu: That's the unity.

Aavani: Multiplicity without unity is impossible, nor unity without multiplicity. They are correlative and complement each other.

Tu: Right. Now, there are two very different images or symbols. Raimundo Panikkar, have you heard about him? Raimundo?

Aavani: Yes, I saw him in Iran.

Tu: You saw him before.

Aavani: He was in Iran before the revolution.

Tu: Yes, we had a dialog.

Aavani: Professor Andrew Lass invited him several times, and I found him to be a very gentle and nice man.

Tu: Ai Bei taped my conversation with him in Barcelona two years before he passed away. This idea is the relationship between Atman and Brahmin.

Aavani: Very important.

Tu: Therefore, it is the relationship between the individual soul and the cosmic soul.

Aavani: *Tat tvam asi.*

Tu: Yes, *Tat tvam asi.* In the classical Hindu notion, it's like water that drops into the ocean.

Aavani: We have the same simile in Islam. It's symbolic. It's not factual; it's symbolic.

Tu: Yes, but I think some Christian theologians worry about the following. What happens to the individuality of the soul? If I die, my soul continues. But what happens to my soul if the idea is that I fall into the ocean and that drop of the ocean now merges with the ocean?

Aavani: You become an ocean.

Tu: I think Panikkar's response to me is quite satisfactory. The important thing for us to think about is whether we focus our attention on the water or we focus our attention on the idea that this water has been shaped into a drop.

Aavani: It's a bubble.

Tu: No, no, no, into a drop.

Aavani: A drop.

Tu: The reason why the water is shaped into a drop is because there are forces that constrain water into a drop. In physics, once a drop of water falls into the ocean, the forces that shaped the water into a drop disappear, so the water becomes an ocean. You can see the ocean becomes the drop.

Aavani: That is, the determined becomes undetermined, absolute.

Tu: However, in Christian mysticism with Rudolph Otto, with Eckhart, there is this idea—I should have asked Mr. Clooney to talk about it—that the real bliss for a Christian devotee with God is in the image of marriage or union. You know there are two terms used.

Aavani: *Unio mystica.*

Tu: Right. One is unity experienced, and the other is union. There is always this consideration that the union experience is more like marriage. The unity experience is that the uniqueness of being human in terms of an incarnated person disappears.

Aavani: Disappears.

Tu: However, from the Hindu point of view or the Daoist point of view—I don't know about the Confucian point of view—unity experience is the highest. Like when you now become part of the Dao or the water.

Aavani: Divinity is very high.

Tu: Yes, very high.

Aavani: Man is very low because we were initially divine, and we separated. But when we return to what we were, there is more luminousness.

Tu: What is it in Sufism?

Aavani: Yes, you have it in Sufism mysticism.

Tu: Sufi mysticism, is it more Daoistic or more Christian?

Aavani: I would explain that a little. They do not have a drop because it is physically the same. They use the example of a bubble and water.

Tu: Oh, the bubble bursts.

Aavani: The bubble is a mere appearance, a phenomenon that appeared from the noumenon. Since it is mere appearance when it becomes the noumenon reality, it becomes its real source, what it was originally. It only had separated itself through manifestation. Manifestation is what you call *Maya*.

Tu: But that's in Sanskrit.

Aavani: In Sanskrit, you have *Maya,* and we have illusion.

Tu: Yes.

Aavani: But this illusion should have a metaphysical source. Why illusion? It is very much explained in Sufi metaphysics. It is the problem of the reality and manifestation of the reality. When a thing manifests to be known, the locus of manifestation becomes a veil. It veils the principle which manifested itself. For example, this wall is a manifestation of God. God manifested himself in this wall, but nobody sees God in this wall, or at least most people do not. Only a very few sages see the manifestation. For most people, though God appeared in this wall, the wall is a veil for them. They see the wall; they do not see God. So, this is the case with a manifestation; it was revealed to make the revealer, the manifester, known.

It is the very image in which the principle appears. The phenomenon that becomes noumenon goes back to the principle of what it was. The principle doesn't lose itself.

Nothing is lost; everything is gained. This reminds me of the sayings of Jesus and Rumi concerning the self. Jesus says in the Bible, "What does a man gain if he loses himself, and what does he lose if he gains himself." Rumi complains about and blames all exoteric *ulama*—not only exoteric *ulama* of his time but of all ages—that they know about the substance of everything, but about their own substance, they're ignorant. Knowledge of self is the highest thing.

Now you mentioned a very, very important point. We are potentially given by Heaven and by God all the names. How do we realize them? This realization is not by book reading alone, but by conceptualization. In religions, only realization is valid, not conceptualization. What is the difference? The difference is this. I know or I've read in books of what is virtue, but I've never read virtuous. I've read only of a concept. But if I realize a virtue like being truthful and wise, not reading about it but being it, then knowledge and Being become one through realized knowledge; this is a higher kind of knowledge, which we call knowledge by realization. Rumi and Ibn Arabi, the great Sufis, believe this is the only knowledge. If knowledge has not reached this stage of realization, it is imitative knowledge.

We have a term concerning great Sufis: they are realizers. Now, the important thing is that the prophets of every religion, the sages of every religion, Confucius and the prophet Mohammed, did not read a scripture, but rather, they were the realization of that scripture. Confucius did not write the *Analects*, but it contains statements about him. So, he was more than *Analects*. If he had lived longer, if people had heard many things about him, they would say things that might not be in the *Analects*. He was more. Our Prophet was not something written. They say that his whole behavior and conduct were the real Quran and were the realization of the Quran.

So this knowledge by this realization and being a realization of this scripture is very important. You have to follow him only. If you follow Confucius truly through realization and not through reading alone, you are linked to Confucius. It is not only enough to read the Quran. It's very good, it's very sacred, but one must realize it as the prophets realized it, as far as humanly possible. This is the essence of faith. You should have faith in the prophets and the books. Of course, not all people can make perfect men, but according to their capabilities, they can become more perfect, and that's very good.

This mere faith is a way to realization, but there are very, very few people in every religious community who are perfect. This is very great because this means that religion is alive in them, lives in them, and religion is realized in them. They become an exemplar, an example for others. Why are we talking about Rumi after so many years, or Ibn Arabi, or many of these people like Mencius? It is because they are a realization, and through realization, they had knowledge, they expressed, they expounded, and still we believe in them after two millennia.

We have the concept of a perfect man. We believe that prophets of every religion, Eastern and Western, were the most perfect men in those religions and were paradigms to be followed. This, I think, is how we can become realized. Of course, all our people are not expected to be perfect men. But so far as they can, they try, and God in the Quran says that God does not obligate anybody except what he can. God is wise: a wise man does not obligate more than one can. He is rewarded completely, because he was not given the ability as the perfect man, because he has no more ability. But this is related to the very important problem of evil. Why is there evil? We need to discuss this.

Generally speaking, there is a difference between the principle and the manifestation of the world and God. The world is not God. God is the most perfect. If the world were like God, you would have two Gods. It should be less perfect if it is to be the world. The lower you come, the more imperfections there are. The spiritual world is a world of unity. Here is the world of multiplicity. There, there is no matter. Here, there is matter. The lower you come, the more there is evil, by definition. This is physical evil. It results from the very nature of the world because it is not God. There should be imperfection. The extent of lack of perfection is the source of evil. Lack of perfection differs at different levels. At the spiritual level, it is much less. The lower down you come, the more matter is mixed in, the more multiplicity there is, and the more imperfection.

As you said very truly and very rightly, man is different. Man is given freedom. Three things distinguish man. First, he knows the absolute and everything through his divine intellect. This is very great and distinguished. Second, he has free will. Perhaps free will is not a very good word because animals have free will. A cow is able to eat this fodder or that straw. Even if it is free, it is not human freedom. Freedom reveals itself in what we call free choice. He's able to choose. An animal is free but not able to choose. That's why we talk about freedom because it's something divine. If we were not given freedom, we would not be in the image of God. God alone is free, and being an image of God has given us freedom. It's a very high quality. Third, he has divine language. The language is very great. We express what we know. So, these three things are language, freedom, and divine intellect.

Some think, "If God had not given us freedom, we would not be made in the image of God because we would lack one of the greatest qualities of God: freedom." He wanted to give us freedom. But since He gave it to us, we must choose between good and bad. Not all people choose good. Some choose bad. This is the source of what we call evil. Also, some mystics say, not to all people but only very privately in their books because people would object, that there is wisdom in the expulsion of man from Paradise. There is some wisdom in this because, here, man has become more perfect. There, he was not free. Moreover, some divine attributes would not be realized without man being here. Some of the divine attributes became realized through his expulsion. For example, man is the forgiver of sins. If there was no sin there, how would there be a forgiver? There would be no forgiver. That is *Al-Ghafur*. Who accepts repentance if there is no sin? Some of the qualities of God would remain in potentiality if man didn't know sin at all.

Another critical point you mentioned is the very, very wise notion—that you said Confucius believes in—of enabling constraints. That's very great wisdom. The constraint, there's a wisdom in that if one ponders. Wisdom becomes evident by reading all wisdoms.

I didn't know about these enabling constraints. We should think and ponder over it. It's very great.

Another problem is multiplicity and pluralism, One-Many. Something wrong with modern pluralism is that it is first secular. Pluralism is a metaphysical principle. Unity can never be without multiplicity, not at all. Multiplicity cannot be without unity. The mistake of modern pluralism is this, especially from the religious point of view. They always talk about plurality, but they never talk about unity. You talk about the plurality of religions. You could also talk about the unity of religion. There is something behind all religions that, at a high level, unites, which is never talked of. They always speak about plurality. Sages have also talked about the unity of religions at a higher level. At the periphery, there is a difference. However, if you delve deeply into the very core, they become very, very close. This is never talked of. Moreover, they do not define religion. Everything we call religion. For example, there are man-made religions now. You have many religious movements now. Should we consider them religions? Do they have foundations? Do they have a virtuous life, divine life, knowledge of the unity of God, and things like that?

I think this problem of pluralism is very good. It deals with the nature of varied things. As you said, we cannot have one language. We should have many languages. We cannot have one religion. We should have many because the world is a multiplicity. There was an argument I gave against exclusivism, a philosophical proof that religion first is a universal term. To limit it in one religion, it needs proof for making a universal a particular. We even need proof of the existence of God and the unity of God. It's a universal clause that we give proof to say that my religion is the religion. Moreover, if a Christian says "religion" is Christianity, is it the case that anyone who thinks about religion in the world should think only of "Christianity." That is not the case. That would be to confine a universal that has many, many particular manifestations.

Religion is not a homonymous term. A homonymous term is one word with multiple meanings. Like "date," for example. There is the date of a palm tree and the date of an event. It's a word with two different meanings. We say that Confucianism is a religion, Islam is a religion, and Christianity is a religion. We mean by "religion," religion. It's not a homonymous term with different meanings. If we delve deeply, religion is a unity with a very, very specified meaning. Of course, we should talk about this meaning, but it's not used homonymously. It's a universal term because this world is plural. Some might think, "Would it not be better if God created one river from which all people would drink?" No. Whenever there is man, God is the most generous and omnipotent. Divine omnipotence requires plurality. If there's no plurality, God is not, because that would mean there are not all possibilities. Omnipotence means he has power over all possibilities; otherwise, God would not be omnipotent at all. To restrict religions, they hate God and deprive Him of omnipotence, wisdom, and every infinite divine quality.

Tu: We shall continue with this. Thank you.

Aavani: Thank you.

https://www.youtube.com/watch?v=Ozf3ZnQpv5o

INDEX

A

Advaita 180
Ai Bei 2, 3, 51, 193, 226
Aiken, Henry 8
All Under Heaven 23
Analects 21, 28, 97, 228
anthropocentrism 109, 130, 187
Aristotle.. 13, 27, 75, 94, 106, 107, 108, 201, 213
atheists 40, 42
Axial Age38, 61, 63, 65, 66, 67, 70, 71, 72, 73, 74, 125, 129
Axial Age civilization 63, 66, 67, 70, 71, 72, 129

B

Babel 225
behavioral inhibition 113
Beijing Forum 169
being-toward-death 190
Bellah, Robert 11, 31, 72, 160, 191
benevolent 114, 118, 122
Berger, Peter 14
Berlin, Isaiah 32
Berthrong, John 195
bias 184, 185
Bosniaks 116, 122
Brahman 136
Brahmin 175, 226
brain 114, 120, 121, 122, 138, 140
Brandeis University 5
Buber, Martin 27, 178, 180, 192
Buchanan 10
Buddhism11, 21, 37, 51, 59, 64, 86, 90, 91, 96, 98, 100, 108, 130, 131, 134, 166, 171, 173, 192, 195

C

Cervantes 145
Châtelet, Émilie du 124, 125
China 5, 7, 11, 14, 15, 18, 22, 23, 24, 25, 32, 33, 41, 51, 52, 53, 54, 58, 63, 64, 77, 90, 91, 92, 93, 95, 96, 97, 98, 99, 129, 142, 143, 144, 152, 153, 154, 156, 157, 161, 166, 167, 168, 169, 170, 172, 173, 174, 180, 188, 189, 191, 201, 202, 203, 204, 213, 218, 219, 221
Chinese5, 6, 7, 8, 22, 24, 25, 32, 38, 39, 41, 45, 47, 50, 51, 52, 53, 54, 55, 56, 57, 58, 59, 62, 63, 64, 92, 93, 95, 96, 99, 100, 103, 104, 105, 115, 116, 118, 119, 122, 129, 131, 133, 139, 143, 152, 156, 157, 161, 167, 169, 170, 172, 173, 175, 180, 188, 189, 191, 192, 196, 201, 202, 208, 214, 217, 220, 223, 224
Ching, Julia 195
Christian theology 99, 184, 222
Christianity .. 38, 39, 40, 51, 60, 63, 72, 91, 168, 174, 202, 215, 230
Clooney 208, 226
communitarianism 6, 14, 34, 153
community6, 14, 16, 17, 18, 20, 21, 22, 24, 26, 48, 51, 53, 54, 65, 66, 70, 95, 97, 105, 107, 108, 109, 110, 111, 114, 115, 118, 121, 123, 125, 126, 128, 132, 133, 134, 136, 137, 138,

139, 141, 144, 149, 155, 156, 158, 159, 160, 161, 162, 167, 174, 180, 191, 194, 195, 196, 202, 212, 228
Confucian... 5, 8, 11, 12, 13, 14, 15, 17, 18, 21, 22, 23, 25, 26, 28, 29, 35, 38, 45, 50, 52, 53, 56, 58, 82, 84, 85, 90, 91, 92, 93, 95, 96, 97, 99, 100, 102, 106, 107, 108, 110, 130, 181, 182, 183, 184, 188, 189, 191, 194, 195, 196, 206, 210, 218, 221, 224, 225, 227
Confucian Christian........................ 195
Confucian humanism 8, 12, 13, 14, 188, 189
Confucianism 21, 55, 57, 58, 63, 90, 91, 92, 93, 95, 96, 98, 99, 110, 166, 172, 175, 181, 184, 188, 189, 195, 202, 208, 216, 230
Confucius..... 41, 51, 52, 58, 81, 92, 99, 105, 115, 184, 191, 202, 203, 204, 206, 215, 223, 224, 228, 229
constitutive.................................. 20, 40
constructed............................. 148, 219
creative transformation........... 154, 172
critical reflection...... 17, 19, 20, 22, 24, 160, 188
Cultural China............................ 24, 99
Cultural diversity...... 96, 153, 188, 225
cultural identity................ 7, 91, 93, 94

D

Dalai Lama 111
Daodejing....................................... 196
Daoism. 5, 51, 63, 91, 98, 99, 166, 175, 227
dark age.. 122
Das Sein.. 189
de Bary, Wm. Theodore 195
Democracy in America.........................7
Derrida, Jacques ...57, 58, 94, 102, 148, 181, 191
Descartes 179, 213, 214, 216
deterministic 123
Dewey, John 31, 32, 33, 192
Dharma 58, 59
Diderot...188
dissent...................19, 20, 23, 170, 171
divinity 17, 89, 153, 184, 197, 225, 227
dogma 81
Dreben, Burton 17
Dreyfus, Hubert................................28
dualism ...180, 192, 209, 214, 220, 223, 224
Durkheim, Emile 7

E

Eckhart 226
economism 129
Einstein..................................135, 174
embodied knowledge.........................80
embodiment......39, 103, 187, 205, 208, 212, 215, 216, 221, 224
Emerson......................................29, 30
Emotivism 8
emptiness 170
Enlightenment 11, 12, 13, 23, 25, 27, 79, 99, 147, 153, 157, 158, 159, 161, 171, 185, 187, 188, 189, 190, 192, 196
Erikson 6, 102
ethic 7, 8, 12, 13, 14, 16, 19, 26, 34, 35, 52, 63, 75, 78, 82, 83, 84, 85, 86, 92, 97, 107, 108, 109, 110, 111, 116, 124, 125, 127, 128, 132, 133, 134, 135, 138, 139, 140, 143, 145, 150,

152, 155, 156, 157, 159, 160, 181, 182, 183, 185, 197, 224
ethic of responsibility 224
eudaimonia 127, 128
extra mile 182, 183

F

Fairbank, John King 8, 9
family 15, 16, 18, 22, 23, 105, 108, 130, 133, 136, 143, 146, 178, 196, 202
Foucault, Michel .. 57, 86, 94, 102, 108, 109, 191, 193
fourfold 196
freedom of speech 76
Friedman, Milton 9
Fukuyama, Francis 10
full moon 193, 197

G

Gadamer, Hans-Georg 99, 107, 178, 179, 180, 181, 184, 185, 189, 190
Galbraith, Kenneth 9, 31
Gandhi 109, 186
Geertz, Clifford 162, 184
Gemeinschaft 7
Gesellschaft 7
geworfen 196
globalization 14, 16, 35, 38, 40, 96, 133, 148, 151, 158, 160, 180, 188
god 39, 40, 41, 43, 46, 47, 52, 60, 61, 108, 117, 118, 122, 124, 125, 131, 135, 136, 144, 171, 174, 204, 205, 206, 207, 215, 217, 220, 221, 222, 224, 225, 226, 227, 228, 229, 230
God 174, 175
Godot 125
Goethe, Johann Wolfgang von .. 75, 187
Golden Rule 29, 84, 85, 182, 183
good life ... 13, 16, 30, 35, 36, 105, 106, 107, 110, 127, 128, 132, 133, 134, 139, 216
Gospel 182
Great Learning 28, 50, 104, 201, 209
guilt 116, 117, 119

H

Habermas, Jürgen 34, 89, 94, 95, 99, 160, 191, 193, 219
Hadot, Pierre 86
Hardin, Garrett 133
harmony ... 39, 40, 47, 60, 97, 114, 126, 136, 150, 214
Hartman, David 25, 26, 28, 29
Harvard 5, 7, 8, 9, 27, 50, 69, 89, 92, 98, 113, 142, 146, 153, 157, 161, 189
Harvard-Yenching 8
Heaven ... 23, 45, 51, 60, 105, 106, 107, 110, 130, 136, 137, 138, 139, 142, 172, 174, 180, 194, 196, 197, 207, 208, 215, 221, 222, 223, 224, 228
Hegel 13, 42, 94, 101, 103, 107, 109, 177, 195, 202, 203, 215
Heidegger, Martin 87, 94, 99, 101, 106, 107, 177, 189, 190, 192, 194, 196, 215
hermeneutics 44, 189
Hinduism 37, 40, 61, 63, 64, 73, 186, 188
historical consciousness 201, 202
Hobbes 12
Homo Sapiens 114
Huntington, Samuel 153
Hutus 116

I

idolatry ... 42
illusion ... 124, 125, 136, 144, 227
immanent transcendence ... 184
intellectual ... 24, 25, 26, 33, 34, 38, 43, 45, 48, 54, 57, 58, 82, 89, 91, 143, 146, 152, 184, 191
Iran ... 50, 54, 199, 200, 201, 202, 225, 226
Islam .. 50, 51, 60, 63, 68, 72, 174, 188, 202, 209, 213, 216, 220, 226, 230
Israel, Jonathan ... 188

J

Jaspers, Karl ... 63, 64, 70, 71, 125
Jesus Christ .. 46, 81, 99, 182, 186, 221, 228
Judaism ... 26, 63, 174
Jung, Carl ... 192
justice ... 9, 11, 13, 19, 26, 82, 123, 144, 161

K

Kant . 5, 12, 13, 14, 27, 34, 85, 94, 109, 124, 181, 213, 215, 220
Kierkegaard, Søren ... 195, 197
Kołakowski, Leszek ... 34
Kuhn, Thomas ... 188
Küng, Hans ... 84, 182

L

Lass, Andrew ... 226
learning to be human ... 114, 125, 224
Leibniz ... 188, 192, 214, 216
Levinas, Emmanuel 21, 27, 28, 94, 183
liberalism ... 5, 6, 11, 12, 13, 29, 31, 33, 35, 109, 148, 219
Liberalism and the Limits of Justice .. 5, 12
linear progress ... 122, 169
localization ... 133, 180
Locke ... 12

M

Madoff ... 128
Maimonides ... 27, 28
Mao Zedong ... 25
market fundamentalism ... 9
Marx ... 68, 94, 212
matter 12, 17, 39, 46, 56, 65, 68, 69, 79, 94, 98, 99, 107, 116, 118, 125, 135, 144, 153, 175, 180, 185, 209, 212, 214, 216, 218, 219, 229
May 4th generation ... 90
Mencius ... 15, 21, 28, 38, 82, 115, 117, 124, 128, 204, 206, 207, 208, 211, 228
merit ... 5, 158
Merleau-Ponty, Maurice. 103, 189, 190, 191, 208
metaphysics ... 8, 50, 53, 54, 57, 66, 80, 81, 87, 188, 213, 214, 216, 218, 220, 227
MIT ... 28, 50, 69
Mohists ... 15, 211
monotheistic ... 40, 107
Montaigne ... 124, 188
moral. 12, 13, 30, 82, 92, 114, 115, 116, 117, 118, 119, 121, 122, 123, 125, 126, 127, 128, 129, 131, 133, 134, 140, 143, 150, 155, 159, 196, 201, 206, 207
morality .. 108, 114, 115, 116, 117, 120, 121, 122, 123, 128, 139, 145, 197
Mote, Fritz ... 184

Mozi 15

N

nation 14, 15, 17, 18, 22, 23, 24, 45, 70, 105, 126, 130, 136, 143, 146, 202, 208
nationalism 95, 148
Neo-Confucianism 55, 57, 95
Neville, Bob 195
Neville, Robert 57, 195
New Testament 45
Nietzsche 87

O

Odyssey 142
Opium War 156, 167
Otto, Rudolph 226

P

Parsons, Talcott 7, 11, 63, 72
particularism 133, 182, 190, 224
patriotic 22, 23, 58, 95
patriotism 17, 19, 20, 24, 135
peace.... 37, 89, 108, 132, 174, 180, 192
Peking University. 24, 96, 98, 152, 157, 162, 169, 199
philosopher. 5, 7, 26, 31, 32, 33, 34, 51, 55, 56, 57, 58, 67, 68, 86, 87, 89, 90, 93, 94, 96, 99, 104, 107, 109, 118, 119, 125, 127, 128, 144, 162, 178, 179, 189, 190, 191, 201, 202, 204, 212, 213, 214, 215, 217, 218, 220
Plato 46, 94, 178, 213, 215, 217, 218
popular philosophy 12
positivistic science 175
postmodern 147, 188, 208, 210
praxis 89, 220
Prejudgments 185
present...... 33, 39, 69, 72, 74, 106, 114, 116, 119, 137, 144, 150, 152, 153, 154, 155, 161, 191, 216, 223
principle 52, 59, 85, 162, 174, 182, 204, 209, 211, 215, 217, 225, 227, 229, 230
psychologist 113, 206
public life 16, 34, 35, 84
public philosophy 31, 34
Putnam, Hillary 26

Q

Quesnay 188
Quine 8

R

R.Balasubramanian 109, 172
Rawls, John 13, 17, 34, 219
reflective dimension 19
regulation of the family 108
Renaissance 140, 141, 142
Ricci, Matteo 52, 56, 57, 189
Ricœur, Paul 99, 187
ritual........ 22, 64, 91, 97, 106, 117, 186
Rockefeller 121, 122
Rorty, Richard..... 20, 31, 111, 193, 210
Rumi 50, 199, 204, 218, 228

S

Sandel, Michael 5, 153, 161
Sanskrit 58, 59, 227
Schelling, Friedrich 103, 192
scholar...... 5, 28, 30, 37, 52, 89, 94, 99, 109, 115, 170, 172, 196, 200, 201, 203
scholar-official 52
Schwartz, Benjamin 8
scientism 161, 175, 188, 189, 219

secular humanism 100, 171, 172
self ... 12, 13, 14, 16, 17, 19, 20, 21, 30, 31, 35, 39, 40, 46, 47, 71, 95, 96, 97, 98, 102, 103, 105, 106, 108, 109, 110, 111, 116, 117, 124, 125, 127, 130, 134, 136, 137, 138, 142, 143, 144, 152, 157, 161, 163, 174, 175, 182, 184, 187, 190, 194, 196, 201, 202, 203, 204, 205, 207, 209, 210, 211, 216, 218, 220, 222, 223, 224, 225, 228
self-awareness......................... 185, 210
self-centered........................... 106, 211
self-consciousness 71, 139
self-critical 175
self-cultivation 185, 201, 202, 203, 209, 210, 220, 224
self-knowledge.................................. 39
self-realization 20, 21, 35, 46, 103, 105, 106, 108, 111, 134, 138, 207, 222, 224, 225
self-reflexivity 46, 97, 98, 163, 184
self-transformation.......... 105, 106, 222
self-understanding 39, 40, 47, 105, 124, 125, 157, 161, 207
Serbs 116, 122
Shaw, George Bernard................... 144
Shia 116
Smith, Adam 127, 128
smoke.................................... 129, 144
socially engaged 89, 195
Socrates.. 86
spiritual exercise..... 152, 203, 210, 220
spiritual humanism 100, 109, 172, 174, 194
Stevens, Wallace..... 124, 125, 127, 140
Stevenson, Charles............................ 8
Sunnis 54, 116

T

T'oegye............................92, 93, 94, 99
Tagore...32
Talmud 25, 26, 27, 28, 29, 183
Taylor, Charles 5, 13, 25, 28, 33, 34, 106, 191, 193
theory of evolution 216
Tocqueville, Alexis de...................7, 17
transformation 7, 38, 39, 66, 70, 92, 105, 106, 147, 154, 155, 157, 160, 171, 172, 175, 184, 222
triff..196
Trinity...........................39, 40, 46, 207
trust.....................................123, 160
Tutsis 116

U

UNESCO 75, 89, 95, 96, 100, 154
United States ..9, 10, 17, 30, 59, 62, 63, 64, 65, 76, 90, 93, 96, 99, 129, 153, 156, 171, 173, 180
universalism . 15, 16, 31, 133, 151, 182, 185, 190, 224
unpatriotic...23

V

Vedanta...180
vital energy...........2, 39, 104, 115, 206
Voltaire....................................23, 188

W

Walzer, Michael 26
Wang Yangming 28
Way of Heaven...............................174
Wealth and power...............90, 91, 194
Weber, Max.......................7, 63, 68, 72
Western Inscription 130, 194
White, Morton 8

wisdom ... 41, 58, 59, 65, 81, 82, 83, 86, 95, 124, 126, 127, 134, 141, 169, 202, 203, 204, 212, 213, 214, 217, 220, 229, 230
Wittgenstein 128, 132, 134, 219
world 13, 15, 17, 18, 30, 33, 37, 38, 42, 43, 45, 46, 47, 48, 50, 55, 56, 57, 59, 60, 61, 62, 63, 64, 65, 66, 67, 68, 70, 74, 75, 86, 87, 89, 90, 92, 93, 94, 95, 96, 101, 105, 106, 107, 108, 109, 115, 122, 123, 124, 126, 127, 129, 130, 131, 132, 133, 135, 137, 141, 142, 143, 144, 147, 148, 149, 150, 151, 152, 153, 155, 157, 158, 159, 160, 161, 165, 166, 168, 169, 170, 171, 172, 173, 174, 175, 177, 178, 179, 183, 184, 185, 186, 187, 188, 189, 190, 191, 192, 193, 194, 195, 196, 197, 200, 201, 202, 203, 204, 206, 207, 214, 215, 216, 217, 218, 220, 221, 222, 223, 229, 230

X

Xunzi 206

Y

Yang Zhu 15
Yulgok 92, 93, 94

Z

Zambia ... 129, 131, 133, 134, 142, 143, 144
Zen 51
Zhang Zai 45, 194
Zhu Xi 28, 51

Made in the USA
Las Vegas, NV
09 June 2026

47993248R00134